D1527179

CONTEMPORARY VIEWS OF ANCIENT JUDAISM: DISPUTES AND DEBATES

Contemporary Views of Ancient Judaism: Disputes and Debates

Jacob Neusner

Academic Studies in the History of Judaism
Global Publications, Binghamton University
2001

Copyright © 2001 by Jacob Neusner

All rights reserved. No portion of this publication may be duplicated in any way without the expressed written consent of the publisher, except in the form of brief excerpts or quotations for review purposes.

Cover artwork entitled "Mystery of the Leaf Quilt" by Suzanne R. Neusner.

Library of Congress Cataloging-in-Publication Data:

Jacob Neusner,   *Contemporary Views of Ancient Judaism: Disputes and Debates*

1. Judaism   5. History of Judaism

ISBN 1-586841-14-9

BM
177
.N466
2001

Published and distributed by:
Academic Studies in the History of Judaism
Global Publications, Binghamton University
State University of New York at Binghamton
Binghamton, New York, USA 13902-6000
Phone: (607) 777-4495 or 777-6104; Fax: (607) 777-6132
E-mail: pmorewed@binghamton.edu
http://ssips.binghamton.edu

ACADEMIC STUDIES
IN THE HISTORY OF JUDAISM

Publisher: Global Publications, State University of New York at Binghamton
Address: LNG 99, SUNY-Binghamton, Binghamton, New York 13902-6000

Editor-in-Chief
Jacob Neusner, *Bard College*

Editorial Committee
Alan J. Avery-Peck, *College of the Holy Cross*
Bruce D. Chilton, *Bard College*
William Scott Green, *University of Rochester*
James F. Strange, *University of South Florida*

CONTENTS

Preface

PART ONE
MY SIDE OF FOUR DEBATES

1. To the Israel Historical Society: Methodology in Talmudic History   1

2. Three Generations of Post-War Study of Judaism in Germany: Goldberg-Schaefer, Houtman, and Becker and the Demolition of Historical Judaism   35

3. Harrington, Stern, and Ilan: Evaluating the Criticism of a New Generation   63

4. Judaism and Christianity in the Beginning: Time for a Category-Reformation? A Review essay in Response to Jack T. Sanders and Stephen G. Wilson   79

PART TWO
FORMATIVE JUDAISM IN ACADEMIC SCHOLARSHIP: BOOKS, DISSERTATIONS, AND MONOGRAPHS OF THE 1990S

5. Donald Harman Akenson, *Surpassing Wonder. The Invention of the Bible and the Talmuds*   93

6. Gabriele Boccaccini, *Middle Judaism. Jewish Thought. 300 B.C.E To 200 C.E,*   103

7.   Markus Bockmuehl, *Jewish Law in Gentile Churches. Halakhah and the Beginning of Christian Public Ethics*   111

8.   Daniel Boyarin, *Intertextuality and the Reading of Midrash*   115

9.   Robert Brody, *The Geonim of Babylonia and the Shaping of Medieval Jewish Culture*   121

10.   Menachem Elon, *Jewish Law. History, Sources, Principles*   127

11.   Menachem Fisch, *Rational Rabbis. Science and Talmudic Culture*   133

12.   Isaiah M. Gafni, *Land, Center and Diaspora. Jewish Constructs in Late Antiquity*   155

13.   Moshe Halbertal, *People of the Book. Canon, Meaning, and Authority*   161

14.   Galit Hasan-Rokem, *Web of Life. Folklore and Midrash in Rabbinic Literature*   165

15.   Christine Elizabeth Hayes, *Between the Babylonian and Palestinian Talmuds: Accounting for* Halakhic *Difference in Selected Sugyot from Tractate Avodah Zarah*   177

16.   Susannah Heschel, *Abraham Geiger and the Jewish Jesus*   197

17.   Catherine Hezser, *Form, Function, and Historical Significance of the Rabbinic Story in Yerushalmi Neziqin*   203

18. Hayim Lapin, *Early Rabbinic Civil Law and the Social History of Roman Galilee. A Study of Mishnah Tractate Baba' Mesi'a'*   209

19. Lee I. Levine, *The Rabbinic Class of Roman Palestine in Late Antiquity*   219

20. Jeffrey L. Rubenstein, *The History of Sukkot in the Second Temple and Rabbinic Periods*   225

21. Ze'ev Safrai, *The Economy of Roman Palestine*   233

22. Rabbinic Sources for Historical Study: A Debate with Ze'ev Safrai   237

23. Michael L. Satlow, *Tasting the Dish. Rabbinic Rhetorics of Sexuality*   267

24. Eliezer Segal, *The Babylonia Esther Midrash. A Critical Commentary*   281

25. Hershel Shanks, ed., *Christianity and Rabbinic Judaism. A Parallel History of their Origins and Early Development*   293

26. David Stern, *Parables in Midrash. Narrative and Exegesis in Rabbinic Literature*   311

27. Sacha Stern, *Jewish Identity in Early Rabbinic Writings.*   319

28. Tal Ilan, *Jewish Women in Greco-Roman Palestine. An Inquiry into Image and Status*   329

29.   Pierre Vidal-Naquet, *The Jews. History, Memory, and the Present*   337

30.   Shaye J. D. Cohen, *The Beginnings of Jewishness. Boundaries, Varieties, Uncertainties*   345

PREFACE

I present two and a half dozen book reviews and Auseinandersetzungen, disputes and debates on the study of formative Judaism. I make the effort to read the dissertations and monographs in that field, particularly as these intersect with my studies on problems I have chosen to solve. Here are some of the results for the decade that has now concluded. These reviews and essays form the counterpart to bibliographies. Let me explain.

A scholarly convention requires appending to a monograph comprehensive bibliographies on the topic of that monograph. These ordinarily are not annotated, and they do not indicate where and how, or even whether, the author has utilized the work in the monograph at hand. Indeed, it is quite common for the bibliography to omit titles frequently cited in the footnotes of the work but to list other items not utilized at all; nowadays, it is becoming customary to publish the bibliography separate from the monograph it supposedly serves. That is a signal of a disjuncture between the scholarship active in the monograph and the politics of the field in which the monograph seeks its location. Cite what is not used, do not cite what is! Include long, formal lists of books that do not pertain to the work actually done, but never indicate why they are logged in. These bizarre procedures call into question the prevailing convention and its rationality.

For several decades I have taken a different approach to situating my *oeuvre* in the larger academic context. I have cited what I actually consult where I consult and engage with the work. Much of the work I have done, beyond translations, addresses problems that have not engaged prior workers, so bibliographical work proves frustrating. In any event, unlike others, I do not compose long lists of works that in fact do not pertain to the problem I take up or the topic I propose to investigate. But I systematically review nearly every title in English that appears in the field in which I work. (I hesitate to review titles in other than my native American language, not trusting my capacity to catch the nuances of expression in a foreign language, even though I can read a variety of foreign languages.)

These reviews focus on dissertations. That is because most of the original scholarly effort in the study of formative Judaism comes to us in dissertations, first books. Alas, few scholars write second books of an equivalently rigorous scholarly character. Beyond the first book, the second and later books in many instances tend to go over ground already explored to begin with. It is uncommon to find scholars pursuing fresh problems in new ways in second and later books. The productive workers are few, and all of them, without exception, find themselves intensely controversial, however routine their findings may be. In trying to read all of the English- and American-language dissertations, wherever written or published, I have been able to keep up with trends and issues in the study of formative Judaism and orient myself to the work of others, even while pursuing my own line of inquiry. That means, while my work defines its own path, I am not unfamiliar with the directions taken by others, both beginners and, where they continue to work, the more mature colleagues.

Every few years I look back on these reviews and choose the ones that seem to me to meet the test of time. In these pages I have collected work of the 1990s, some longer review-essays, some somewhat briefer reviews of single titles. In my judgment these endure and deserve a review. In this way I maintain an ongoing dialogue with other scholars as they progress in their work. I gain from this perspective both on the field as it develops and also on my definition of what is worth investigating in the study of formative Judaism. It seems to me a more appropriate way of a systematic *Auseinandersetzung* than simply collecting titles of books in bibliographies and pretending to engage with them when in fact I have not read, let alone studied, them at all.

Continuing a long series of *Auseinandersetzungen* in the form of essays and reviews,[1] then, I commence with four essays on method, encompassing these issues: [1] how we derive from our sources information of a historical character; [2] how we derive from the texts of Rabbinic Judaism an account of the religious system that animates those texts and the context and contents of those texts; [3] the documentary reading of the canonical texts and its critics; and [4] the appropriate category-formations for the study of formative Judaism in the engagement with earliest Christianity.

[1]   THE USE OF RABBINIC TEXTS FOR HISTORICAL PURPOSES: I begin with a paper written nearly two decades ago, in 1983, upon the invitation of the Israel Historical Society. It was to be given at their fiftieth anniversary celebration of the journal, *Zion*. I took the invitation as an honor and in return determined to pay the Society the compliment of taking seriously the scholarly requirements of the

---

[1] *Ancient Judaism. Debates and Disputes.* Chico, 1984: Scholars Press for Brown Judaic Studies; *Ancient Judaism. Debates and Disputes. Second Series.* Atlanta, 1990: Scholars Press for South Florida Studies in the History of Judaism; *Ancient Judaism. Debates and Disputes. Third Series. Essays on the Formation of Judaism, Dating Sayings, Method in the History of Judaism, the Historical Jesus, Publishing Too Much, and Other Current Issues.* Atlanta, 1993: Scholars Press for South Florida Studies in the History of Judaism; Ancient Judaism. Debates and Disputes. Fourth Series. Historical, Literary, Theological, and Religious Issues. Atlanta, 1996: Scholars Press for South Florida Studies in the History of Judaism; Rabbinic Judaism in the Formative Age: Disputes and Debates. Atlanta, 1994: Scholars Press for South Florida Studies in the History of Judaism.

occasion. That meant the highest compliment I know: serious engagement with matters of substance of broad general interest, criticism and argument. My contribution was meant to be, to stimulate an exchange of viewpoints and perhaps clarify the state of learning in the field under discussion. This compliment on my part took for granted what was simply not the case, which was, that rational inquiry was at issue. My lecture, sent well in advance for translation into Hebrew, provoked an immediate dis-invitation, by return mail. The Israel Historical Society would not offer a platform for the criticism of *Zion's* treatment of the field in which the keynote speaker works. I wrote to Menachem Stern, then the President of the Historical Society to complain, and he never had the decency to respond to my letter; nor did I ever hear about the dis-invitation from any part to the invitation. It could not have been conceived so weighty an occasion as I stupidly interpreted it to be.

Such Bolshevik suppression of dissenting opinion should not have surprised me. It is all I have ever known from those circles of Judaic learning. I was naïve to interpret the invitation in the way I did. I should have understood it as an effort to engage, even though it was on political, not academic, terms of engagement. I was expected to pay compliments to my hosts in response to the compliment of their invitation. I assumed, as readers of the rejected address will immediately grasp, that the change marked by the invitation represented a statement of interest in debate and argument. That would have represented a considerable political shift, and I should have accepted it as such. I did not understand that merely inviting me represented a massive capitulation on the part of the Israel Historical Society. For until that moment, it had been unthinkable to do so. People had to die, a whole generation had to pass away, for such an invitation to be issued!

For the prior quarter-century, it had been forbidden to cite my books or articles in Israeli monographs and dissertations; they were not to be reviewed; they were kept under lock and key, along with the pornography, in the Hebrew University Library. This campaign of *Totschweigen* denied two generations of Israeli scholars access to a corpus of work that was making its way everywhere else. It was in that context that the invitation, essentially a political statement, was issued. Had I known it was merely political, not intellectual, I would have declined. Instead, I took it for what it was not and a public scandal resulted.

Lest the matter pass from memory, I reprinted the essay every five years, to give it the hearing denied by the Israel Historical Society. This is the last such reprinting, for now times change. First, much, though by no means all, of the coming generation of Israeli scholars, even in Jerusalem, have adopted the critical program vis-à-vis the Rabbinic sources that, for a long time, I advocated in isolation. The reviews reprinted here pick up lapses, but much of the Israeli work on Talmudic history has made its peace with the critical historical program of the Enlightenment. Second, in the nearly twenty years since the famous dis-invitation, the younger Israeli scholars have engaged with my work, and a perceptible change in the framing of questions and in the interpretation of pertinent evidence and argument has registered. Citing work of mine no longer endangers careers, and many of my books can be located and consulted in the academic libraries of the state of Israel.

The dis-invitation of 1983 did not accomplish its goal, which was to suppress criticism of regnant methods and approaches instead of confronting and dealing with it. But dis-inviting me was the best the hosts could do: they had no answer and could not meet the challenge I meant to lay before them. They could not keep up and so have been left behind.

The other essays require a simple description of what is at stake.

[2] THE TEXTUAL INTEGRITY OF THE RABBINIC CANON: I here survey German-Dutch scholarship. Chapter Two moves from the Israeli to the German setting in the study of ancient Judaism, and I offer perspective on the character of the scholarship on Rabbinic Judaism produced in the three generations from World War II. It is not a heartening account. The reconstruction has failed.

[3] THE DOCUMENTARY READING OF THE RABBINIC CANON: I proceed to the English-speaking world and take up the criticism of the documentary hypothesis as set forth in three books written in that language, by an American, a British, and an Israeli scholar. These have in common an interest in debating with me on propositions of mine that intersect with research of theirs.

[4] CATEGORY-FORMATION: "JUDAISM" AND "CHRISTIANITY:" In Chapter Four I point to a profound flaw in the category-formations put forth by New Testament scholars of formative Judaism.

Then I proceed to a long sequence of systematic book reviews of important titles of the 1990s. Some are ambitious Auseinandersetzungen with their authors, some are more conventional reviews. I conclude, in Chapter Thirty, with an assessment of the scholarly oeuvre of a more advanced scholar, who over a quarter-century now has published three books of his own (not taking account of edited titles), [1] a dissertation, [2] a text book, and [3] a collection of essays. Here we see an interesting pattern in the trajectory of a scholarly life.

The academy does not settle issues through popularity contests, and a fair amount of quite violent language — not academic criticism at all — has been directed against me by such colleagues as Solomon Zeitlin, Saul Lieberman, Morton

Smith, and lesser figures such as Daniel Boyarin, S. J. D.
Cohen, and the like. These reviews for their part rarely win
the warm thanks of the authors of the books subject to discussion, though in some instances they have, with productive
results for both parties.

   That reviews of the kind set forth here make their
mark is shown in the (futile) effort to suppress them. That is
made manifest, in a representative case, by the arbitrary decree barring me from the book review columns of the *Journal
of Biblical Literature* for all eternity, a decree issued in 2000 by
the then-book editor of the *Journal of Biblical literature*, Marvin
A. Sweeney, confirmed by the then-executive director of the
Society of Biblical Literature, Kent Richards. It was conveyed
to me when I volunteered to review some rather routine
items listed by Dr. Sweeney on the SBL web page as requiring
reviewers. To three initiatives on my part, involving three different titles, I received no response whatsoever. Seeing the
books still listed months later, I inquired. I was then told by
Dr. Sweeney that because I had earlier had the effrontery of
submitting a review to him — it concerned the title by Shaye
J. D. Cohen treated in Chapter Thirty — I was singled out for
his special handling. In this *Sonderbehandlung* accorded to me,
he never bothered to reject the review or return it or inform
me of his decision of it. But, specifically, he decided *in peccato*
that I would never again be invited — or even permitted —
to review a book in the *Journal of Biblical Literature*. This he finally revealed, when I asked the Executive Director what had
become of the matter. Predictably, I had no problem placing
the review elsewhere. It was published. After decades of
membership, and with regret, I dropped my membership in
the society.

   Cui bono? The Society of Biblical Literature cannot
foreclose public discussion of scholarly issues or even much
impede it. It cannot protect this one from the criticism of that

one or adopt a bill of attainder against unwanted criticism and those that advance it. A learned society lacking a monopoly in its field can do some good, but it cannot do harm. If a review is not printed in one place, it will appear somewhere else; academic debate cannot be stifled in a free society. To be sure, my books have not been reviewed by the *Journal of Biblical Literature* under Dr. Sweeney's editorship. Then they have been reviewed elsewhere and have found their audience.

I do think Dr. Sweeney's and Dr. Richards' decree of academic excommunication reflects poorly on the academic integrity of the Society of Biblical literature and politicizes its journal. But times change. I remember better days for the SBL and the JBL and I am confident in due course a more enlightened attitude toward public debate and disagreement will prevail.

In that context I express my pleasure at the vigorous support for my intellectual ventures accorded by Bard College through the professorship I hold, by my colleagues, both at Bard College and at many other places, who sustain my work through dialogue and criticism, and by Global Publications, which has succeeded the now-defunct Scholars Press in the work of academic publishing of short-run scholarly monographs. The damage done to the academic study of religion by the closing of Scholars Press by its board of directors under Kent Richards' chairmanship can never be fully repaired. But firms such as Global Publications and University Press of America and Oxford University Press for the American Academy of Religion have come to the rescue of humanistic study of religions and have done much to secure a continuing public forum for learning in this corner of the academy.

JACOB NEUSNER
Research Professor of Religion and Theology, Bard College
Annandale-On-Hudson, New York 12504

neusner@webjogger.net

1.

TO THE ISRAEL HISTORICAL SOCIETY: METHODOLOGY IN TALMUDIC HISTORY

[Written for the Historical Society of Israel. Conference in celebration of its journal, *Zion,* on the occasion of its fiftieth volume. Jerusalem, Israel. Scheduled for July 2, 1984. This paper was mailed to Jerusalem on January 27, 1984, and the invitation to present it was withdrawn in a letter dated March 5, 1984. The facts speak for themselves, but I prefer not to suggest what they say. Then again, I don't have to — everybody now knows.]

I
METHODOLOGY

When we speak of methodology, we may mean many things. To specify the very few things under discussion here, let us begin with the simplest possible definition. The method by which we work tells us the questions we choose to pose and the means we use to find the answers. Our method tells us what we want to know and how we can find it out. Method then testifies to the point at which we begin, the purpose for which we work. A sound method will guide us to questions both pertinent to the sources under study and also relevant to broader issues of the day. The one without the other is merely formal, on the one side, or impressionistic and journalistic, on the other. Proper method will tell us what sources we must read and how to interpret them. Above all, sound method will match the issues we raise to the information at hand, that is, will attend especially to questions of historical epistemology: what we know and how we know it.

We cannot raise in the abstract the issues of historical methodology in Talmudic history. Talmudic history is a field that people practice. We cannot ignore what people actually do in favor of some preferred theory of what we think they should do. It furthermore would defy the honorable occasion at hand, to speak about Talmudic history without paying appropriate attention to the journal we celebrate here and now. Accordingly, let us first of all turn our attention to Zion itself and ask how Talmudic history is practiced in its pages: the methodology demonstrated here.

The answer is in three parts. First, Talmudic history constitutes a strikingly unimportant field in Zion. From 1935 (Vol. 1) to 1983 (Vol. 48), the journal published 476 articles, at the rate of approximately 10 per volume. Of these, no more than 28 in all fall into the category of Talmudic history, approximately one article for every two volumes. Talmudic history accounts, in all, for little more than 5% of all articles published in the 50 years we celebrate — a strikingly small proportion.[1] Yet, in fact, these figures overstate the impor-

---

[1] My student, Paul Flesher, supplied the following footnote:

A list of all the articles of Talmudic History appearing in the journal, Zion, since its inception. I have divided the articles into two categories, General Talmudic history, and the use of the Rabbinic literature for the study of the second Temple period.

I. Talmudic History
1.   E. Bickermann, "Notes on the Megillath Taanith," vol. 1.
2.   G. Allon, "How Yabneh became Rabbi Johanan ben Zakkai's Residence," vol. 3.
3.   M. Stein, "Yabneh and her Scholars," vol. 3.
4.   A. Kaminka, "Rabbi Johanan ben Zaccai and his Disciples," vol. 9.

5. G. Allon, "Concerning the History of Juridical Authorities in Palestine during the Talmudic Period," vol. 12.

6. E.E. Urbach, "Political and Social Tendencies in Talmudic Concepts of Charity," vol. 16.

7. E.E. Urbach, "Halakhot Regarding Slavery as a Source for the Social History of the Second Temple and the Talmudic Period," vol. 25.

8. M. Beer, "The Exilarchs in Talmudic Times," vol. 28.

9. B.Z. Dinur, "The Tractate Aboth (Sayings of the Fathers) as a Historical Source," vol. 35.

10. J. Florsheim, "The Establishment and Early Development of the Babylonian Academies, Sura and Pumbeditha," vol. 39.

11. J. Geiger, "The Ban on Circumcision and the Bar-Kochba Revolt," vol. 41.

12. Moshe David Herr, "The Causes of the Bar-Kokhba War," vol. 43.

13. S. Safrai, "Kiddush Ha-Shem in the Teachings of the Tannaim," vol. 44.

14. M.D. Herr, "Continuum in the Chain of Torah Transmission," vol. 44.

15. Z.W. Falk, "On the Historical Background of Talmudic Laws Regarding Gentiles," vol. 44.

16. A. Wasserstein, "Rabban Gamaliel and Proclus the Philosopher (Mishna Aboda Zara 3.4)," vol. 45.

17. D. Goodblatt, "New Developments in the Study of the Babylonian Yeshivot," vol. 46.

18. I. Gafni, "On D. Goodblatt's Article," vol. 46.

19. O. Irsai, "R. Abbahu said: If a man should say to you 'I am God' — He is a Liar," vol. 47.

20. B. Rosenfeld, "The Activity of Rabbai Simlai: A Chapter in the Relations Between Eretz Israel and the Diaspora in the Third Century, vol. 48.

21. R. Kimelman, "The Conflict Between the Priestly Oligarchy and the Sages in the Talmudic Period (An Explanation of PT Shabbat 12:3, 13C = Horayot 3:5, 48C))," vol. 48.

II. The Use of Rabbinic Literature for the Study of Second Temple Times

1. G. Allon, "The Attitude of the Pharisees Toward Roman Rule and the Herodian Dynasty," vol. 3.

tance accorded to Talmudic history in the journal. How so? Of the 28 articles at hand, seven deal with Second Temple times, using Rabbinic literature for the treatment of the period before 70 (five of the seven by Y. Baer, as a matter of fact). Now since a vast range of sources, outside of the Talmud, pertain to the period before 70, and since the bulk of the Talmudic writings do not speak of that period, we can hardly concur that that period falls into Talmudic history at all. Strictly speaking, Talmudic history encompasses the period from the second century A.D. onward. Accordingly, when we ask how many articles in Zion dealt with problems on which the Talmuds and related documents provide first-hand evidence, rather than merely referring to things that happened long ago of which the authors have no direct knowledge of their own, and on which (by definition) the Talmuds constitute the principal corpus of evidence, the figures change. Specifically, only 21 of the 476 articles — four percent of the total, at the rate of somewhat less than one article every two years — attend to the field at hand. So we see in a rather dramatic way that Talmudic history — the history of the Jewish people in its formative centuries beyond 70 and

2.   I.F. Baer, "The Historical Foundations of the Halacha," vol. 17.
3.   I.F. Baer, "On the Problem of Eschatological Doctrine During the Period of the Second Temple," vol. 23-24.
4.   I.F. Baer, "The Historical Foundations of the Halakha," vol. 27.
5.   J. Amir, "Philo's Homilies on Fear and Love in Relation to Palestinian Midrashim," vol. 30.
6.   Y. Baer, "Jerusalem in the Times of the Great Revolt," vol. 36.
7.   I.F. Baer, "The Service of Sacrifice in Second Temple Times," vol. 40.
Zion began in 1935. This study begins with volume one and ends with number 3 of volume 48 (1983). The total number of articles in these volumes is 476.

up to the rise of Islam — enjoys little attention in Zion.[2] I need hardly add that were we to examine other scholarly journals3 in this country [viz., the State of Israel, where the paper was supposed to be presented] and overseas, the proportions might change somewhat, but the picture would emerge pretty much the same.

The second and third observations about the status and methodology of Talmudic history in Zion require less exposition.

The second is that when people practice Talmudic history in Zion, they limit their discussion to Talmudic history in particular. The field does not encompass its period, but only one set of sources emergent from its period. While many of the scholars represented in Zion draw upon sources outside the Talmud, none of the articles deals with a problem outside the Talmud. Accordingly, Talmudic history in the journal at hand finds definition as the study of historical problems pertinent to a given source, rather than to a chronological period to which that source attests. (In this regard, Baer's articles form an exception to the rule.) It follows that Talmudic history severely limits itself, in Zion, to literary evidence. While, once again, we may find allusion to archeological data, no article in the past half-century has entered the category of inquiry in which archeology, as much as literature, defines the problem or contributes to its solution.

The third observation is that the methodology of reading the literary sources, which define the problems and solutions of Talmudic history in Zion, begins in an assumption universally adopted by the scholars of the journal (and not only there). Whatever the Talmud says happened hap-

---

[2] We note that no articles on the period from ca. 70 to ca. 640 deal with any topic outside of Talmudic history, as defined in Flesher's catalogue in n. 1. So Talmudic history is the only history of the Jews as a group in the period at hand on which Zion published articles as all

pened. If the Talmud attributes something to a rabbi, he really said it. If the Talmud maintains that a rabbi did something, he really did it. So among the 21 articles under discussion, I find not a single one that asks the basic critical questions with which historical study normally commences: how does the writer of this source know what he tells me? How do I know that he is right? On the contrary, the two Talmuds serve, in Zion, as encyclopedias of facts about rabbis and other Jews in the Land of Israel and Babylonia. The task of the historian is to mine the encyclopedias and come up with important observations on the basis of the facts at hand. The work of the historian then is the collection and arrangement of facts, the analysis of facts, the synthesis of facts. It is not in the inquiry into the source and character of the facts at hand. Just as, for the literary scholar, the text constitutes the starting point of inquiry, so for the historian, the text at hand defines the facts and dictates the character of inquiry upon them. This is the case, beginning and end, from Allon to Kimelman.

Whether it is Allon, telling us what Yohanan ben Zakkai meant in his conversation with Vespasian in August 70, on the assumption that Vespasian and Yohanan were attended by secretaries who wrote down their every word, or whether it is Kimelman, telling us about the politics of the priesthood and exilarchate as reported by a story in Yerushalmi Shabbat 12:3, the method is the same. Now I hasten to add that the prevailing assumption need not deprive of all interest and value a given study in Zion. For instance, where the meaning of a story is subject to interpretation, without attention to whether or not the story took place, the article stands on its own, as in the case of Wasserstein on Gamaliel and Proclus and Israi on Abbahu's saying. Again, when the author deals with events on which the Talmud by definition constitutes a primary source, as in the case of Goodblatt's study of the Babylonian Yeshivot, we deal with a very high level of critical acumen. But the bulk of the articles could not have been written in the way that they were written had the authors first of all taken up the critical program of contemporary historical scholarship.

II
THE FIRST CENTURY OF TALMUDIC HISTORY

No one should suppose that the work of Zion met a lower standard of critical acumen than articles and books published elsewhere. The contrary is the case. My impression is that the great Gedaliahu Allon, to name the premier Israeli Talmudic historian of all time, published his best work in Zion. In fact, from the beginning of Talmudic history in modern times, things scarcely have changed. The work of Talmudic history began with three books, all of them completed within approximately one decade, from 1850 to 1860: A. Geiger's Urschrift und Uebersetzungen der Bibel (1857), an effort to correlate the history of biblical translation with the history of Israelite sects in the period at hand; Z. Frankel's Darkhei HaMishnah (1859), a collection of thumbnail biographies of Talmudic rabbis and some other historical observations; and H. Graetz's History of the Jews, volume 4, on the Talmudic period (the first book to be published of his general history of the Jews) (1853). These were the first systematic inquiries into the Talmud as a historical document, as distinct from an interest in the Talmud as a source of law for Judaism.

From the very beginnings of Talmudic history, the critical program of ancient history and of biblical studies remained remote. By the 1850s, biblical studies had attained a quite critical program. From the time of Geiger, Graetz, and Frankel, down to nearly our own time, by contrast, it has been taken for granted that a story in a holy book about an event accurately portrays exactly what happened. The story itself has no history, but it is history. No special interests or viewpoints are revealed in a given historical account. Everything is taken at face value. Since historians and story-tellers stand together within the same system of values, it was unthinkable that anyone would either lie or make up a story for his own partisan purposes. No one ever would wonder, Cui bono? To whose interest is it to tell a given story? Obviously, if a learned rabbi told a story, he said it because he knew it to be so, not because he wanted to make up evidence to support his own viewpoint.

In modern times — beginning long before the Enlightenment — by contrast, people learned to take a skeptical position vis-à-vis the sacred histories and holy biographies of the earlier generations. They asked about the tendencies of stories, the point the storyteller wished to make, and wondered not about whether a story "really" happened, but rather, about the situation to which a given story actually supplies accurate testimony. They asked how the storyteller knew the facts of the case. Who told him? If he was an eyewitness, on whose side did he stand in a situation of conflict? No reporters were present to take down verbatim what was said and done at the various incidents recorded in the Rabbinic traditions. If that is so, then all we have are traditions about such events, given both form and substance on some other, later occasion than that of which they speak. But often we have not traditions but mere legends, fabrications quite unrelated to the events they purport to report.

Such a skeptical attitude had been well established in biblical studies done by non-Jews by the early nineteenth century. Western scholarship in these and related fields had furthermore shown the necessity of analyzing the components of stories and asking how each element took shape and where and when the several elements were put together. But with

Rabbinic materials, aside from some reservations about obvious miracles, one rarely discerns among nineteenth or even
most twentieth century scholars an appreciation of the necessity to understand the historical background of texts in a
manner other than that narrated in the texts themselves. And
when the Rabbinic scholars tried to stand outside the presuppositions of the texts, they did so chiefly for exegetical, not
historical purposes.

III
EXAMPLES OF ESTABLISHED METHODOLO-
GIES

One cannot, however, attempt to refute histories
made up on the basis of Talmudic tales. One can only point
out that such histories are seriously deficient, because they are
wholly uncritical and gullible, omit all reference to the internal
evidence revealed by the Talmudic sources, and exclude from
discussion the literary evidence available in cognate literature.
Nor need one refute the nineteenth- and twentieth-century
historians, who, using the Talmudic materials, go on to rein-
terpret them, to posit new "postulates" about their meaning,
to reject one detail of a story in favor of another — in all, to
lay claim to a "critical" position toward a literature whose historical usefulness is never in the end called into question. In
such histories we have the pretense of critical scholarship but
not its substance. The bulk of the work of nineteenth and
twentieth century historians must be regarded as pseudo-
critical, critical in rhetoric but wholly traditional in all its presuppositions; and in the main, primitive and puerile. Like the
"critical" fundamentalists, who agree that the whale did not
really swallow Jonah, but only kept him in his cheek, or like
the pseudo-orthodox who say it was for three hours, not
three days, the "critical" scholars of the modern period have

scarcely improved upon the traditional picture. They have merely rearranged some of its elements. "Plus ça change, plus c'est la même chose." Nothing has changed, but much is made of the changes.

Two specific examples of the primitivism of the scholarship of so-called "scientific" scholars will suffice.

First, Zecharias Frankel, the founder of the modern study of the Mishnah, the first component of the Talmud, is still taken seriously, as shown by the reprinting of his books and their use in contemporary Israeli scholarship to this day. But Frankel operates in a world of private definitions, circular reasoning, and capricious postulates. For him it is unnecessary to prove much, for one may, through defining things properly, obviate the need for proof. For Frankel medieval commentaries constitute primary sources for the study of the Mishnah. He furthermore claims that Seder Toharot is old because it is the largest order (!); that the ancient Jews were all students of the Rabbinic Torah; that the structure of the Mishnah was revealed by divine inspiration; and numerous other marvels. In what way then is he to be regarded as "modern"? The reception of his book supplies the answer. His enemies accused him of treating the Mishnah in a secular spirit and not as a divinely revealed document, the Oral Torah. They said he regarded the Mishnah as the work of men and as a time-bound document. He even explained Mishnaic laws otherwise than through the Babylonian Talmud. For this Frankel was condemned by the traditionalists of his day. That his work today is taken seriously among traditionalists tells us that what is said in the name of tradition changes from one century to the next. But scarcely a line of his Darkhei Hammishnah can be taken seriously as history.

Second, H. Albeck, in his Mabo Lammishnah (1959) looks upon the Mishnah and Talmud as the culmination of the process of "oral tradition" beginning in ancient times. He takes for granted that anything reflective of non-Scriptural (= oral) tradition, whether in biblical or apocryphal, pseudepigraphic, or Septuagintal literature, is The Oral Tradition of Pharisaic-Rabbinic Judaism. While Albeck is critical of earlier students of the history of the Oral Torah, he does not depart from their frame of reference. Indeed, Albeck takes pretty much the position of Sherira Gaon, founder of Talmudic history in the ninth century, altering details but not the main points. What is striking is that for Albeck the scholarly agenda formulated by Sherira remain uncriticized and unchanged: "When was the Mishnah written?" He extensively reviews and criticizes the ideas of earlier scholars, as if they had supplied him with viable agenda. So we find ourselves once again in the midst of debates on the work of the Men of the Great Assembly, although we have not the slightest shred of evidence about what they had actually done, let alone a document produced by them or in their days. While Y.N. Epstein demonstrated for example, in his Introduction to Tannaite Literature (1957) that the tractate Eduyyot was produced by the disciples of Aqiba at Usha — they are explicitly named throughout — Albeck takes seriously what the traditions from Talmudic times assert, that Eduyyot was produced at Yabneh: "It was ordered according to the names of the sages and the work was done at Yabneh." But he never proves this is so. One may easily show that Eduyyot is different from other tractates, but that difference does not mean it is earlier than the others. Whatever a Talmudic tradition alleges about a tractate is taken as fact. Albeck seldom looks in a thorough and critical way for internal evidence. Again and again one finds circular reasoning. For example, Albeck holds that Rabbi Judah the Patriarch, author of the Mishnah, arranged the material he had received according to a single principle, content, and he did not change anything he had received. How do we know this? Because Judah ordered the material only according to the content of the laws and any material not collected according to this principle was formed into units before Judah received them. We know that they were formed into units in Judah's sources because Judah ordered his material only according to the content of the laws. Likewise, Judah did not change any of the material he received because the sources are not changed. We know the sources are not changed because Judah did not change any of the sources. And so forth. Albeck further disputes the view of Epstein that the Mishnah yielded numerous variations in texts. He says once the Mishnah was edited, it was never again changed. I am not clear on how Albeck understands the work of the early Amoraim, for they seem not only to have changed the Mishnah, but to have stated explicitly that they changed the Mishnah.

Though separated by a century, Frankel and Albeck exhibit the same credulousness and lack of critical acumen. Considering the achievements of scholarship in the intervening hundred years, one may be astonished at how little Albeck's perception of the critical task and definition of the problems has been affected. But Frankel, too, exhibits little mastery of the critical conceptions of his own day.

IV
PRINCIPAL ERRORS OF PREVAILING METHOD-OLOGIES
IN TALMUDIC HISTORY

Let me now generalize from these two examples. I focus discussion on the concrete errors that render useless for historical purposes nearly all work on the Talmud, with the two exceptions specified earlier, namely, interpretation of Talmudic texts in historical context, typified by Wasserstrom's splendid article, and study of Talmudic institutions in historical reality, exemplified by that of Goodblatt. The bulk of the articles in Zion, as well as elsewhere, have taken for granted that the numerous specific stories concerning what given rabbis and other Jews actually said and did under specific circumstances — on a given day, at a given place, in a given setting — tell us exactly the way things were. I speak, then, of a species of the genus, fundamentalism.

The philological fundamentalists have generally supposed that once we have established a correct text of a Rabbinic work and properly interpreted its language, we then know a set of historical facts. The facticity will be proportionately greater the earlier the manuscript and the better its condition. These suppositions are correct. But these facts will concern only what the compiler of the text wished to tell us. Whether or not the original text was veracious is to be settled neither by textual criticism nor by philological research, valuable though both of these ancillary sciences are for the historical inquiry.

The fundamentalists further suppose that any story, whether occurring early or late in the corpus of Rabbinic literature, may well contain valuable information, handed on orally from generation to generation, until it was finally written down. I cannot accept the unexamined opinion held in rabbinical circles, both scholarly and traditional, that all rabbinical material was somehow sent floating into the air, if not by Moses, then by someone in remote antiquity (the Men of the Great Assembly, the generation of Yabneh); that it then remained universally available until some authority snatched it down from on high, placed his name on it, and so made it a named tradition and introduced it into the perilous processes of transmission. By this thesis nothing is older than anything else: "there is neither earlier nor later in the Torah."

Synoptic studies of the traditions of Yohanan b. Zakkai and of the Pharisees before 705 indicate that versions of a story or saying appearing in later documents normally are demonstrably later than, and literarily dependent upon, versions of the same story or saying appearing in earlier documents. This is important, for it shows that what comes late is apt to be late, and what comes in an early compilation is apt to be early. Admittedly, these are no more than probabilities — extrapolations from a small number of demonstrable cases to a large number in which no demonstration is possible. But at least there are grounds for such extrapolation.

I therefore suggest that the fundamentalists' convictions about the nature of the historical evidence contained in the Babylonian Talmud are likely to be false. Whether true or false, the primary conviction of fundamentalism is that the story supplies an accurate account of what actually happened. It is difficult to argue with that conviction. A study of Rabbinic sources will provide little, if any, evidence that we have eyewitness accounts of great events or stenographic records of what people actually said. On the contrary, it is anachronistic to suppose the Talmudic rabbis cared to supply such information to begin with. Since they did not, and since they asserted that people had said things of which they had no sure knowledge, we are led to wonder about the pseudepigraphic mentality. By the time we hear about a speech or an event, it has already been reshaped for the purpose of transmission in the traditions. It is rarely possible to know just what, if anything, originally was said or done. Sometimes we have an obvious gloss, which tells us the tradition originated before the time the glossator made his addition. But knowing that a tradition was shaped within half a century of the life of the man to whom it was attributed helps only a little bit. It is very difficult to build a bridge from the tradition to the event, still more difficult to cross that bridge. The fact is that the entire Babylonian Talmud is a completely accurate record of the history of those who are responsible for it. But the specification of those people, the recognition of the viewpoint of a particular group, place, and time to which the Talmud's various facts pertain — these remain the fundamental task still facing us.

V
TOWARD A RECONSIDERATION OF APPROPRIATE METHODOLOGY

I now wish to offer an alternative set of problems and solutions, a program of inquiry in my judgment more appropriate to the sources under study and to the sort of information we may ask those sources to supply us. In order to offer such a fresh program, I naturally have to begin at the beginning. Let us start with the character of historical study — the field of history itself, the place of Talmudic history within the historical field. History is the noun, the genus, Talmudic history the adjective, the species. Before we can deal with the species, we surely must first attend to the genus.

A subdivision of the vast realm of historical learning marked off solely by information contained in a particular book finds the definition of its program and tasks in the pages of that book. The field of historical study bearing the adjective "Talmudic" covers the age in which the Talmudic canon took shape and to which it refers. That field of history attends to the places in which the people of that document flourished. So the time and place conform to the limits set by the principal source of historical study. The boundaries of topics, too, fall within the bindings of one book. Now to those who study other realms of historical learning, the one at hand must appear artificial, merely theological. In general people define a range of historical inquiry through limits posed by geography, political change to denote beginnings and endings, surely in addition national or ethnic traits that include some and exclude others. More to the point, the pertinent historical information will derive from many different sources, not from a single book. Accordingly, anyone opening a book of history will find puzzling the particular sort of historical study under way here. Specifically, such a person will ask what sort of history may bear the adjective "Talmudic," as distinct from "American," "medieval," or "African," thus national, chronological, or regional, not to mention economic, social, or political. Indeed, who has ever heard of a field of historical study defined by a particular book, unless it is what is in the book that is studied, e.g., constitutional history or the history of New England as seen through Cotton Mather's sermons!

By "the Talmud," all agree, we mean the entire canon of writings of the Jewish sages of Babylonia and the Land of Israel ("Palestine"), a canonical corpus beginning with the Mishnah, closed at ca. A.D. 200, and ending with the Talmud of Babylonia, completed at ca. A.D. 600. These documents to be sure refer to events spread over a longer period of time, specifically from the creation of the world onward to the end of history. They cover, in their scope of commentary, things that are supposed to have happened throughout much of the known world of their day. But in chronology, the account becomes particular to the first-hand knowledge of its authors and editors at ca. A.D. 70 or so, and, in geographical area, it covers the affairs of the Jews in the specified provinces, the one under Iranian, the other under Roman, rule.

In all, Talmudic history cannot be said to deal with great affairs, vast territories, movements of men and nations, much that really mattered then. Even the bulk of the women and men of Israel, the Jewish nation, in the time of the composition of the canonical writings at hand, by the testimony of the authors themselves fall outside of the frame of reference. Most Jews appeared to the sages at hand to ignore — in the active sense of willfully not knowing — exactly those teachings that seemed to the authors critical. To use the mythic language, when God revealed the Torah to Moses at Mount Sinai, he wrote down one part, which we now have in the Hebrew Scripture ("the Old Testament"), and he repeated the other part in oral form, so that Moses memorized it and handed it on to Joshua, and then, generation by generation, to the contemporary sages. Now, to the point, the contemporaries of the sages at hand did not know this oral half of the Torah, only sages did, and that by definition. Only sages knew the whole of the Torah of Moses. So, it follows, the Talmudic corpus preserves the perspective of a rather modest component of the nation under discussion.

How could we define a subject less likely to attract broad interest, than the opinions of a tiny minority of a nation, about the affairs of an unimportant national group living in two frontier provinces on either side of a contested frontier? Apart from learning, from the modest folk at hand, some facts about life on the contested frontier of the ancient world — and that was only the one that separated Rome from Iran, the others being scarcely frontiers in any political sense — what is to be learned here that anyone would want to know must seem puzzling.

VI
LATENT AND MANIFEST HISTORY IN THE TALMUD

Self-evidently, no one can expect to find stories of great events, a continuous narrative of things that happened to a nation in war and in politics. The Jews, as it happens, both constituted a nation and sustained a vigorous political life. But the documents of the age under discussion treat these matters only tangentially and as part of the periphery of a vision of quite other things. But if manifest history scarcely passes before us, a rich and complex world of latent history — the long-term trends and issues of a society and its life in imagination and emotion — does lie ready at hand. For the Talmudic canon reports to us a great deal about what a distinctive group of people were thinking about issues that turn out to prove perennial and universal, and, still more inviting, the documents tell us not only what people thought but how they reasoned.

That is something to which few historians gain access, I mean, the philosophical processes behind political and social and religious policy, class struggle and popular contention. For people do think things out and reach conclusions, and for the most part, long after the fact, we know only the decisions they made. Here, by contrast, we hear extended discussions, of a most rigorous and philosophical character, on issues of theory and of thought. In these same discussions, at the end, we discover how people decided what to do and why. That sort of history — the history of how people made up their minds — proves particularly interesting, when we consider the substance of the story. The Jews in the provinces and age at hand adopted the policies put forward by the sages who wrote the sources we consider. The entire subsequent world history of the Jews — their politics, social and religious world, the character of the inner life and struggle of their community-nation — refers back to the decisions made at just this time and recorded in the Talmud.

A further aspect of the character of the principal sources for Talmudic history, moreover, will attract attention even among people not especially concerned with how a weak and scattered nation explained how to endure its condition. The Talmudic canon bears the mark of no individual authorship. It is collective, official, authoritative. Now were it to hand on decisions but no discussion, that collective character would not mark the literature as special. We have, from diverse places and times, extensive records of what legislative or ecclesiastical bodies decided. But if these same bodies had recorded in detail how they reached their decisions, including a rich portrait of their modes of thought, then we should have something like what the Talmud gives us.

But the points of interest scarcely end there. The Talmudic corpus stands in a long continuum of thought and culture, stretching back, through the biblical literature, for well over a thousand years. Seeing how a collegium of active intellectuals mediated between their own age and its problems and the authority and legacy of a vivid past teaches lessons about continuities of culture and society not readily available elsewhere. For their culture had endured, prior to their own day, for a longer span of time than separates us in the West from the Magna Carta, on the one side, and Beowulf, on the other. If these revered documents of our politics and culture enjoyed power to define politics and culture today, we should grasp the sort of problem confronting the Talmud's sages. For, after all, the Talmud imagined as normative a society having little in common with that confronting the sages — isolated, independent, free-standing, and not — as the sages' Israel was — assimilated in a vast world-empire, autonomous yet subordinate, and dependent upon others near and far.

VII
TOPICS FOR TALMUDIC HISTORY

Proceeding from the explanation of why the species Talmudic belongs in the genus history to the logical next question, we ask ourselves just what sort of history we may expect to compose. The Babylonian Talmud and related literature contain two sorts of historical information: first, stories about events occurring within an estate of clerks; second, data on the debates of those who produced the Talmud. How are these to be used for historical purposes? It is important to specify what those purposes are. We must at the outset recognize that there are many kinds of information we simply do not have, and never shall have, on Jews and Judaism in late antiquity. The Talmud contains very little information on such questions, for instance, as the nature of the inner life, the consciousness and personal hopes of Jews of the day. It has no autobiographical materials, no record of what people thought and felt as private individuals. No one person stands behind a simple sentence. All has been refracted through a shared prism. The whole is a public record, publicly redacted and communally, hence politically, transmitted. Few individuals play a manifest part in the redaction of their own thoughts, much less in their transmission. This seems to me a significant fact: autobiography, letters, the records of individual life are simply not present. It means at the outset that we cannot ask questions about the motives of individuals, their feelings and intentions — the essence of historical inquiry. But there is, in compensation, the record of the collectivity of sages, and, as I have argued, that permits a remarkably contemporary kind of historical study.

Our information on various kinds or groups of Jews, moreover, is limited. The Talmud is not a historical document and was never intended as such. It is the record of the laws and logic, exegesis and episodic theology, of a relatively small group of Jews. One may estimate that about three hundred names of Babylonian Amoraim are mentioned, yet we may guess that a minimum of two hundred thousand, and probably more like half a million, Jews lived in Babylonia and Mesopotamia in Parthian and Sasanian times. Whatever judgments one may make about the rabbis' being "normative" or "more significant" than others are fundamentally theological, not historical. Moreover, when we take seriously the facts of rabbinical life — that the rabbis lived within a relatively limited institutional framework, somewhat like the contemporary monastic communities of Mesopotamian and Babylonian Christianity — we may wonder how far what we do know represents what we do not know. Whatever archaeological data we have of the same place and period — the Dura synagogue and the magical bowls — bear little obvious relationship to what we learn in the Babylonian Talmud. So we cannot ask a great many questions about Jews who are other than rabbis, except in relationship to the rabbis themselves.

The third and most important specification is this: We must at the outset isolate and identify the viewpoint of the texts we study and attempt to separate ourselves from that viewpoint for the purposes of historical inquiry. As I said earlier, we must always wonder, Cui bono? Who is served? What interest advanced? If we neglect to do so, we simply repeat, in modern language, the viewpoint of our sources, rather than attempt to understand and evaluate that viewpoint. When, for example, we concentrate attention on the issues set by the texts, when we merely generalize in historical language the specific stories and ideas presented by the text, then we are doing little more than repeating what is before us in the same propagandistic, tendentious, and partisan spirit in which it was originally composed. This will not serve any useful purpose, for if all we hope for from history is to participate in the world-view of the documents that supply us with information, why study history at all? Why not remain in the tradition of the classical and modern exegetes, who may add their episodic philological hiddushim (artificial refinements, fictional distinctions that make no difference, and other artifices) but contribute nothing new and comprehend nothing more than they are told by the discrete texts they study?

What purposes then do we have in reading the Baby-lonian Talmud for the writing of history? It will not suffice, alas, to say we want to know just how things were. This is na-ive, since "things" encompasses information about trivialities as well as important matters. We must acknowledge at the outset the values and interests shaping our mind and imagina-tion and isolate what we regard as important issues. We must criticize those values and interests. And then we may proceed to the historical problems. What we must seek to know is not just how things were, but just how those things were which interest us, and which the documents in their present state may reveal. What interests us is, naturally, a reflection of our, and not their, situation. So the we is decisive. And we who read the Babylonian Talmud for historical purposes are mod-ern historians, who want to know things of no interest what-ever to classical Jews, or who want to know the same things but in different ways, in ways congruent to our knowledge and understanding of all aspects of reality.

What I want to know, first, is how a community actu-ally functioned: the dynamics of the relationships among various power-groups, and between those groups and the in-choate masses. In many ways my History of the Jews in Baby-lonia6 is an essay not merely in historical knowledge — though that lies at the foundation of everything historians do — but an essay in power. What earlier interpreters saw as eth-ics I see as power. What they saw as objective and eternal truths I see as statements of a particular viewpoint, serving a particular group and its interest; statements reflecting the val-ues and ideals, the imagination, of the special interest groups represented in the documents available to us.

Alongside concern for power is an interest in myth: namely, the stories people told, the beliefs they held, to verify and justify the power-relationships they experienced. Why did people do what they did? Earlier, I denied that we can inves-

tigate individual motivation. But we can ask many questions
about ideas widely held, characteristics of specific groups; issues investigated by historians of religion: What were the beliefs that people referred to in order to understand and explain reality? What were the fundamental convictions about
reality that underlay all their actions? How did they justify
themselves to other people — Israel, gentiles — and before
God? In line with my earlier emphasis on the record of the
collective consensus of individuals, I further want to know
what happened to many people so as to present as self-
evident the mythic world at hand. How do we account for the
formation of the consensus of myth and of power, expressed
in a distinctive mode of powerful discourse, achieved in an
iron consensus within the estate of the clerks, but then,
among the nation at large.

These two, then, power and myth, represent the theoretical interests of our day, these and still a third — function:
How did things work? Granted the existence of power, the
ability of some men to coerce others to say and do their will,
either by force or, more amiably, by moving them through an
internalization of values; and granted the knowledge of the
imagination of those men and their community, knowledge of
their mythic life — granted these two, we ask ourselves, how
did the system work? What defined adaptive behavior in such
a power-structure? What sort of history took place? What institutions embodied the power and the myth, what programs
carried them forward, what was their thrust and dynamism,
and what were the events that at specific times and places
embodied these abstract forces of power and of myth in historical facts?

These then are the questions in my mind as I do my
work. I should confess that at the outset I could not have
specified them. On the contrary, it was in response to the materials I found pertinent to my History that I began to discern

what I wanted to know. I began with chaos, the chaos of the texts and of my own limited historical understanding. Whatever order and sense emerged came forth unanticipated and uninvited.

VIII
FOUNDATIONS OF TALMUDIC HISTORY

But does the Babylonian Talmud serve to answer these questions, and if so, how? What are the principles of historical knowledge by which I can justify historical results? First, it seems to me important to form a view of the whole, rather than to allow oneself to be paralyzed by the exegesis and eisegesis of the discrete texts within the whole that historians supposed were historical, primarily because of their contents and themes. Earlier historians of the Talmud took for granted that what a man was said to have done is what actually was done. What was attributed to him is what he really said. What people claimed happened actually took place. And the record before us is the accurate, detailed, account of what really was said and done. The legal scholar or textual exegesis is interested in the content of the texts; it would not matter to him whether a man really said what is attributed to him, for he wants only to know the legal principles at issue and to trace the rabbis' discussion of those principles through legal literature. The literary critic — and the classical scholars produced brilliant literary criticism of a kind — takes at face value the text before him. He so concentrates on the meaning of words and sentences and their relationships to other words and sentences, that he cannot but accept their content as true. The exegesis and explication of texts, whether by Talmudists or by Biblical scholars, in the very nature of things, tend to produce a fundamentalist spirit.

But if it is time to attempt a critical characterization of the whole, not merely a gullible reprise of suggestive parts, what to characterize? Here, as I said earlier, we need to locate questions both pertinent to our own imagination and appropriate to the Talmud. These questions obviously could not concern what the Talmud purports to tell: Was Aqiba really ignorant until he was forty? Did Rabbah b. Nahmani really get taken up to heaven because his Torah was needed in the heavenly academy? On the other hand, the Talmud does accurately tell what those responsible for compiling it thought about the world around them. It contains substantial materials given en passant, not in a polemical or tendentious spirit. For example, it preserves numerous reports of what rabbinical courts decided in specific cases. These seem to me to possess great historical value, for, while we may never know whether such a decision was actually made on a given day concerning a given litigation, the fact that the tradents certainly believed such decisions could be made is of some sociological interest. The shape of such beliefs, after all, cannot have greatly diverged from the configuration of everyday life, if no polemical or theological interest intervenes.

While the beliefs of the rabbis about times past may be of slight consequence for the description of those times, the belief of the rabbis about what they themselves did every day in their courts seems to me very important in analyzing what the courts actually did. So I do not know whether a man named Samuel really decided thus-and-so in court. But I think the conviction of the generation and school responsible for shaping the story that he had done so accurately portrays how they saw things, and therefore provides us with valuable information on how they viewed the state of their courts and the range of their authority and power. And if, further, we find evidence of a consistent picture, extending for several hundred years, we may then conclude that the courts in general could accomplish pretty much what the rabbis claimed in their behalf. If a picture of an effective court-system emerges, we may then proceed to speculate on the basis for the ability of a group of men to force others to do what they wanted. Obviously, we must take into account not only how the rabbis explained things, but also the facts known to us from quite separate sources of information. In the case of Babylonian Jewry, we need to know about the policies of successive Iranian governments toward the minority communities and their government, and also about other groups and institutions within the Jewish community likely to be able to exercise authority, which are not described in much detail in rabbinical sources.

When it comes to the mythic life of the rabbinical group, we are on still firmer ground, for the Talmud is a rich resource for information on how the rabbinical circles in particular viewed reality. Here again, we may well have the record only of the final period of Talmudic literature. Only through specific and careful investigation can we distinguish what is peculiarly characteristic of the last group of Talmudic tradents and redactors, and what also characterized earlier groups in sequence.

IX
THE PROMISE AND PROSPECTS OF TALMUDIC HISTORY

What will persuade someone primarily interested in historical study, rather than in continuities and changes in culture and society, that the document at hand demands sustained attention in particular as a problem for historians? It is the simple fact that the Talmud provides a striking example, for close analysis, of a problem of acute interest in historical debates even in our own day. I refer to the debates on how we study not the individual but human societies, organized groups, that engage historians from the Annales of the 1920s through Social Science History today. Let me explain.

In describing and interpreting the life of peoples, we seek to generalize about attitudes and shared conceptions, using the French word, "mentalité," for example, to explain that about which we speak. Specifically, we want to know how people form a shared conception of themselves, so as to see themselves as a group, and how, further, what they conceive in common relates to how they each, as individuals, confront and experience life. Louise A. Tilly, writing on "People's History and Social Science History"[3] frames matters in terms of shared emotions and, citing Lucien Febvre, founder, with Marc Bloch, of the Annales, quotes Febvre as follows:

> [Emotions] imply relations between men, collective relationships. They are doubtless born within the organic depths specific to a given individual... [B]ut their expression is the result of a series of experiences of common life, or similar and contemporaneous reactions to the shock of identical situations and encounters of the same nature... [L]ittle by little... by linking many participants in turn as initiators and followers — [these] end by becoming a system of interindividual motivations that differ according to circumstances and situations... [and] a true system of emotions is built. They become something like an institution.

Febvre copes with the deep problems of how peoples' emotions so take shape as to fit a common pattern. That is why he speaks of experiences of common life, identical situations, encounters of the same nature. Now if we take up the same issue framed in terms not of feelings but of the ideas and doctrines that give expression to attitudes and feelings, we find ourselves raising exactly the same questions.

---

[3] Social Science History, 1983:7, 458.

The thesis at hand, that collective relationships expressed through mutually comprehensible emotions emerge, not from what is specific to the given individual, but from what is shared and common, becomes all the more pertinent. Specifically, we take up the social expression of attitudes. We turn then to matters of doctrines and institutions, and issues of governance of groups based on a compact of common values. These all together constitute politics, for the secular world, and theology, for the religious one. In the setting of Judaism, with its interest in what people do as much as in what they think, the whole reaches the surface of everyday life in what we call halakhah, the rules and laws of life. If, then, we can trace the context of consensus and the progress through which consensus is achieved, we find ourselves providing an exceptionally suggestive example for the inquiry into the interplay between the individual and the group, specifically the formation of collective attitudes out of individual experiences.

In the Talmudic corpus we have the end result of half a millennium of the process of attaining concurrence, the achievement of what was at first a caste and class consensus but what was at the end a national compact and agreement. Israel, the Jewish people, in late antiquity produced a minority, the sages under discussion, which to begin with coalesced on its own, and then won adherence to its views, through coercion and persuasion alike, among the nation as a whole. So when we ask what sort of history we may expect from the sources at hand, we find a remarkably relevant sort of discourse. We deal with an example of the long-term formation of collective doctrine, social theory shared among people in diverse times and places, subject to transmission, moreover, from the special circumstances in which the theory took shape to distant and wholly other conditions confronted by the Jewish nation later on. The sources at hand come down

from late antiquity because people agreed to copy and preserve them. They came to that agreement because what they
found in the sources laid claim to truth and authority. The
fundamental thesis of the sources attained that status of utter
self-evidence that made possible debate on everything but the
fundamental issues. These were settled in late antiquity.
Where, when, how they were settled, what sort of "experiences of common life, of similar and contemporaneous reactions to the shock of identical situations and encounters of
the same nature," in Febvre's language, produced these components of a common consensus and endowed them with
self-evidence — these are the issues at hand.

In the conditions of contemporary debate on the nature of historical study, the interest in generalization and the
analysis of collectivities, the concern for comparison of group
to group, the interest in small details and how these typify
large trends, the concern for politics and the influence of ideology — in these conditions the Talmudic historian finds remarkably relevant what in itself is remote, particular, and
rather special. What we have is a collective biography of a
well-organized political and religious estate. But the constant
reference to individual opinion characteristic of the sources at
hand allows for attention to the individual as well. The vigorous debate, the close study of modes of argument as much as
of substance, likewise allow us to address the formation of
shared modes of thought. Self-evidence, in the documents at
hand, is not conferred by politics alone but achieved by argument. Professor Tilly concludes her article with the following words:

> The genius of social science history is twofold. First, its
> central method — collective biography of one kind or
> another — preserves individual variability while identi-
> fying dominant social patterns. Second, its focus on so-
> cial relationships rather than psychological states re-

> mains our surest guarantee of reconstructing how ordi-
> nary people of the past lived out their days and made
> the choices that cumulate into history. Social science
> history, properly conceived, is the ultimate people's his-
> tory.

So far as we wish to trace collective biography, our documents exemplify precisely the sort of sources that make that
work feasible. So far as we take up the issues of social relationships, both within a social group and also between that
group and the outsider, the sources of the Talmudic canon
address precisely the issue at hand. That is why I claim that,
by criteria of contemporary historical debate, the kind of history that bears the adjective "Talmudic" and that emerges
from a rather circumscribed body of sources indeed falls
smack in the center of historical learning today.

X
MY OWN PROGRAM

Let me close with a few remarks about how I have
tried to carry out the program outlined here. Since my work
has never been read and reviewed in this particular setting —
in Zion, I mean — or indeed in any other journal in this important center of Jewish learning, it is surely appropriate to
introduce it to people who do not know it.8 My work began
with precisely the methodology I have rejected, with a history
of the Jews in Babylonia and some parallel studies, all of
which rest upon the givens that the sources mark the beginning of study, not the focus, and that their facts define the
task at hand.

From all that has been said, the reader will realize that
there is not a page, not a paragraph, not a sentence in my
early books that I could write today exactly as I did twenty-
five or even fifteen years ago. The very fundamental category

at hand — "the Jews in Babylonia" — yields a program that stands entirely asymmetrical with the characteristics of the sources. The division by particular periods, for instance, is simply implausible. In order to speak of "the Parthian period" or "the early Sasanian period," I have to take for granted that stories told about events before the rise of Sasanian rule, in the early third century, really took place in the time and circumstances in which the story teller narrates them. What is attributed to rabbis of the period before 200 really was said, before 200, by those rabbis. None of this has been or can be either demonstrated or disproved. And, it goes without saying, in those early studies everything Josephus tells us is fact, pure and simple. But Josephus was not eye-witness to the stories cited here, and we do not know how he found out about these events. To state matters simply, I here assume as data for the composition of manifest history what in fact serve as constituents for that very different, latent history I described earlier.

More to the point, the sources at hand — stories and sayings — cannot be read distinct from the documents that contain those sources. We begin from the whole and work back to the parts. We start with, not the Jews in Babylonia in Parthian or Sasanian times, but Josephus, the Mishnah, the Tosefta, the Talmud of the Land of Israel ("Yerushalmi") and the Talmud of Babylonia ("Bavli"). Let me state with appropriate emphasis. Each of the components, the documents, of the Talmudic canon requires attention as a whole and on its own terms. And if we pay attention to the documents, we shall not find interesting the remnants and shards that these documents contain on the history of the Jews in Babylonia in Parthian times. The documents tell their own story. It is to that story that we must teach ourselves to listen. The documents (except for Josephus) constitute artifacts of culture, testimonies to the inner life of people who expressed their consensus through them — facts of politics, indicators of collective doctrine and dogma, expressions of a small community of clerks and their imagination. So I think it quite correct to say that we need to find out just what happened, what came first and what came afterward. But what happened is not what I described, analyzed, and interpreted in my earlier books. It is the documents that constitute the principal events: social events, cultural and intellectual events. The history must then be the history of the cultural life of a well defined social group and its encounter with the politics and condition of the larger nation of which it formed an active and aggressive component. When we know how the community of sages framed its ideas in the context of its historical and social setting, we shall have learned from the books that community endorsed and transmitted precisely the kind of history they allow us to recover. And, as I argued at the outset, that is exactly the sort of historical inquiry that in our own day proves urgent and compelling.

Let me conclude by referring to the two trilogies that bring to fruition twenty years of reflection and further study of exactly the same texts and problems of historical description, analysis, and interpretation, on which I worked at the outset.

These are, first, the trilogy on the reading of each of three individual documents as historical testimonies: Judaism: The Evidence of the Mishnah, Judaism in Society: The Evidence of the Yerushalmi and Judaism and Scripture: The Evidence of Leviticus Rabbah (all: Chicago, The University of Chicago Press, 1981, 1983, and 1985, respectively). Second is the trilogy in which, reading documents as a whole on critical issues, I carry out the first work of stage-by-stage restoration and renewal: Foundations of Judaism: Method, Teleology, Doctrine, as follows: I. Midrash in Context: Exegesis in Formative Judaism, II. Messiah in Context: Israel's History and Destiny in Formative Judaism, and III. Torah: From Scroll to Symbol in Formative Judaism (all: Philadelphia, Fortress Press: 1983, 1984, and 1985, respectively). The double trilogy shows rather strikingly that Talmudic history enjoys prospects unimagined in its first century, the one that began with Geiger, Graetz, and Frankel, and ended with my History. So let the old — whether in Zion or in my History of the Jews in Babylonia — find its way as a model, not of what to do, but of what not to do. Alas, since most of the historical work on the documents at hand even now remains bound to the old ways, the claim that my History of the Jews in Babylonia marks the epitaph may appear premature. But in fact it is where things indeed did end, and it marks the point from which the future began.

2.

THREE GENERATIONS OF POST-WAR STUDY OF JUDAISM IN GERMANY: GOLDBERG-SCHAEFER, HOUTMAN, AND BECKER AND THE DEMOLITION OF HISTORICAL JUDAISM

I. FIFTY YEARS OF RECONSTRUCTION AND WHAT HAS COME FORTH

A religion without determinate texts, religious texts out of all context, and texts without contents — that is how Judaism is represented in scholarship produced in the German universities in the three generations — master, disciple, the disciple's disciples — since the end of the Holocaust in 1945. The results of fifty years of reconstruction by three generations of scholarship have now come in. They call into question the cultural capacities of German scholarship plausibly to construct an academic account of formative Judaism. I refer to the Judaism of the first six centuries of the Common Era and the enterprise of studying that Judaism in the context of the history of religion. From what the Germans do well, we learn what they cannot do at all.

Why so? Because, for three generations of scholars who have never engaged with the religion in its living expression — a religion realized in the social order as a cultural phenomenon — I shall show here in concrete cases that Judaism and its texts represent a matter of theory alone. And the results of that representation to date call into question whether people who have never seen a religion in actuality, in

35

social reality can ever study any age, remote or contemporary, of that religion cogently and coherently: as a plausible option for the social order. For a religion is not the same thing as a book, and — so it now seems to me — someone who has encountered a religion only in libraries finds exceedingly difficult the act of social imagine required to represent that religion as a cogent social construction.

Those results call to mind the fantasy of turning out surgeons educated in books, who have never seen a real corpse for dissection, let alone performed, an actual operation. They make one think of ethnography by tourists. For pre-Kristalnacht Germany's vital Judaism, the principal source and driving force everywhere of all modern theology, philosophy, and sociology of, and much academic scholarship on, Judaism from the end of the eighteenth century to 1939, was wiped out in the National Socialist period, and in the half-century since 1945 no community of Judaism took shape. If before 1939 nearly all the great works of academic scholarship and theology in late antiquity came out in German, from 1945 onward, for tragic reasons, no one has expected important scholarship or theology to emerge from German Judaism, and none has. The great tradition ended, its heirs and continuators working in the USA and Canada, Britain and the state of Israel.

What happened in the age of remorse and repentance, expressed also in the selection of the topic, Judaism, as an act of cultural contrition? In that context, scholarship on ancient Judaism was left in the hands of scholars who knew Judaism not as a coherent religious culture but as a shelf of library books. And the post War scholars, pursuing Judaic learning as an act of benevolent condescension, perhaps to expiate collective shame, if not collective guilt, quite naturally treated Judaism as something to be read about in books, where nothing of human interest was at stake. They never saw a native, living Judaism in Germany, in the cultural idiom of Germany, and in the state of Israel, they encountered, in their year or two or three of study, nothing coherent and accessible, no Judaic construction of humanistic valence worthy of respect and even emulation.

And in their scholarship Judaism in no way flourishes; it lies inert, a dead religion, not a soaring construction of culture and society in response to divine revelation that formed the center and source of life of a vital community of the faithful. That is what I shall show, for the first three generations, in a reprise of three issues: [1] whether formative Judaism is represented by determinate texts, deriving from a particular time and place, or merely by variant versions of we know not what? [2] Whether the texts of ancient Judaism belong to a particular literary context, or may be read out of all cultural continuity? And [3] whether the "parallels" or variant readings of texts permit identifying the contents of those texts or prevent the description of the religious system and structure that animate the documents at hand?

The first generation is represented by Arnold Maria Goldberg, an apostate Jew, who converted from Judaism to Catholicism; the second generation is embodied by his disciple, Peter Schaefer, also a Catholic; the third and current generation by Schaefer's disciples, Alberdina Houtman (Dutch, not German, for whom Schaefer was a principal dissertation adviser in her Utrecht degree), and Hans-Juergen Becker (doctorate in Berlin with Schaefer).[4] A clear pattern emerges from the principal work (Goldberg-Schaefer) or respective dissertations (Houtman, Becker) of the German school of ancient Judaism. In the works I shall examine the religion, Judaism, is represented as a set of textual problems (Goldberg-

---

[4] The theory of this paper can be tested by the doctoral dissertations of Schaefer's students at Princeton, if and when any degrees are completed there.

Schaefer), who deny that formative Judaism is even accessible through determinate texts. The normative texts of formative Judaism are represented as a set of formal problems, lacking all content (Becker). And the texts are treated as both inchoate and lacking canonical context (Houtman). Represented by the Goldberg-Schaefer-Houtman-Becker school, German scholarship on formative Judaism in the half-century since World War II has demolished the claim in behalf of that Judaism set forth by the scholarly tradition of Wissenschaft des Judenthums down to 1939, to take shape at a particular place and time, in response to a particular set of challenges: texts in context and bearing contents. Rather, in these works, Judaism is denied a history, the status of a social culture. In its formative writings Rabbinic Judaism exhibits no signs of religious vitality, theological cogency, historical presence. It is inaccessible, its writings are comprised by meaningless glyphs, and its texts bear no meaning at all.

The post-National Socialist German academic culture alone can have sustained this mortuary-scholarship, which has offshoots but no corporate counterpart in any other community of scholarship on Judaism, not in Britain, not in France, not in the USA and Canada, and not in the state of Israel. For the Judaism now studied in Germany is that very same dead religion that, beyond the walls of the universities, National Socialism had left in ruins, beyond all reconstruction. The scholars, reducing the religion to a set of textual and philological variants, with all the good will in the world, come along merely to complete the burial. My experience as a visiting professor for a semester at Frankfurt and against at Goettingen, and also as lecturer in many other German universities, yielded not a single encounter with a student who took seriously the religious and historical realities of Judaism — or took an interest in them. Judaism is everywhere a theoretical construct. Whether Lutheran or Catholic or secular, whether in faculties of theology or philology, the students and professors of formative Judaism imagine a dead religion, represented by manuscripts, not a living religion that values and draws nourishment from those manuscripts and their meanings — and that imposes its own hermeneutics on its holy books.

The study of Judaism in Germany at best gives Judaism a decent burial. It lays to rest, in collations of variant readings of texts lacking all consequence, the last remains — the textual monuments — of a once-vital religious structure and system. Denying to it the possibilities of text in history, context in religion, and contents in theology, the German school of ancient Judaism demolishes that intellectual construction that the Jewish School of ancient Judaism in Germany created in the nineteenth and twentieth centuries. It is that historical Judaism that was the discovery and the glory of the great Reformers and their opposition, Zunz and Geiger, Frankel and S. R. Hirsch, Hoffmann and Cohen and Baeck and others beyond listing. The German School of ancient Judaism dismisses Judaism not out of anti-Semitism (though the anti-Semitic tradition represented in the study of Judaism by Emil Schuerer's notorious chapter, "Life under the Law," continues to flourish), but out of incomprehension. That is, the social facts of post-War Germany have offered no other possibility. And those Jewish scholars of ancient Judaism who see matters otherwise gain slight hearing for an account of matters deemed, prima facie, simply implausible.

II.   ARNOLD MARIA GOLDBERG AND PETER SCHAEFER: JUDAISM WITHOUT TEXTS

Professor at Frankfurt University, Arnold Maria Goldberg and his student, Peter Schäfer, Professor, successively, at Frankfurt, Cologne, Berlin, and Princeton, have found themselves so impressed by the obstacles put forth by a fluid and sparse text tradition for some of the Rabbinic canonical documents as to claim we have no documents at all, only masses of variant readings. These they then collect and classify, with no heuristic consequence for the reading of the documents themselves. That nihilistic position defines the task of learning as the assembly of variant readings and the publication, with virtually no critical judgment, of a mass of this and that. Work of a historical and cultural character simply loses its bearings, if we have no documents at all.

Arnold Maria Goldberg, "Der Diskurs im babylonischen Talmud. Anregungen für eine Diskursanalyse," in *Frankfurter Judaistische Beiträge* 1983, 11:1-45 states (in the translation of Peter Schaefer), "Once it has been written, every text is exclusively synchronic, all the textual units exist simultaneously, and the only diachronic relation consists in the reception of the text as a sequence of textual units whose 'first' and 'then' become 'beforehand' and 'afterwards' in the reception of the text...The synchronicity of a text is...the simultaneous juxtaposition of various units, independent of when the units originated."[5]

In his exposition of the matter Schäfer proceeds, "This emphasis on a fundamental synchronicity of the texts of Rabbinic literature is completely consistent with Goldberg's methodological approach. The text as it stands is exclusively synchronic and, since we cannot go back beyond this state, there remains only the classifying description of that which is there...A historical differentiation is deliberately excluded, because in effect the texts do not permit it. Whilst analysis of the forms and functions of a text makes its system of rules transparent, 'the comprehension of Rabbinic texts through habituation and insight could be superseded by a

---

[5]Cited in Peter Schäfer, "Research into Rabbinic Literature," *Journal of Jewish Studies* 1986, 37:145.

comprehension of the rules of this discourse as competence...."[6]

Goldberg's dogmatic definition of matters notwithstanding, a sustained examination of the various documents leaves no doubt whatsoever that we can identify not only "beforehand" but "first," showing that the formation of composites out of fully-articulated compositions took place prior to the definition of a document's distinctive traits. Had Goldberg read my *The Formation of the Jewish Intellect. Making Connections and Drawing Conclusions in the Traditional System of Judaism*. Atlanta, 1988: Scholars Press for Brown Judaic Studies, he would have found ample grounds, based on the logics of coherent discourse alone, to reconsider his position.

The data that prove the exact opposite of Goldberg's premised position emerge fully and completely, for the Talmud, in my *The Talmud of Babylonia. An Academic Commentary*. Atlanta, 1994-5: Scholars Press for *USF Academic Commentary Series*, and in its companion, *The Talmud of Babylonia. A Complete Outline*. Atlanta, 1994-1995: Scholars Press for *USF Academic Commentary Series*. Why Goldberg takes the positions that he does I cannot say, since they contradict the facts of the characteristics of the documents that he purportedly discusses. The facts that are set forth in *Academic Commentary* and *Complete Outline*, indicate that Goldberg certainly cannot have known through his own, first-hand analysis, a great deal about the literary traits of the Rabbinic literature as exemplified by the Bavli. For he seems to have confused a kind of abstract philosophizing with the concrete acts of detailed learning that scholarship requires. That explains why he left no imposing legacy of scholarship to sustain his opinion, which is at once doctrinaire and eccentric.

---

[6] *ibid., ad loc.*

I do not share Goldberg's nihilistic position, because I have shown, on the exactly same basis of phenomenology on which he lays out his view, that the contrary is the fact. Having completed the work on the Talmud of Babylonia, I only now begin the equivalent academic commentary and complete outline for the Yerushalmi, and comparison of the outlines of the Bavli and the Yerushalmi,[7] with the plan of proceeding to the score of Midrash-compilations, so I cannot say what I shall find in continuing a uniform analysis. But the naked eye suggests that Goldberg's position will not find in the other documents any support at all. The documents as we know them certainly encompass not only materials that serve the clearly-manifest program of the framers or compilers of the documents, but also the self-evident interests of authors of compositions and framers of composites who had other plans than those realized in the documents as we have them. But the question is, how do we identify components of a composition, or of a composite, that took shape outside of the documentary framework and prior to the definition of the documentary traits of a given compilation? Unless we take at face value the attributions of sayings to specific, named authorities at determinate times and places, we must work by paying close attention to the material traits of the compositions and composites.

This brings us to the disciple's explicit statement of Peter Schäfer that we have no documents, just variant readings.[8] Lest I be thought to caricature or exaggerate the full confusion that envelopes his position, let me cite his exact language, beginning with his critique of Goldberg and pro-

---

[7]*The Two Talmuds Compared*. Atlanta, 1995-7: Scholars Press for South Florida Studi

[8]"Research into Rabbinic Literature," *Journal of Jewish Studies* 1986, 37:145ff.

nouncement of a still more extreme position; I number those
paragraphs that I shall discuss below.

1. The question that arises here is obviously what is
meant by 'texts.' What is the text 'once it has been written' — the Babylonian Talmud, the Midrash, a definite
Midrash, all Midrashim, or even the whole of Rabbinic
literature as a synchronic textual continuum whose inherent system of rules it is necessary to describe? Indeed, in such a description, neither the concrete text
concerned, nor the form a particular textual tradition
takes, needs to be important. Every text is as good —
or rather as bad — as every other, the 'best" being presumably the one representing the latest redactional
stage.
2. But this is precisely where the problem begins.
Goldberg himself must finally decide on one text, and,
in doing so...must decide against or several other texts.
Whether he wants to or not, he inevitably faces historical questions. This problem can be elucidated by the
second line of research within the 'literary' approach.
3. This second line of research...is that of the interpretation immanent in the work. Complete literary
works are analyzed as a whole, as literary systems so to
speak, and are examined for their characteristic arguments...Neusner has ...sent to press such analyses...The
plane on which this research approach moves...is the
final redaction of the respective work...Two closely related problems arise from this.
4. The approach inevitably disregards the manuscript
traditions of the work in question. But especially in the
case of Rabbinic literature, this is essential. Thus, to
give an example, both Vatican manuscripts of the
Bereshit Rabba...represent texts which are quite different from that of the London manuscript...The variations are sometimes so great that the redactional identity of the work is debatable. Is it meaningful to speak
of one work at all, or rather of various recensions of a
work? But then how do these recensions relate to one
another? Are they different versions of one and the
same text...or are they autonomous to a certain extent,

and is Bereshit Rabba' merely an ideal or a fictitious entity? What then constitutes the identity of the work 'Bereshit Rabbah'? Any preserved manuscript or the modern 'critical' edition by Theodor-Albeck...
5.   The problem becomes more acute when the question of the boundaries of works is taken into consideration. To remain with the example of Bereshit Rabba, the problem of what relation Bereshit Rabba and the Yerushalmi bear to one another has been discussed since the time of Frankel...How are Bereshit Rabba and Yerushalmi related to one another...? Does Bereshit Rabba quote Yerushalmi, i.e., can we regard Bereshit Rabba and Yerushalmi at the time of the redaction of Bereshit Rabba as two clearly distinguishable works, one of which being completed? Did the redactor of Bereshit Rabbah therefore 'know' with what he was dealing and from what he was 'quoting'? With regard to the Yerushalmi, this conclusion is obviously unreasonable, for we immediately have to ask how the Yerushalmi of the Bereshit Rabba is related to the Yerushalmi existent today. The Yerushalmi cannot have been 'complete' at the time of the redaction of Bereshit Rabba since it is not identical to the one we use today.[9]
6.   A brief reference to Hekhalot literature will constitute a last example. This is without doubt the prototype of a literature where the boundaries between the works are fluid. Every 'work' in this literary genre that I have investigated more closely proves to be astonishingly unstable, falls into smaller and smaller editorial units, and cannot be precisely defined and delimited, either as it is or with reference to related literature. This finding is of course valid with regard to the works of Hekhalot literature to a varying degree, but can be generalized as a striking characteristic feature of the whole literary genre....[10]
7.   The questioning of the redactional identity of the individual works of Rabbinic literature inevitably also

---

[9]Schäfer, pp, 146-147.
[10]*ibid., ad loc.,* p. 149.

disavows the research approach to the work at the level of the final redaction. The terms with which we usually work — text, "Urtext," recension, tradition, citation, redaction, final redaction, work — prove to be fragile and hasty definitions that must be subsequently questioned. What is a "text" in Rabbinic literature? Are there texts that can be defined and clearly delimited, or are there only basically "open" texts which elude temporal and redactional fixation? Have there ever been "Urtexte" of certain works with a development that could be traced and described? How do different recension of a "text" relate to one another with respect to the redactional identity of the text? How should the individual tradition, the smallest literary unit, be assessed in relation to the macroform of the "work" in which it appears? What is the meaning of the presence of parts of one "work" in another more or less delimitable "work"? Is this then a quotation i work X from work Y?

8.   And finally what is redaction or final redaction? Are there several redactions of a "work" — in chronological order — but only one final redaction? What distinguishes redaction from final redaction? What lends authority to the redaction? Or is the final redaction merely the more or less incidental discontinuation of the manuscript tradition?[11]

Enough of Schäfer's presentation has now been quoted to permit a simple statement in response.

It is simply put forth: the "text" loses its quotation-marks when we describe, analyze, and interpret recurrent formal properties that occur in one document, but not in some other, or, in the particular congeries at hand, not in any other. To state matters as required in the present context, we simply reverse the predicate and the subject, thus: a writing that exhibits definitive traits of rhetoric, logic, and topic, that occur in no other writing constitutes a text.

---

[11]*ibid., ad loc.*, pp. 149-150

That simple definition permits us to respond to the long list of questions and to sort out the confusion that characterizes Schäfer's conception of matters. Let me systematically respond to Schäfer's unsystematic formulation of his position, which, as we see at the end, rests heavily on his observations of an odd and unrepresentative writing, which may or may not originate in the Rabbinic canon at all.

[1] I shall stipulate that my "document" corresponds to Schäfer's "text." The rest of this paragraph is unintelligible to me. I do not grasp the distinctions that Schäfer thinks make a difference, e.g., between "a definite Midrash, all Midrashim, or even the whole of Rabbinic literature...." Here Schäfer seems to me to shade over into sheer chaos. How the several following sentences relate to one another I cannot discern. I am baffled by the sense of his allegation, "Every text is as good — or rather as bad — as every other, the 'best" being presumably the one representing the latest redactional stage." It is not clear to me whether this is his view or one he imputes to someone else, and, as is clear, apart from Goldberg, I know no one to whom these words even pertain.

[2] Goldberg's comments leave no doubt on his meaning; he denies all possibility of historical or cultural research. This he says in so many words. As I said, in the context of German academic culture, such a result condemns the Rabbinic classics to the dustbin.

[3] Schäfer's characterization of my description ("for their characteristic arguments") proves uncomprehending. I define a document by appeal to the standard indicative traits of classic literary analysis: rhetoric, logic, topic. Rhetoric covers the forms of expression; logic the principles of coherent discourse; topic pertains to the prevailing program, hermeneutics, or even proposition of a given piece of writing. (Not all compilations can sustain such documentary analysis, Mekhilta — dubiously assigned to late antiquity to begin with —

— standing apart from all the other items in the Rabbinic canon, for instance.) Still, Schäfer is correct in his main point: I do focus on what in his terms is "the final redaction of the work," and, in my terms, the definitive congeries of traits distinctive to this complex of composites and no other.

[4] Here Schäfer spells out what he means by disregarding manuscript traditions, and he gives as his example the diverse versions of Genesis Rabbah. But he would do well to address more directly the question of the occurrence of a single pericope in two or more documents. When we find such a case, are we able to identify the document to the definitive traits of which the pericope conforms? If we are, then we can safely describe the pericope within the framework of one document and not the other(s) in which it appears.

When in the mid-1980s Schäfer made these statements, they formed a set of fair and pertinent questions. But they have been answered, and whether or not Schäfer has found the answers persuasive (or has even understood them) I cannot say, since so far as I know, he has not followed up on this point at all. Indeed, his astonishing silence on this matter since he printed the paper at hand suggests that Schäfer appears quite oblivious to work that raised precisely the question he asks — and answered it. I refer in particular to *From Tradition to Imitation. The Plan and Program of Pesiqta deRab Kahana and Pesiqta Rabbati.* Atlanta, 1987: Scholars Press for Brown Judaic Studies. I raised that question when I reflected on Schäfer's problem and systematically addressed the challenge he set forth; that is why it is so disappointing to seek evidence of his serious response to the answer. There I am able to show that pericope common to both compilations conform to the definitive traits that characterize Pesiqta deRab Kahana and do not conform to those that characterize those pericopes of Pesiqta Rabbati that do not occur, also, in Pesiqta deRab Kahana. It is not clear that Schäfer follows the scholarly literature on the very matters on which he passes his opinion.

[5] Here Schäfer wanders a bit, and his problem with "boundaries of works" suggests he cannot hold to a single subject. For the problem of the peripatetic pericope has nothing to do with that of the shared pericope. The entire range of questions he raises here reveals an underlying confusion, which can be overcome by detailed work, an examination of the specifics of matters; this Schäfer has never done for the matter at hand. But, at any rate, for reasons already stated, his questions have nothing to do with the documentary method.

[6] Schäfer here talks about that on which he is expert. His allegation about generalizing from the document he knows to those on which he has not worked therefore hardly demands serious consideration. He can be shown to be wrong in treating the one as in any way analogous, or even comparable, to the other. What he does not know and cannot show, he here simply assumes as fact.

[7] This is the most egregious break in the strain of coherent argument, for here Schäfer confuses the pre-history of documents with the documents as we now know them. What I have said about the phenomenological inquiry into the pre-history of documents suffices to answer the questions that he raises. His questions are probably meant, in his mind, to form arguments in behalf of his fundamental proposition. In fact they are susceptible to clear answers; his labor-saving device of sending up obscure clouds of rhetorical questions accomplishes no good purpose. But for his instruction, let me take up his questions and address those that pertain to the documentary method.

[A] What is a "text" in Rabbinic literature? A text in Rabbinic literature is a writing that conforms to a distinctive set of definitive traits of rhetoric, topic, and logic.

[B] Are there texts that can be defined and clearly delimited, or are there only basically "open" texts which elude temporal and redactional fixation? The Rabbinic canon (with only a few exceptions) contains texts that can be defined and clearly delimited (from one another) by reference to the distinctive congeries of rhetoric, topic, and logic, characteristic of one but not the other, or, as I said, characteristic solely of the one. We can establish sequence and order among these documents, determining what is primary to a given document because it conforms to the unique, definitive traits of that document. What Schäfer means by "open" texts I cannot say, so I do not know the answer to his "or"-question, but what I do grasp suggests he is reworking Goldberg's position.

[C] Have there ever been "Urtexte" of certain works with a development that could be traced and described? The answer to this question remains to be investigated, text by text (in my language: document by document).

I do not know the answer for most of the documents. I have done the work to state the answer for some of them. The Mishnah, it is clear, proves uniform through all but two of its tractates, Eduyyot and Abot. All the others conform to the single program of formulary traits, logical characteristics, modes of exposition and argument. That does not suggest within the Mishnah are not already-completed compositions, utilized without much change; the contrary can be demonstrated on formal grounds alone. Forming compositions by appeal to the name of a single authority, as in Mishnah-tractate Kelim, or by utilization of a single formulary pattern, as in Mishnah-tractate Arakhin and Megillah, or by illustration through diverse topics of a single abstract principle, — all these other-than-standard modes of composition and composite-making do occur. But these ready-made items take up a tiny proportion of the whole and do not suggest the characteristics of an Urtext that would have held together numerous compositions and even composites of such an order. We may then posit (and many have posited) the existence of documents like the Mishnah but in competition with it, formed on other rhetorical, logical, and even topical bases than the Mishnah. But these do not stand in historical relationship with the Mishnah, e.g., forming a continuous, incremental tradition from some remote starting point onward to the Mishnah as we know it.

[D] How do different recensions of a "text" relate to one another with respect to the redactional identity of the text? This repeats Schäfer's earlier question, e.g., concerning Yerushalmi and Genesis Rabbah. Here by text he seems to me, a given saying or story that circulates from one document to another. Part of Schäfer's problem is imprecision in the use of terms, e.g., employing the same word when he means different things.

[E] How should the individual tradition, the smallest literary unit, be assessed in relation to the macroform of the "work" in which it appears? The answer to this question is both clear and not yet fully investigated. It is obvious that we move from the whole to the parts, so the individual composition (Schäfer's "tradition," whatever he can mean by that word) finds its place within the framework of the document's definitive characteristics. But the investigation of the traits of compositions and composites that stand autonomous of the documents in which they occur has only just begin, and only with the continuation and completion of my Academic Commentary will the data have been collected that permit us to deal with this question document by document. For the Bavli we have a set of viable answers; for no other document do I claim to know the answer. For the Mishnah, as I said, I do not think that this is an urgent question, though it is a marginally relevant one.

[F] What is the meaning of the presence of parts of one "work" in another more or less delimitable "work"? Is this then a quotation in work X from work Y? The question of the composition or even composite that moves hither and yon is a variation of the question just now considered. My preliminary probe is in *The Peripatetic Saying: The Problem of the Thrice-Told Tale in Talmudic Literature*. Chico, 1985: Scholars Press for Brown Judaic Studies. Reprise and reworking of materials in *Development of a Legend; Rabbinic Traditions about the Pharisees before 70* I-III. Schäfer does not appear to know that work, which appeared long before the article under discussion here. Here again, he sets obstacles in the path of scholarly progress when he ignores work already in print at the time of his presentation.

[G] And finally what is redaction or final redaction? Are there several redactions of a "work" — in chronological order — but only one final redaction? What distinguishes redaction from final redaction? What lends authority to the redaction? Or is the final redaction merely the more or less incidental discontinuation of the manuscript tradition? These questions suggest only more confusion in Schäfer's mind, and since I cannot fathom what he wants to know, or why he frames matters as he does, I also cannot presume to respond. If Schäfer spelled out with patience and care precisely what he wishes to know, others could follow his line of thought, e.g., what he means by "authority...redaction?" When we look at such unintelligible sentences as, with his underlining, <u>And finally what is redaction or final redaction? What distinguishes redaction from final redaction?</u> we wonder, indeed, whether Schäfer is not simply saying the same thing over and over again.

Schäfer's inattention to how others have responded to precisely the problems he highlights finds its match in the case that comes next, which draws our attention to a failure even to grasp the sorts of data that yield the results of form-analysis.

III.   ALBERDINA HOUTMAN: TEXTS OUT OF CONTEXT

Alberdina Houtman, *Mishnah and Tosefta. A Synoptic Comparison of the Tractates Berakhot and Shebiit.* Tübingen, 1996: J.C.B. Mohr (Paul Siebeck). 225 pp.

Alberdina Houtman, *Mishnah and Tosefta. A Synoptic Comparison of the Tractates Berakhot and Shebiit.* Appendix Volume. *Synopsis of Tosefta and Mishnah Berakhot and Shebiit.* Tübingen, 1996: J.C.B. Mohr (Paul Siebeck). 92 pp.

Alberdina Houtman's monograph claims to set forth "a new way of dealing with the problematic relationship between the Mishnah and the Tosefta." In prior work she finds the faults that the Mishnah is given "higher religious status," research has focused "on a single relationship in terms of unidirectional dependence," and "most of the comparative research was done on the textus receptus of the texts." That prior research has in fact identified multiple relationships she does not concede; had she done so, she would have had no dissertation, no "new methodology." But Houtman insists that she has worked out what she proclaims to be "a new methodology," "a computer-assisted analysis of the texts on the basis of the most important manuscript material, and a computer program was made for the compilation of different synopses. The program can take the Mishnah as a running text to which the Toseftan material is synoptically arranged, but it can also reverse the procedure. This enables an unbiased comparison of the two texts." She then applies this methodology to Mishnah- and Tosefta-tractates Berakhot and Shebiit.

Her thesis is "the texts are interwoven so closely that it is almost possible to consider them as a single literary work." That opaque statement will have pleased our sages of blessed memory, who, after all, did set forth the Mishnah, the Tosefta, and the Yerushalmi, or the Mishnah, the Tosefta, and the Bavli, as single literary works; that is how they wanted us to see the Halakhah, and they were absolutely right. My presentations in Chapters Three through Five show how we may read the Halakhah from the Mishnah through the Bavli as a seamless, unfolding statement. But Houtman has not set forth to prove our sages to have been right about what they created, namely, the Halakhic corpus. She wants the computer to settle some scores of her own, to do so without reference to the contents of the documents. That is something that our sages cannot have approved, because in their view, the Halakhah, not the media of the Halakhah, is what mattered.

Houtman does not seem to grasp that that study has produced, without computers, a much more systematic and complete analysis of the two documents — not two tractates but all tractates! — than her work on two tractates has yielded, and her results (though not her claims for her results, let alone her interpretation) replicates existing work. Nor does she grasp that others, before her, have concluded that if the Mishnah is a highly crafted document, the Tosefta by the same criteria is not. In her own right, then, she presents the diverse relationships between statements in the two documents, some are called "parallel," some "supplementary," some "additional." But as is obvious, all she is doing is recapitulating published findings of long-available work, which she clearly has not dealt with in a scholarly manner. That is why what is important in the dissertation is not new, and what is new is trivial and mechanical — and in the end, chimerical, for, as I said, she wants us to pretend we do not have the Mishnah, but we do.

Clearly, Houtman writes in haste, wishing to establish that she has something new to say, even at the cost of a shoddy and slipshod reading of the prior literature — not the mark of mature scholarship. Now to what Houtman wishes to do on her own. She wishes to attempt a "two-way intertextual comparison." That sounds mysterious, but all she means by that mantric word, "intertextual," is "comparison between two text corpora." She wants to prepare two sets of textual comparisons ("synopses"), one with the Mishnah as running text and one with the Tosefta: "For the one the arrangement of the Mishnah was accepted and the Tosefta material was arranged to it; for the other, the Tosefta was the point of departure and the Mishnah material was synoptically arranged to it. Only after studying both synopses could it be decided which synopsis illustrated the relationship in the best possible way."

Here we come to what has gone wrong, the treatment of Judaism as a religion that is all form, not substance. Specifically, to identify those instances of systematic clarification, the Tosefta by the Mishnah, formalities such as a computer identifies hardly suffice. Rather, one has to pay attention to the context of the Tosefta in relationship with the Mishnah, let alone the contents of the Mishnah and to the substantive, not merely formal, relationship of what the Mishnah says to what the Tosefta says. This Houtman does not do, and her monograph never suggests that she could have conducted Halakhic analysis had she recognized the need to do so. Her grasp of the Halakhah is superficial, seldom transcending the capacity merely to paraphrase the words that are before us and perfectly clear on their own. When, then, I characterize the Tosefta as the Mishnah's first talmud, what I mean is that the Tosefta stands in relationship to the Mishnah as the two

Talmuds (sometimes) stand in relationship to the Tosefta, as I shall illustrate in Chapter Two. These are judgments based on the study of the Halakhah, the logical relationship of one statement to another.

None of this makes an impact on Houtman's formulation of matters, because, so far as I can see, she has a very limited understanding of the documents she claims to study, being able at best to paraphrase what they say, but not to analyze their contents, the logic of what is said, and how the logic of one document's statement relates to that of the other document's statement. I do not see how one can claim to analyze the relationship between two Halakhic documents, if one knows so little of the Halakhah. Only if she reduces the whole to a matter of formalities can the computer do any work at all for her, but only if to begin with she brings to the Halakhah an infirm grasp of matters could she conceive of doing what she has done, which is simply to ignore the substance of matters and to let the computer dispose of formalities.

She undertakes, then, to compose a "hierarchy, parallels, supplementary, then additional material." Forthwith the computer program emerges: "The material can be treated according to this inherent hierarchy: for a given sentence in the basis [sic! read: basic] corpus, the reference corpus can be searched for a complete parallel. If there is a complete parallel, it is placed in a parallel column at the same level as the sentence of comparison. If there is no complete parallel, the reference corpus is searched for supplementary material. If there is, it is placed in the parallel column one level lower than the sentence of comparison. Subsequently, the reference corpus is searched for additional material. If there is any, it is placed one level below the supplementary material. If there is no supplementary material, the reference corpus is still searched for additional material. If there is additional material, it is placed one level below the sentence of comparison. The same procedure is followed if there is indeed parallel material." There follows "a decision tree," leading to this conclusion: if there is both supplementary and additional material, the supplementary material is given first and then the additional material. if there is only supplementary material, or only additional material, then it is reproduced one level below the sentence of comparison." And so on and so forth.

When she reaches the tractates themselves, she wants to know whether the Tosefta tractate "proves readable and intelligible as it is, without falling back on the Mishnah." Had she asked me, I would have answered, [1] some is, [2] some isn't, [3] some may be. Others who have worked on the problem have produced the same results, though worded differently. Consulting completed research would have told her that some passages are readable and intelligible as is, some are not, and some are intelligible as is but still more consequential in dialogue with the Mishnah. She does not pay attention to content, as I said, and therefore she cannot deal with that third possibility at all, even though, I have shown, fully half of the Tosefta falls into that interstitial category of rhetorical independence, but substantive dependence. In other words, Houtman wants to pretend that the Mishnah does not exist, except when she concedes that it does.

Houtman's "synoptic reading of Tosefta and Mishnah Berakhot," consequent upon her reading of each as autonomous literary productions, concludes, "Both works were indeed independent in that each work could be read and understood without the help of the other. At the same time, however, each work presented some literary difficulties. They were comprehensible at a Halakhic level, though there were some scars and irregularities at a literary level." Now comes the issue of relationship: "By considering the synopsis as if the two columns form one compound work — [her footnote:

consisting of either a basic text with explanatory additions and supplements or of two parts of an originally larger corpus] — we will try to establish whether this premise [that the two works have relations with each other] is tenable."

Now to return to our problem: post World-War II scholarship on ancient Judaism in Germany, or, here, under German direction. The scholars can contemplate the opposite of reality because they conceive no governing reality. Specifically, Houtman has the odd notion that we may invent a condition contrary to fact and then conduct research to prove that that condition describes the fact. She asks, How would we read the Tosefta if we did not have the Mishnah? Would it make sense? Yes, it would, she concludes. But so what? For we do have the Mishnah, and its traits continue to make all the difference in forming a theory of the Tosefta. Here is what happens when the ancient texts are taken out of context. Houtman wishes to show that we may read the Tosefta as a free-standing document, as though there were no Mishnah. She finds the Tosefta mostly intelligible, and she is happy with the arrangement of the Tosefta, which she sees as well ordered in its own terms. So if there were no Mishnah, the Tosefta would serve for the same purpose, the presentation of the law.

In fact we do have the Mishnah, and no plausible theory of the Tosefta — if that is what she intends — can be formulated in contradiction to that fact. Not only so, but Houtman as much as admits that fact. Much of the evidence by her own analysis indicates that the Tosefta must be read in relationship to the Mishnah. That is because, she admits, the Tosefta is comprised by various types of material, some of it free-standing, some not, but dependent on the Mishnah, and some of it citing the Mishnah in so many words. Further, some of it is arranged in intelligible composites, some of it set forth in composites that derive cogency only from their relationship to the Mishnah (but that is something else that Houtman does not notice). In producing these results of hers, moreover, she recapitulates work complete and in print twenty years ago, part of which she knows but has not understood, part of which she does not appear even to have examined at all.

Houtman moreover simply ignores the substance of the documents and concentrates on the form — hence texts without contents! At no point does she ask about the relationship, as to logic and premise, between the law set forth in the Mishnah and the law set forth in the Tosefta. Had she done so, she would have noticed that the Mishnah's formulation of the halakhah invokes a principle that is logically prior to, and that is presupposed by, the Tosefta's formulation of the same, corresponding halakhah. But to do so, she would have had to study the halakhah of the documents — pay attention to matters of substance. She would, in other words, have had to enter into, to master the interiorities of the halakhah. Apart from her power to paraphrase what is clear in the text itself, however, she shows no Halakhic acumen or perspicacity. That is why she can treat the Mishnah and the Tosefta as simply co-equal statements.

But had she looked at the sequence of statements of a Halakhic character on a given topic (from the Mishnah to the Tosefta to the Yerushalmi to the Bavli, or, if she liked, from the Tosefta to the Mishnah and so on), she would have noticed that the Mishnah consistently sets forth what is logically, Halakhically primary and fundamental, the Tosefta consistently amplifies, instantiates, and extends the Mishnah's generative halakhah, the Yerushalmi adds only little halakhah but much analysis, and the Bavli, less halakhah but still more analysis. For the Tosefta, Yerushalmi, and Bavli set forth only new details about the Halakhic topic with its interior logic that the Mishnah has defined in its basic characteristics. The subsequent documents carry forward the exposition. As a matter of fact the Halakhic structure — topics, problematics — emerges nearly whole and complete in the Mishnah, to be refined and amplified and complemented later on, but never to be vastly reconstructed as to its generative categories. Reading the Tosefta outside out of relationship with the Mishnah — as if we had no Mishnah — as Houtman does proves possible only if we ignore all questions of content, as Houtman, alas, has done. Scholarship that simply ignores the substance of the texts that are studied exhibits nihilism. Like others of the Goldberg-Schäfer School, by ignoring the substance of the documents in favor of their formal traits, Houtman treats with contempt the religion, Judaism, that values the contents, the substance of these documents, not only the formal problems they manifest. So Houtman ignores questions of history and context. She does not prove that the framers of compositions and composites in the Tosefta did not have the Mishnah in hand. She takes a simpler route. She simply posits a condition contrary to fact — the Tosefta read without the Mishnah — and then *tout court* conducts a massive exercise in illustrating the result of a premise contrary to fact.

IV.   HANS-JÜRGEN BECKER: TEXTS WITHOUT CONTENTS

Hans-Juergen Becker, *Die grossen rabbinischen* **Sammelwerke Palaestinas. Zur** *literarischen Genese von Talmud Yerushalmi und Midrash Bereshit Rabba.* Tuebingen, 1999: J. C. B. Mohr (Paul Siebeck). 218 pp.

Hans-Juergen Becker, newly-appointed Professor of New Testament and Ancient Judaism at Goettingen, here presents his dissertation, devoted to relationships between Genesis Rabba and the Talmud of the Land of Israel. Specifically, he compares the wording of passages that occur in both documents, not the documents as a whole, which are essentially autonomous of one another, except at a handful of intersecting passages. More exactly, Becker takes four points at which comparable compositions occur in both documents:[1] narratives of Creation at Y. Hag. 2:1 and Gen. R. 1-12; [2] Halakhic texts in Genesis Rabbah with parallels in Yerushalmi, [3] Genesis Rabbah parallels in the Babottractates of Yerushalmi, and [4] the narratives of the death of R. Samuel bar R. Isaac. At each point he identifies "parallels," undertakes analysis of components of those parallels ("einzelanalysen"), and attempts then to draw some conclusions. These conclusions of his, alas, are uniformly indeterminate, e.g., "In Bezug auf die Schoepfungs-Aggadot insgesamt ist festzuhalten, dass unsere Textvergleiche nicht zu der einen Quelle gefuehrt haben, aus der alle diese Traditionen fliessen, sondern zu mehreren verschiedenen Quellen, von denen widerum verschiedene Fassungen existierten" (p. 60). Given the deplorable condition of MS evidence and text traditions, what other conclusion can have been anticipated? So too, "...ein wichtiges Ergebnis unserer Einzelanalysen festgehalten werden, dass eine dirkete Uebertragung der untersuchten Texte aus dem Y in der BerR oder umgekehrt in allen Faellen ausgeschlossen ist" (p. 101) — I wonder who thought otherwise? On the relationships of Gen. R. parallels to the Babas: "die jeweiligen Versionen sind nicht direkt voneinander abhaengig; die verwendeten Traditionen lagen Y und BerR bereits in verschiedenen Fassungen vor...," and so forth (p. 132). And finally, on the diverse readings of the story of R. Samuel's death, "Die unvollstaendige Textevidenz, die einen direkten Vergleich zwischen Vorlage(n) unter Bearbeitung ausschliesst, tragt aber ihr Teil dazu bei, die redaktionskritische Arbeit auch an einzelnen Punkten dieser fluktuierenden Ueberlieferung beinahe unmoeglich zu machen" (p. 148).

The upshot is, a great deal of industrious work of detail has produced some unsurprising conclusions about the indeterminacy of readings of compositions and composites shared among kindred documents. I do not think anyone who has worked on these documents over the past century will find that conclusion astonishing. The explanation of the project is equally puzzling: "Diese Arbeit behandelt rabbinische Texts als Texte" (p. 1), something I thought pretty commonplace. Who thinks otherwise?

Then to what end? Becker directs the entire project into a critique of the documentary reading of the Rabbinic classics, a matter that, his discussion and bibliography indicate, he grasps imperfectly, if at all. None of the pertinent documentary analyses nor their companions appears in Becker's bibliography. But that bibliography does include a sizable proportion of items not cited in the text. The upshot is infelicitous. Becker does not seem to understand what is alleged, and not alleged, in that documentary theory that he has written an entire dissertation to disprove but that he has to begin with not conscientiously researched. This is not the old German tradition of a thorough Auseindersetzung with traditions of research. But that his data have slight bearing on the documentary hypothesis in no way deprives the dissertation of considerable value in its own terms. Despite the indeterminacy of his diffuse results, his dissertation contains many useful observations about this and that. Anyone interested in the texts he addresses will find indispensable his presentation of the variants and other text problems.

But in the context of this essay, that net-result once again illustrates what has not happened in the post-World-War II reconstruction of scholarship in Germany on formative Judaism. That is, to lay the foundations for the study of formative Judaism as a historical and religious phenomenon and problem. The Germans only deal with texts, not their context or their contents. Stated otherwise, they are proficient at collecting, but not interpreting, manuscript-variants: all form, no substance.

3.

HARRINGTON, STERN, AND ILAN

EVALUATING THE CRITICISM OF A NEW GENERATION

Part of the task of systematic learning requires address to the criticism of colleagues, young and old alike, and, over the years, I have undertaken in various books and articles, not only in casual footnotes, to take seriously the comments of others. Three young critics call attention to perspectives I might otherwise have missed, and I hasten to address their comments on various books of mine. As a long-time professor in graduate education and director of scores of doctoral dissertations, masters theses, and undergraduate honors papers, I am used to grading students' work. So, in the American system, I assign grades to the initial published work of today's future scholars, whose work wins them a C-, a D, and a B, respectively.

As I shall demonstrate, the three have in common a deplorable ignorance of that about which they pass their opinions. All undertake to criticize a hypothesis and method, an entire *oeuvre* and a fully-spelled out position that have been imperfectly mastered, to say the least. None has had the interest in directly addressing questions to me about impressions formed on the basis of this or that. I do answer my mail and should have been pleased to set them straight had they inquired. In my judgment, therefore, all mark themselves as poor, impatient readers and slovenly scholars, rushing into print on the base of half-baked impressions of we know not what. But one of the three, at the very least, has a glimmer of what is at stake, and that one won the grade of B for herself.

I.

HANNAH K. HARRINGTON ON
JUDAISM: THE EVIDENCE OF THE MISHNAH

Reviewing my PURITY IN RABBINIC JUDAISM,[12] Hannah K. Harrington, Patten College, devotes most of her attention to a book not announced as subject to review, which is my JUDAISM: THE EVIDENCE OF THE MISHNAH.[13] The review cannot be classed as an important one, but it makes a mistake that is both elementary and common among beginning scholars: she forgets the title of the book subject to her review.

Harrington starts with the announced title. She begins with a brief comment on the Purity-book. She states, "Neusner is unclear whether uncleanness is a 'natural' or 'unnatural' condition." I find it hard to understand what she means by "natural" and "unnatural," as distinct from natural and unnatural without quotation-marks, which ordinarily signal an unconventional meaning. The issue she raises is not spelled out. But a simple reply seems appropriate. Uncleanness comes about in part through natural processes, so I should take for granted it is a natural condition, but I do not know whether it is a "natural" condition.

It is at this point that she changes the subject of her review, moving from PURITY IN RABBINIC JUDAISM to JUDAISM: THE EVIDENCE OF THE MISHNAH, when she then proceeds with the following:

---

[12]*Purity in Rabbinic Judaism. A Systematic Account of the Sources, Media, Effects, and Removal of Uncleanness.* Atlanta, 1993: Scholars Press for South Florida Studies in the History of Judaism, writing in *Religious Studies Review* 1995, 21:340

[13]*Judaism. The Evidence of the Mishnah.* Chicago, 1981: University of Chicago Press.

> Second, he asserts that the Mishnah has developed independently of Scripture but that 'as soon as it gets underway' the Mishnaic system 'turns naturally to Scripture' for its fundamental data. What caused the Mishnah to 'get underway'?
>
> Third, Neusner portrays the Mishnah as a philosophy without morality or theology. He overlooks the legal genre of the Mishnah; it is no more a philosophical treatise than a theological one. Additional, to assume that any community, let alone a 'Judaism,' can be adequately characterized solely by the rituals of the Mishnah is implausible.

These two points are worth attention, even though they have little to do with the book under review, because they represent commonly-expressed questions about my work on the Mishnah.

What caused the Mishnah to "get underway"? I take for granted that, in general terms, since the Mishnah, coming at the end of the second century, lays heavy emphasis on the relationship of the sanctity of Israel the people to Israel the land, and since, it is broadly agreed, the document came to closure at the end of the second century, the work on the Mishnah's system as a whole was precipitated by issues of that time and circumstance. That is, the Mishnah as a complete system, coming to full exposure after the Bar Kokhba War, responds to one fundamental issue facing Israel in the aftermath of that war, which is the question of what remains of the foci of sanctification that had formerly centered in, and emanated from, the Temple. The Mishnah's systemic answer affirms that what survives endures in the condition of sanctification.

As to the genre to which the Mishnah is alleged by Dr. Harrington to belong, I am puzzled by two matters, first, her certainty of the genus of the document, second, her confidence that the document belongs to an identifiable genus. I think it is sui generis.. For, as I have said in my replies to E. P. Sanders's often-repeated allegation, echoed her, about the generic classification of the Mishnah, a book is not a genre, and to show that a book belongs to a genre, we need more than a single example of the alleged genre. But I do not know how a genre can be defined by a single book, and I also do not know of a single document among ancient Judaisms that compares with the Mishnah in any way whatsoever, whether in language, or in program, or even in size.

The next document in the history of Judaism that may fall into the genre defined by the Mishnah is Maimonides' Mishneh-Torah. Dr. Harrington declares that the Mishnah is not a philosophical treatise. She ought to examine the arguments and evidence set forth in *Judaism: The Evidence of the Mishnah, Judaism as Philosophy, the Philosophical Mishnah,* and a variety of other monographs of mine, which may change her opinion on that matter.[14] As to the documents in which standard theological issues are addressed (as distinct from philosophical ones), I turn her attention to *Transformation of Judaism,* which traces the movement from philosophy to relig-

---

[14]*The Philosophical Mishnah.* Volume I. *The Initial Probe.* Atlanta, 1989: Scholars Press for Brown Judaic Studies; *The Philosophical Mishnah.* Volume II. *The Tractates' Agenda. From Abodah Zarah to Moed Qatan.* Atlanta, 1989: Scholars Press for Brown Judaic Studies; *The Philosophical Mishnah.* Volume III. *The Tractates' Agenda. From Nazir to Zebahim.* Atlanta, 1989: Scholars Press for Brown Judaic Studies; *The Philosophical Mishnah.* Volume IV. *The Repertoire.* Atlanta, 1989: Scholars Press for Brown Judaic Studies; *Judaism as Philosophy. The Method and Message of the Mishnah.* Columbia, 1991: University of South Carolina Press. I have now carried this matter forward, with interesting results, in *Jerusalem and Athens: The Congruity of Talmudic and Classical Philosophy.* Leiden, 1997: E. J. Brill. *Supplements to the Journal for the Study of Judaism.*

ion;[15] as to the movement from religion to philosophy, this is adumbrated in a variety of later work of mine. On the matter of the movement from philosophy to theology, she ought to open JUDAISM STATES ITS THEOLOGY.[16] The upshot is, if she is going to review the author rather than the book, she ought to be sure she knows the oeuvre of the author she claims to review.

I share her view that the Judaic religious system of a community of Judaism is to be described through all of the evidence, in all of the media, that we have. I have not done so in the work to which she makes reference. I describe the Judaism of the document, not the Judaism of the time of the document, not the Judaism of the Jews of the period of the document. The entire intent is contained within the title, JUDAISM: THE EVIDENCE OF THE MISHNAH. The title makes clear that I have subjected the Mishnah to a systematic systemic description, analysis, and interpretation: the system of *that* document, that alone. At several points in that book I explicitly stated that the Mishnah stands only for itself; it does not tell us about the condition of all of the Judaisms of its age, let alone of all Judaisms in all places or times (for such a single, encompassing, coherent, linear, harmonious Judaism never has existed in time and space, but only, perhaps, in theologians' minds); it does not inform us even about all of the ideas that its framers may have had in mind but did not include in their document; the book promises, and delivers, what it says, which is, a systemic analysis of a single, vast

---

[15] *Jerusalem and Athens: The Congruity of Talmudic and Classical Philosophy.* Leiden, 1997: E. J. Brill. *Supplements to the Journal for the Study of Judaism.*

[16] *Judaism States its Theology: The Talmudic Re-Presentation.* Atlanta, 1993: Scholars Press for South Florida Studies in the History of Judaism. My initial effort in this area is *From Literature to Theology in Formative Judaism. Three Preliminary Studies.* Atlanta, 1989: Scholars Press for Brown Judaic Studies, but, predictably, she knows nothing of that book either.

document. From the earliest publication of the book, all reviews have imputed to the book a program that the book explicitly declares does not define the problem undertaken in its pages.

I do not think Dr. Harrington has grasped what documentary description entails — or what such an account does not claim to set forth. Her characterization of matters in the language "rituals of the Mishnah" is puzzling; the Mishnah vastly transcends narrow ritual questions, and I am surprised that Dr. Harrington has not understood that fact. Her again, she need not focus on my claims to that effect; she need only study Maimonides.

Finally, I find it odd that in reviewing one book of mine, she has preferred to pass her opinion on another one, and I wonder at the willingness of her editor, Dr. Martin Jaffee, who assigned the book to her and who did his doctorate with me, to permit such confusion, for, if she does not know the difference between the one title and the other, he certainly does. Her review should get a D, but we shall award her a C- for exemplary effort; and her editor gets a flat F.

II

SACHA STERN ON

JUDAISM AND ITS SOCIAL METAPHORS
ISRAEL IN THE HISTORY OF JEWISH THOUGHT

In his work on "Jewish identity" in ancient times,[17] Sacha Stern, Jews College, London, devotes a unit of his introduction to "Neusner on Jewish identity." Here I find myself puzzled, never having written a line on that subject, which is peculiarly modern in its provenience. He refers, in

---

[17] *Jewish Identity in Early Rabbinic Writings*. By Sacha Stern. Leiden, 1995: E. J. Brill. *Arbeiten zur Geschichte des antiken Judentums und des Urchristentums*. Edited by Martin Hengel, Peter Schäfer, Pieter W. van der Horst, Martin Goodman, and Daniel R. Schwartz, Volume 23.

fact, to JUDAISM AND ITS SOCIAL METAPHORS,[18] a study of
the meaning of the theological category or concept, "Israel,"
in various documents of Rabbinic Judaism, each read as a
free-standing statement, all read in the conventional sequence
that scholarship today assigns to them.

His summary of the results hardly wins confidence,
for here is what he has learned from the work:

> "Neusner identifies a chronological develop-
> ment in the Rabbinic perception and use of the term
> 'Israel' — and hence by implication, in the perception
> of Rabbinic self-identity."

Nothing could be further from the truth; Stern makes several
gross errors. First, I am baffled to know how Stern leaps
from "the term Israel" to "Rabbinic self-identity," since by
"Israel" our sages of blessed memory mean, all Israel, the entire holy people of God, children of Abraham, Isaac, and Jacob. "Self-identity" is simply no issue in that work. Second, I
do not identify a chronological development in Rabbinic
perception and use of the term, I identify a documentary sequence of presentations of the term and further claim to correlate one presentation with the systemic traits of one corpus
of documentary representations, and another presentation
with the temporal context (as defined by contemporary conventional dating) of another corpus of documentary representations. I do not claim that these representations stand in sequence, nor, obviously, do I maintain that the documents at
hand contains all opinions held by their compilers, let alone
everyone in their day. I allege only that, in these documents,
this is what the compilers chose to say, and I attempt, then,
to relate what they say about the category at hand to the
broader systemic program of said documents. None of this

---

[18]*Judaism and its Social Metaphors. Israel in the History of Jewish Thought.* N.Y., 1988: Cambridge University Press.

emerges in the flaccid summary that Stern supplies. But it gets worse. For Stern wishes to translate everything into the one thing that he has defined as his focus of interest. His summary of my results wins still less confidence, since he has reduced a rather substantial and nuanced discussion to the following:

> "He distinguishes between an earlier period, 70=300 CE, where 'Israel was only viewed in Rabbinic sources as a taxonomic abstraction which hardly represented social reality, and the post-Constantinian period of circa 300-600, where Neusner suggests that in reaction against Christianity, 'Israel' took on the vividness of a real social group, as a family, a chosen people, or as a nation."

The picture of the earlier period, as I draw it, yields by Israel a taxonomic component of a system of hierarchical classification; that utilization of "Israel," coherent with the Mishnah's system throughout, serves only within the systemic context; it forms no social judgment, no account of the here-and-now. And neither does the reconstitution of "Israel" in the next set of documents, which forms an equally systemically-bound construct and serves the interests of the system-builders of the later period. I do not think Stern understands that fact.

Stern is troubled by the conception that documents provide a determinate point for the reading of their data. I maintain that if a document has reached closure (as the generality of scholarship may assume) in ca. 200, then the document tells us the state of opinion of its own framers as of that date. The document does not tell us the state of public opinion, nor does it indicate who else, at that time, or at any earlier time, held that view. The document provides one heuristic setting, but excludes none. No one alleges that a story told in the third century was not told in the first; we have no information on that subject. All I maintain is that, in the context of our document, the story attests to views held by some framers of a piece of writing at that time.

Echoing the complaint of Harrington, Stern is troubled, also, by the "generic nature" of the sources, in that the materials of the Mishnah-period "consist exclusively of Halakhic material...His second period is documented exclusively with Aggadic material." He could not more drastically misrepresent both sets of writings and I wonder whether he can mean what he has said. Let me state very simply that he has drastically misrepresented the character of the contents of the documents he claims to describe. No one who has opened the Mishnah, Tosefta, Sifra, Sifré Numbers, Sifré Deuteronomy, or Mekhilta Attributed to R. Ishmael can concur that these documents consist "exclusively" of Halakhic material, and how he can allege that the Yerushalmi is "exclusively Aggadic" defies my powers of explanation. He is simply wrong, and, since he is not an ignorant man or a charlatan but presented this dubious dissertation for a doctorate at Oxford University and now finds employment at Jews College, London, we shall have to suppose he has been carried away by his youthful enthusiasm and inexperience. In time to come he will write more carefully. He goes on to allege the following:

> This leads Neusner to the illusion that the earlier concept of 'Israel' was only abstract and taxonomic, and that 'Israel' came to be perceived as a concrete reality only in the post-Constantinian period.

In so stating, Stern shows he not only writes in a slovenly way, but he reads impressionistically as well. What I maintain is that the documents of the earlier period represent matters in one way, and the documents in the later period, in a different way. I further propose an explanation for why framers of documents of a later period will have found important for their systemic work considerations that the framers of the earlier writings did not deem consequential for their writings. That is a far cry from "came to be perceived," and it appears that Stern misconstrues the entire claim of the documentary hypothesis. He seems to think only in within the limits of a gross and vulgar historicism.

That that is the case is shown in the sentences that follow the allegation just now cited:

> In fact, this 'change' may not reflect a histori-cal development, as Neusner concludes, but rather a literary, generic difference between his sources; indeed, Halakhic sources are most likely, as legal works, to refer to 'Israel' as a 'theoretical' category rather than as ac-tual, lived reality; whereas Aggadic passages would be most likely, by nature, to relate to Israel a concretely experienced in lived reality.

But I do not use the language of "development" at all, since even in 1987, when I wrote that work, I had abandoned the last shards of historicism as a medium of learning. So here he goes again. I discern no "historical development," only a se-quence of portraits deriving from sequential writings, just as he says.

But at this point, Stern shades over into gibberish — language that sounds nice but says nothing. For Stern's allega-tion that Halakhic sources will refer to Israel as a theoretical category rather than as actual lived reality, etc., is simply fab-ricated for the occasion; he offers no evidence, nor argument, in behalf of his surmise. He could have framed matters in precisely the opposite way with the same degree of enthusi-asm, on the one side, and absence of rigorous argument, on the other. Here is a case of making things up as one goes along, and I am startled by the thought that his doctoral su-pervisor at Oxford did not notice and call his attention to the routine requirements of academic learning: evidence and ar-gument, not merely allegation. Finally, Stern states in conclusion:

> ...it would be absurd to conclude that aggadah,
> and hence the Aggadic concept of 'Israel,' did not exist
> in this [the Mishnaic] period. The virtual absence of
> references in the Mishnah to "Israel" as a real people
> does not imply that the authors of the Mishnah were
> unaware of this notion. In this respect, Neusner relies
> on a fallacious argument a silentio.

Here is more gibberish. Indeed, once more, we find Stern
imputing to me opinions I do not hold and positions I have
never expressed. I do not say, in the book that he claims to
have read or anywhere else, that the authors of the Mishnah
were "unaware of this notion." I do say that I accurately
characterize what the authors of the Mishnah state. I do not
know what they knew or did not knew, let alone what anyone
else in their day knew or did not know. I do not even know
what he means when he speaks of "the virtual absence of references in the Mishnah to 'Israel' as a real people"! If Stern
imagines that the framers of the Mishnah did not deem their
"Israel" to form a real people, in a palpable, this-worldly
sense (as, for instance, Philo seems to have), then he once
more gives evidence of never having read a line of the Mish-
nah/

In sum, Stern attributes nonsense to me, and he then
proposes to refute nonsense by a flood of more nonsense. I
find myself puzzled by his haste to publish silly things. Here
is a case of a young man rushing into print without doing his
homework carefully. His treatment of "Neusner on Jewish
Identity" rates a D.

III
TAL ILAN ON *A HISTORY OF THE MISHNAIC LAW OF WOMEN*

Now we come to less dismal scholarship. In her work on women in ancient Judaism,[19] Tal Ilan, Hebrew University of Jerusalem, summarizes (p. 17-18) the main point of my *History of the Mishnaic Law of Women*[20] in the following language:

> "the Mishnah's purpose is to enable every Jew who is not a priest to live a life of holiness comparable to that prescribed for priests… Furthermore, he stated, the Mishnah does not concern itself with everyday life but rather tries to regularize the very marginal situations in which the distinction between purity and impurity is not obvious, in order to preserve the holiness of the Jewish people against any mitigating defect. Accordingly, the tractates of the Order of Women treat those stages in a woman's life…in which, because her personal status is not clearly defined, she endangers the holiness of the men with whom he comes into contact…"

Further, she states,

> Neusner also offered his existential justification for studying the Order of Women — or any other work — in isolation, without reference to any other contemporary work, in the case of women or any other matter. Neusner determined that it is in fact impossible to write the true history of women and that all that the historian can do is study the history of a particular source and its attitude towards a particular subject, in this case women. In the end, Neusner neither wrote nor tried to write a history of women, but he did help

---

[19]Tal Ilan, *Jewish Women in Greco-Roman Palestine. An Inquiry into Image and Status. Texte und Studien zum antiken Judentum 44*. Tübingen, 1995: J. C. B. Mohr (Paul Siebeck).

[20]*A History of the Mishnaic Law of Women*. Leiden, Brill: 1979-1980. I-V. I. *Yebamot. Translation and Explanation*; II. *Ketubot. Translation and Explanation.*; III. *Nedarim, Nazir. Translation and Explanation*; IV. *Sotah, Gittin, Qiddushin. Translation and Explanation. V. The Mishnaic System of Women.*

clarify how the sources relate to them.[21]

She concludes (p. 19):

> Neusner and his students have made real con-
> tributions but their work reveals also the weaknesses of
> Neusner's system, which can inform directly and in
> great detail about the treatment of women in each indi-
> vidual sources but reveals nothing about the actual
> condition of women during the period in which the
> source was written.

Ilan has rather general impressions but no precise
understanding. Let me correct her mistakes.

I do not maintain the view of the Mishnah's purpose
that she attributes to me, though I do maintain that part of
the program of the Pharisees, as represented by the Mishnah's traditions attributed to pre-70 authorities, is exactly
what she says.

I do not think Ilan grasps the English of my discussion, at which I speak of not the marginal situation but the interstitial situation, and she evidently thinks these are the same.
But they not only are not the same but stand for quite differ-

---

[21]She further has my students following in my footsteps, speaking of W. C. Trenchard as an outstanding one. I published Trenchard's
Ben Sira's View of Women in Brown Judaic Studies, but he never studied
with me, and, in fact, I do not believe I have ever met him. I published his
work because I thought it was good. She further refers in the same context to a woman who did complete a doctorate with me, Judith Wegner,
Chattel or Person: The State of Women in the Mishnah. But I reject any responsibility for the published boo, which was vastly revised. Much in the published book is to be deplored. On this matter, see Herbert Basser's
trenchant criticisms of her reading of Rabbinic law in his essay, "Femi-
nism and Mishnaic Law," in Jacob Neusner and Alan J. Avery-Peck, editors, *Judaism in Late Antiquity.* Volume Three. *Where We Stand: Issues and
Debates in Ancient Judaism* (Leiden, 1999: E. J. Brill). Basser further has set
forth his views elsewhere in this volume.

ent relationships. I hold that as a classifying and hierarchizing system, the system of the Mishnah focuses especially on the problems of classification, therefore hierarchization, inherent in interstitial classes of persons or objects.

Worse still, I never imagined that woman "endangers the holiness of the men with whom she comes into contact," and I do not know where Ilan formed such a strange impression. Once more, the imprecision of her reading probably derives from a hazy knowledge of the English language. Scholarly Hebrew often leaves the impression of

Her summary of the documentary hypothesis as accurate so far as it goes, but none of the governing considerations and principles of that hypothesis emerges in her superficial statement of matters.

To her credit, Ilan has understood the difference between systemic analysis of documents and historical description of the everyday world of ancient times. For her main point is quite valid: we can study what the sources tell us and try to find the systemic context, within a document, for its treatment of the various subjects addressed in that document, including, in this context, women. It remains to demonstrate how we may move from what a document alleges about the world beyond its words to the actualities of that world.[22]

---

[22]I dealt with this problem in two major projects. The first is *From Text to Historical Context in Rabbinic Judaism: Historical Facts in Systemic Documents*. I. *The Mishnah, Tosefta, Abot, Sifra, Sifré to Numbers, and Sifré to Deuteronomy*. Atlanta, 1993: Scholars Press for South Florida Studies in the History of Judaism; *From Text to Historical Context in Rabbinic Judaism: Historical Facts in Systemic Documents*. II. *The Later Midrash-Compilations: Genesis Rabbah, Leviticus Rabbah, Pesiqta deRab Kahana*. Atlanta, 1994: Scholars Press for South Florida Studies in the History of Judaism; *From Text to Historical Context in Rabbinic Judaism: Historical Facts in Systemic Documents*. III. *The Latest Midrash-Compilations: Song of Songs Rabbah, Ruth Rabbah, Esther Rabbah I, and Lamentations Rabbah*. Atlanta, 1994: Scholars Press for South Florida Studies in the History of Judaism. The second is still more de-

tailed: *The Judaism Behind the Texts. The Generative Premises of Rabbinic Literature.* I. *The Mishnah.* A. *The Division of Agriculture.* Atlanta, 1993: Scholars Press for South Florida Studies in the History of Judaism; *The Judaism Behind the Texts. The Generative Premises of Rabbinic Literature.* I. *The Mishnah.* B. *The Divisions of Appointed Times, Women, and Damages (through Sanhedrin).* Atlanta, 1993: Scholars Press for South Florida Studies in the History of Judaism; *The Judaism Behind the Texts. The Generative Premises of Rabbinic Literature.* I. *The Mishnah.* C. *The Divisions of Damages (from Makkot), Holy Things and Purities.* Atlanta, 1993: Scholars Press for South Florida Studies in the History of Judaism; *The Judaism Behind the Texts. The Generative Premises of Rabbinic Literature.* II. *The Tosefta, Tractate Abot, and the Earlier Midrash-Compilations: Sifra, Sifré to Numbers, and Sifré to Deuteronomy.* Atlanta, 1993.:

Since English is obviously not her native language, Ilan may be forgiven her imprecise and impressionistic reading of my work. Still, even taking her linguistic incapacities into account, Ilan's précis of my discussion of *Women* rates a C+. But her grasp of what is at stake is commendable, so her final grade is a good solid B — by far the best of the lot. And her subsequent writing has shown marked improvement at

---

Scholars Press for South Florida Studies in the History of Judaism; *The Judaism Behind the Texts. The Generative Premises of Rabbinic Literature*. III. *The Later Midrash-Compilations: Genesis Rabbah, Leviticus Rabbah and Pesiqta deRab Kahana*. Atlanta, 1994: Scholars Press for South Florida Studies in the History of Judaism; *The Judaism Behind the Texts. The Generative Premises of Rabbinic Literature*. IV. *The Latest Midrash-Compilations: Song of Songs Rabbah, Ruth Rabbah, Esther Rabbah I, and Lamentations Rabbati. And The Fathers According to Rabbi Nathan*. Atlanta, 1994: Scholars Press for South Florida Studies in the History of Judaism; *The Judaism Behind the Texts. The Generative Premises of Rabbinic Literature*. V. *The Talmuds of the Land of Israel and Babylonia*. Atlanta, 1994: Scholars Press for South Florida Studies in the History of Judaism. The upshot of the whole is spelled out in *The Judaism the Rabbis Take for Granted*. Atlanta, 1995: Scholars Press for South Florida Studies in the History of Judaism. It goes without saying that of these works Ilan knows nothing.

that.

4.

Judaism and Christianity in the Beginning: Time for a Category-Reformation?

A Review Essay in Response to Jack T. Sanders and Stephen G. Wilson

Schismatics, Sectarians, Dissidents, Deviants. The First One Hundred Years of Jewish-Christian Relations. By Jack T. Sanders. Valley Forge, 1993: Trinity Press International.
Related Strangers. Jews and Christians. 70-170 C.E.. By Stephen G. Wilson. Minneapolis, 1995: Fortress Press.

Covering the same subject in the same way, these two books, the one incompetent, the other exemplary, present a striking contrast but also share a massive flaw.[23] Since, as I shall explain, we cannot attribute the flaw to individual idiosyncrasy, we must assign its origin to a common source. Both books turn out to ask questions that can be imagined, then investigated, only if we adopt premises and presuppositions that, in fact, contradict the character of the evidence. Neither book can have been written if the author did not invoke categories that, in fact, do not apply, in the investigation of questions the sources do not answer, for a purpose the ancient au-

---

[23] The journal in which this essay originally appeared invited Sanders and Wilson to respond, with the proviso that I would add a surrejoinder. They declined.

thorities will not have comprehended to begin with.

Asking about relationships between Jews and Christians, each author shows what he can do. Wilson writes elegantly and lucidly, presenting a clear and compelling account; Sanders writes like a barbarian, loses his way constantly, and ends up casting his never-to-be-tallied ballot in every contested opinion. The one is controlled, civil, interesting, well-conceived, and nicely crafted. The other wanders purposelessly hither and yon, shamelessly declaring at the end that this entire piece of academic busy-work served as an utter self-indulgence. So Sanders confesses, "It has been a long road from the Apostolic Conference to social evolution...I hope that I have left a reasonably legible map and that others can now take the journey with greater ease. But if that should prove not to be the case, probably such following is not the most important thing. I had loads of fun finding the way. Why else do we undertake historical investigations?" The answer is, to learn something important — and that must mean, more than the author's casual, space-filling opinions about everything and its opposite.

Let us begin with the bad book. Sanders shows his hand at the end: "This study began with a historical problem that I had: Why did the author of Luke-Acts portray Jews generally in such a negative way?...I concluded that the answer must lie in the author's own environment, in some aspect of Jewish-Christian relations in his own place and time...Other scholars have tended to avoid this question...." That allegation must astonish, among a legion of scholars, Lloyd Gaston, "Anti-Judaism and the Passion Narrative in Luke and Acts," R. I. Brawley, Luke-Acts and the Jews, not to mention Wilson himself, "The Jews and the Death of Jesus in Acts."

To portray "Jewish-Christian relations," Sanders proceeds to describe "Palestine before 70," with attention to literary evidence (Acts, Paul, the Synoptics), Jewish literature, and material remains; then the situation between 70 and 135, Christian literary evidence comprising the Fourth Gospel, "the stoning of Jewish-Christian missionaries," and later Christian writers; then Jewish literature, birkat hamminim (the curse of sectarians), and Rabbinic (Tannaitic literature). After "material remains," comes a long chapter of "explanations," in these rubrics: cultural (theological) explanations (Christianity increasingly gentile, the unity of holiness, Jesus as magician, Christology, criticism of the temple and of Mosaic tradition); social science perspectives (social science approaches not useful for this problem, sect movements, conflict theory, defiance, with attention to Howard Becker, Kai Erikson, "on the universality of the principle," early Christian deviance and its punishment, and test cases, Samaritans and Chinese Jews. Next comes a chapter on Syria and Asia Minor, followed by Greece and Rome, and "further explanations" (chapter six matching chapter three), in these parts: Jewish denunciations of Christians: perverting Jewish traditions, self-protection, Jewish-Christian opposition to the gentilizing [sic!] of Christianity, the response of deviants, the middle — on the way to the Grosskirche. This chapter treats new religious movements, with stress on the example, for Sanders's theory, of Soka Gakkai, gradual accommodation of new religious movements, early Christianity as a new religious movement, and, finally, the evolution of social groups. Clear, Sanders treats an enormous agendum here.

But the book presents much less than meets the eye, for at each point, Sanders's method is the same: introduce a topic, identify a scholar who has written on the topic, set forth a meandering, stream-of-consciousness commentary to that scholar's findings, then pass judgment on the matter and go on to the next item. This procedure makes for a very boring book, one that is hard to follow unless the reader knows the item under discussion and what it actually says and why it matters. Then Sanders's discussion takes on some interest. As I shall explain with a specific case, where I know first-hand the sources and the scholarly literature treated by Sanders, I found his discussion uninformed, inaccurate, and misleading. But Sanders covers many topics, and I have worked on only a few of them; I suspect that every other reader will find himself in the same uncomfortable position: believe or walk away. Alas, Sanders simply does not succeed in winning for himself that position as arbiter and final judge of all questions that he aspires to hold. For having investigated only a tiny portion of the problems on his own, he ends up setting forth one unsustained and often inane opinion after another. Anyone who doubts it should try to follow his uncomprehending and often incomprehensibly obtuse expositions and then critiques of Bruce Malina, on the one side, and Mary Douglas on the other — among many!

Scroggs, Lüdemann (many times), Malina and Douglas and pretty much everyone else maligned ("criticized") by Sanders may speak for themselves on whether or not Sanders accurately portrays and pertinently addresses their views. But in the area in which I work, I can say, he does not know the territory. A single instance of his failure to acquire first-hand scholarship suffices, in my case, predictably, involving the use of Rabbinic evidence for historical purposes. Here he announces, "When we turn to Tannaitic literature, by which I mean the Mishna and other literature approximately contemporary with it, we shall be able better to fill out the picture that we have been able to draw of Jewish-Christian relations in Palestine between the time of the destruction of Jerusalem and Bar Cochba's revolt." But the Mishnah reached closure approximately a century after that period, so Sanders has to explain why he deems it a valid account of things actually said and done one hundred years earlier, or how stories and sayings have been formulated and transmitted to preserve those historical facts. This he does not even pretend to do. But the problem proves still more ominous, when a second glance shows that Sanders treats not the Mishnah, but the Tosefta. Now that document, as everyone who has opened it (and not just consulted a handbook of stories, as Sanders admits by giving credit to Herford (Our canvassing of this literature is greatly facilitated by the existence of Travers Herford's compendium of relevant passages"!), depends upon the Mishnah, cites the Mishnah verbatim and glosses it, and reached closure some time after the Mishnah. So if the Mishnah stands a century after the events under discussion, the Tosefta must come from a still later period.

Why both documents should not tell us about the age in which they came to closure and viewpoints held at that time, rather than the long-ago times of which they speak Sanders does not say. For instance, they describe the Temple and its cult, for example, and no one in contemporary scholarship opens the Tosefta for a picture of exactly how things were two or more centuries earlier. But that does not stop Sanders from citing the composite (treated as two separate stories, not a unit) at Tosefta Hullin Chapter Two that narrates two stories about rabbis' views of Jesus. The former involves an Ishmael and Jacob in the name of Joshua ben Pantera, the latter the trial of Eliezer on the charge of *minut*. Now, as scholarship has long recognized, *minut* may stand for a variety of matters, depending on the context. But with no ado at all, Sanders leaps to these conclusions: "Herford argues that the setting of this story must have been the time of a general Roman sweep of the area for Christians....We therefore have before us evidence of an innocent Galilean rabbi accused of being a Christian in the process of a general persecution of Christians during Trajan's reign." (I cannot explain why Sanders has moved Eliezer from Lud, to which all pertinent sources assign him to Galilee.)

And, in a further leap of enthusiasm, Sanders proceeds, "If rabbis of only modest prominence have to be coaxed back from contact with Christians by the most eminent of the sages, what will have been the situation with the common people?" I find the characterization of Eliezer (if that is Sanders' focus at all) puzzling, since all stories identify him as one of the two most prominent figures of his day, and make Aqiba, who figures in the story, his disciple. But those are minor quibbles, important only to those who have examined and studied the actual sources in vast detail, not only what people say about them. The upshot is, Sanders finds in the stories at hand a stenographic report of what was actually said in court; he even knows the private conversations that supposedly took place among masters and their disciples. Outside diminishing circles of the faithful, attempting a kind of pseudo-scholarship for an apologetics lacking all plausibility, no body works that way any more in these documents, any more than, for two hundred years, biblical scholarship has pursued the chimera of what Moses really said to Pharaoh that day. So if the title of the book, *Schismatics, Sectarians, Dissidents, Deviants,* leaves the reader puzzled about Sanders's proposition, the title accurately captures the quality of the work: utter confusion, the intellectual chaos brought about by pretentious omniscience about everything in general, but nothing in particular.

Everything bad about Sanders' book finds its mirror-image in Wilson's work. If the one is disorganized and aimless, opinionated, vacuous and in the end indeterminate, the other is well-organized and purposeful, rich in reflection and well-focused. Let me start with a specific chapter of remarkable lucidity and compelling argument, which can then stand for the whole. I state flatly that anyone who wants to know about the Jews and Judaism in the Gospels (Mark, Matthew,

Luke-Acts, and John) had best start with Wilson's chapter on that subject, which clearly states the facts and astutely lays out a coherent and comprehensible picture of what they mean. This model of scholarly exposition and argument, written with grace and intellectual poise, shows us how mature learning reaches its final statement. And the rest of the book follows suit. The program is as cogent as Sanders's is diffuse: the political and social context; Jews and Judaism in the canonical narratives; apocrypha; supersession: Hebrews and Barnabas; Jewish Christians and gentile Judaizers; Jewish reactions to Christianity; Gnostics and Marcionites; patterns of Christian worship; dialogue and dispute: Justin, and an overview.

Wilson's treatment of the Jewish evidence is judicious and informed, beginning with the obvious point: "there are, even on the most optimistic count, very few allusions to Christianity or its founder in Rabbinic literature, and most of these are uncertain and obscure." A sample of Wilson's discussion reveals the quality of his mind. In explaining why we have so little evidence, he offers paragraphs beginning in the following sentences: "First, the rabbis...address themselves in a highly idiosyncratic fashion to a limited range of issues...In addition...there would have been much less reason for Jews to concern themselves with Christians than the reverse...A third obstacle is that Rabbinic traditions were censored by both Jews and Christians...It has been noted, fourthly, that the inherent problems of Rabbinic traditions have been compounded by the simplistic or false assumptions that scholars have frequently brought to them. A common error, for example, is to assume that Rabbinic Jews = Judaism...

Even if we are alert to the drawbacks of the evidence and the weaknesses in its interpretation, there is still the broader methodological issue to confront: Of what value is Rabbinic evidence, dating in its earliest written form from ca. 220 CE, for reconstructing Judaism in the first two centuries?" Clearly, we find ourselves in reliable hands. But that does not prevent Wilson from expatiating on the birkat hamminim, citing the enigmatic story behind the equally-enigmatic curse as the Talmud of Babylonia, ca. 600 CE, tells it. Now all of his judicious warnings about the difficulty of utilizing stories in later Rabbinic documents as evidence of the period of which they speak fall away, and the remainder of the discussion goes over familiar ground as though critical considerations need not apply. Wilson would have done better to study the solid scholarship of Judith Baskin, whose *Pharaoh's Counselors: Job, Jethro, and Balaam in Rabbinic and Patristic Tradition,* which I published in Brown Judaic Studies in 1988 does not appear in his index, and who has produced results that are not only pertinent to the issue but also solid and well-crafted.

What a contrast! Two books, the one abysmal, the other incandescent! Yet they have in common a crippling flaw. Both take for granted a single set of premises, which render the results of each indeterminate and inchoate. That is the three-part assumption: [1] we may speak of Judaism and Christianity as coherent religious entities; [2] we also may speak of "the Jews" and "the Christians" as coherent social entities, subject to generalization; [3] we may derive from literary evidence facts concerning not the opinions of the writers but the social world beyond the pages of the documents.

In order to write books on "Jewish-Christian relations" or on "Judaism and Christianity" as coherent religions that once were the same but then parted company, people must hold these assumptions. If we do not know in advance that two free-standing and cogent religions, Judaism and Christianity, may be defined and described, we also cannot formulate as a problem how the two religions related, one on one so to speak, and where, when, and why the two parted company. If we do not take for granted that "the Jews" and "the Christians" constituted well-delineated social groups, we cannot speak of how the two "groups" related at all. And if we do not take as our generative principle the notion that documents report not the author's opinion (e.g., theology, viewpoint, perspective, and the like) but the facts of the social order beyond the limits of the writing, we cannot write books about how things were and opinions widely held, only about how various bits and pieces of evidence portray matters.

Wilson may rightly claim that he does read the evidence piece by piece, and it is his portrait of each piece that forms the principal ornament of his elegant book. But Sanders does the same, if gullibly and often stupidly. Both intend to join the parts into a coherent account: "Jewish-Christian," "Judaism-Christianity," "parting of the ways," and similar usages abound. Both scholars moreover in the end have in mind an account of how things really were, and each provides an account of not the evidence but the social world to which, both assume, the evidence in some way or other attests. For both, the categories "Judaism" and "Christianity" assume the reality of givens, and those data, however subtly refined as they are by Wilson, remain paramount. And neither could have undertaken his study without the clear aim of account for the division of Judaism and Christianity. That, after all, is the point of both books.

Here it is Wilson, not Sanders, whose flaw gapes, for he announces at the outset a position that he ignores for the rest of the book, which is, that there was no single Judaism or Christianity. He says in so many words that matters are far more complex: "There have been attempts to reduce the story of Jewish-Christian relations to a core issue...[Rosemary Ruether's fine study]...has been rightly criticized because...it underestimates the extraordinary range of ideological and pragmatic reasons why Jews and Christians parted company. If I began with a conviction, it was that the story is far more complex and interesting than is suggested by the identification of any single issue as the key to all else. Not surprisingly, perhaps, it has been confirmed..." Now here we find two contradictory positions: [1] there were Jews and Christians, treated as diverse, but there also is a "they" that "parted company." The use of the language "parted company" proves plausible only if we deal with two coherent groups, originally joined, that ultimately separated. Otherwise the formulation is gibberish.

Wilson proceeds with language that I find stunningly inept: "Thus if I use the singular terms 'Judaism' and 'Christianity,' or their equivalents, it is only because the plurals ring unmusically to my ears. In almost all instances the plural should be understood, as I think the context usually makes clear." But that is a distinction that, in the actuality of Wilson's presentation, really makes no material difference. I shall now show that a passage (among a great many) in which "Jewish" stands for "the Jews, Judaism" and Christian for "the Christians, Christianity," loses all sense when we follow Wilson's counsel and introduce the dissonant, but real, Judaisms and Christianities:

> Yet the events surrounding the Jewish revolts were only one aspect of the political context of Jewish-Christian relations. The broader picture must take into account the overall standing of Jews and Christians in the Roman worlds...To find a niche in the world was thus, for the Christians, an uphill struggle against Jewish superiority and Roman suspicion. The Christian apologists consciously attempted to present their case in terms comprehensible to the outside world, and in the process explicitly contrasted themselves with the Jews."

Now that paragraph, I maintain, becomes senseless if we do what Wilson has counseled and inserted the equivalent of Ju-

daisms and Christianities, e.g., "the political context of relationships among Judaisms and Christianities." Surely that is
not what Wilson can possibly intend, and his initial pronouncement that he sees only Judaisms and Christianities
merely throws dust in the eyes of the scholars.

Nor do matters become simpler when we turn to the
social groups, Jews and Christians. Here too, whatever Wilson says at the outset, in the end he has "the Jews" against
"the Christians," as in the following:

> When we shift our attention from the political
> setting, the variety of responses of Christians and Jews
> to each other becomes even more pronounced. ...That
> the Jews often reacted with hostility and suspicion to
> Christians is indicated not only by the evidence for
> their involvement in public harassment, but also by the
> generally negative attitude recorded in stray Rabbinic
> traditions....

Here again, if Wilson really meant what he said, he could not
have framed matters in this way at all. Using "the Jews" for
"Judaism" improves matters only slightly. "That Judaisms often reacted with hostility...to Christianities...," yields nonsense
— something so obvious as to shade over into stupidity; and
how else Wilson can speak of "the Jews" and afford full recognition to the fact he affirms, that not all Jews look, act, or
think, alike, I cannot say.

But more: the evidence itself is not so much over-
interpreted as misconstrued and misrepresented, to say the
least. For Wilson in all accuracy should portray the evidence
and its results only in words such as these: we have very late
stories, recorded centuries after the event, that indicate that
(some) sages, centuries later, took a hostile view of what appears to be some teachings attributed to Jesus and told stories
about how earlier sages, closer to the time of Jesus, disputed
about them (some favoring, some opposing, Jesus's power to

heal). The stories prove that, much later on, when Christianity had achieved world-dominance, rabbis told such stories about their long-dead predecessors. Such an accurate portrayal of the authentic facts — what the source, in its day, has to say about a much earlier time — yields nothing relevant to the categories under discussion, "the Jews, the Christians," let alone "Judaism, Christianity."

How shall we explain these remarkable failures of intellect? It is not because Wilson generalizes wildly. He forms the model of the judicious scholar. It is because bits and pieces of we know not what in the end can leave no room for discourse about "the Jews" "Judaism" "the Christians" or "Christianity" at all. But then how Judaism parted company from Christianity ceases to form a viable category of inquiry, and if we frame matters with the correct and accurate, atomistic representation of the sources — how (some) Judaisms parted company, at diverse times and places and under diverse circumstances, from (some) Christianities — matters lose all cogency. The evidence itself is diverse — Wilson's splendid book demonstrates that fact on every page. But then the evidence speaks only for the people behind it, not for the people (if any) beyond it. And then a book such as this cannot be composed. For (to return to the exemplary case at hand) the "stray Rabbinic traditions" are just that, not evidence for "Judaism" let alone for "the Jews."

Consequently, the evidence does not sustain the categories we use for the analysis of the evidence but contradicts those categories. That accounts for the utterly indeterminate, though certainly not inane, conclusion that Wilson reaches: "If variety marks the way Jews and Christians related to each other and envisaged their respective futures, it is also the hallmark of the ideological and social tensions that separated them." This I find to be true but pointless, a device for masking the simple fact that the evidence supplies support for every conceivable proposition and its opposite. And that is solid reason for insisting, as I do, that it is time for a category-reformation. When categories draw together evidence that produces either contradictory conclusions or vacuous and self-evident but inconsequential ones, then it is time to ask why we are asking the wrong questions. For where, when, and why Judaism and Christianity parted company, how anti-Semitism originated, and similar questions of acute contemporary interest turn out to distort our perspective on the questions the evidence can answer.

Indeed, not only have the available category-formations drastically distorted the character of the evidence, they also have predetermined that we ask the wrong questions to begin with. The documents attest to the world of their authors (in the case of the writings of individuals) or of their authorships (the textual communities that collective and anonymous writings represent) — that alone.

5.

DONALD HARMAN AKENSON, *SURPASSING WONDER. THE INVENTION OF THE BIBLE AND THE TALMUDS*. NEW YORK, SAN DIEGO, AND LONDON, 1999: HARCOURT BRACE & CO.

No one before has ever tried to tell as a single, unfolding narrative the story of the formation of the Scripture of ancient Israel, the diverse Judaisms of Second Temple times, the formation of Christianity, and the development of Rabbinic Judaism. In this vast, remarkable and ambitious work, written with rollicking good humor and grace, a historian whose prior credits focus upon Irish history, Donald Harman Akenson has done just that. He lays matters out in four parts, "inventing the covenant," which deals with the return to Zion and the formation of the Hebrew Scriptures from Genesis to Kings; "inventive fecundity and Judahist multiplicity: the later Second Temple Era;" "the invention of Christianity;" and "the invention of the Jewish faith." While in each case he conducts a vigorous dialogue with the literary evidence, he has composed much more than a history of the diverse documents of ancient Judaisms in their unfolding. This is narrative history in the grand style.

What makes Akenson's book unique is the fourth section, on Rabbinic Judaism, because the prior histories — and they are many — stop with 135, that is, the conventional date for the end of the Jewish chapter of Christianity. Without that section, "the invention of the Jewish faith," moreover, Akenson cannot have accomplished his goal, which he explicitly states at the end. He "is willing to deal with the Tanakh, the 'New Testament,' and the Rabbinic literature with an open mind and a desire to learn." He aims "to encourage a form of Jewish-Christian ecumenism," by which he means, specifically, to bring "present-day Christians and Jews into a more intelligent and more sympathetic relationship with each other:"

> This will not occur…by minimizing the differences between the two sister-faiths. Instead, one simple set of parallel cognitions must be encouraged: the recognition that Christians will not understand their own faith until they are at least modestly familiar with the basic texts that form the modern Jewish faith, not just the Tanakh, but the great Rabbinic texts and especially the massive, glorious Bavli; similarly, adherents of modern Judaism should recognize that they cannot understand their own faith unless they are conversant with the Christian scriptures…

That is why Akenson presents the primary texts of Rabbinic Judaism, Christianity, and "the ancient Yahweh-faith," with texts as the focus in all three cases, because "it would be false to distinguish between the invention of each of their sacred texts and the invention of their specific religions." Akenson sees discontinuities between Scripture and the Rabbinic texts, so too, between Scripture and the Christian ones: "each went through massive disorientation in the post-70 CE years, and each was such a radical re-invention of older ideas that neither one can legitimately share a single label with its ancient predecessor." But while distinct, "the texts of the three faiths intertwine with each other. Sometimes this interweaving is direct and obvious, at other times, complex and convoluted." Akenson holds that what they have in common is "a common bank of reflexes in dealing with the catastrophes of 70

CE." The author of Genesis-Kings, after the first destruction, set the pattern: [1] "the details of the now-dust Temple are set down...; [2] the author-editor of Genesis-Kings does not permit himself to be trapped in the belief that the physical manifestation of the Almighty was the sole and complete meaning of the Temple; [3] in responding to the crisis engendered by the Temple's destruction, the author-editor of Genesis-Kings brought together for the first time the previously-disparate portions of the great narrative theodicy...we call Scriptures." Then comes Akenson's principal thesis: "The Jewish religion and the Christian each reacted in exactly the way one would have predicted, given a knowledge of the earlier pattern of response to the destruction of Solomon's Temple. Separately, but in a strikingly parallel fashion, the leaders of the Jesus-faith and of embryonic Rabbinic Judaism re-invented the religion of the Temple, but without a physical Temple being required. The faithful did not re-establish a Temple on this earth, but in their hearts, in the heavens, and in each home."

This account of Akenson's generative thesis hardly does justice to the complexity of his execution of the shank of the book, which is massively detailed and shows broad and deep reading of both sources and contemporary scholarship. Experts in the four fields he here brings together, Tanakh-studies, Second Temple sectarian writings, the Gospels, and the Mishnah-Tosefta-Yerushalmi-Bavli and Midrash-compilations, will have to form their own judgments on the details of his presentation. My sense is, where scholarship is strong and well-articulated, Akenson stands on solid foundations, and his reflections prove dense and engaging. Where scholarship is elementary and even primitive, there the work loses its vitality and trails off into episodic observations. Certainly the first and third sections show Akenson at his most certain, the treatment of earliest Christianity being imaginative and stimulating, not just a reprise of familiar exercises on the historical Jesus. The work is original and demands attention in its own right with his observation:

> The Christian scriptures are an impressively coherent, wondrously successful entity, because the 'New Testament' honors the ancient Hebrew grammar of religious invention, and does so at three levels, each of which is best approached by its own metaphor. Specifically, at the level of macro-structure...the 'New Testament' canon was organized like a successful piece of architecture. Second the 'New Testament' achieved another level of unity between the various books through the 'interdigitation' of motifs, symbols and icons. And third, at a verse0-by-verse level, the author-editors of the 'New Testament' achieved yet another form of unity, by shaping their individual phrases so that they resonated with those of the Hebrew scriptures...

Equivalently magisterial writing characterizes Akenson's treatment of the earlier phases of Second Temple Judaism, when the Tanakh was taking shape. By contrast, his discussion of the later Second Temple times, especially of the apocalyptic writings, loses coherence just as the sources do, and the evidence of the Dead Sea scrolls does not yield a clear and cogent account at all. Here Akenson's powerful mastery of narrative rhetoric ("Inventive fecundity and Judahist multiplicity: the later Second Temple Era," yielding "Siloam's Teeming Pool") does not fully mask the incoherence of the sources and the failure of scholarship to come to grips with them in a massive, field-theory. That is work left for another generation to undertake. As to Akenson's treatment of Rabbinic Judaism, most of it comes directly from my work, though Akenson is much stronger on the description of the character of the documents than on the analysis of the religion, Rabbinic Judaism, that those documents adumbrate. A great part of the presentation of "the hermetic, perfect

Mishnah," "taming the Mishnah: tractate Aboth, the Tosefta, Sifra, and the Yerushalmi," and "the bounteous Bavli and the invention of the dual Torah," recapitulates my work and its implications. I found it quite coherent.

The real question raised by Akenson's undertaking is, does he accomplish his goal, that is, do we emerge with a picture of "parallel histories"? Others have toyed with the same motif, most recently Hershel Shanks. While Shanks and the dozen scholars he assembled announce and then ignore the problem they promise to work out, viz., how Judaism and Christianity run along parallel lines (Shanks's project really ignores Judaism as a religion altogether!), Akenson has tried both to narrate the story of the literature and the history that it yields, and also to demonstrate the proposition he has taken for himself. And yet if we ask ourselves whether he has shown that Rabbinic Judaism and the Christianity portrayed by the New Testament really do what Akenson says they do, which is, "re-invent the religion of the Temple" — his unifying conception of "parallel histories" — we must respond, for the moment, with the verdict "not proved." I do not think Akenson has shown that the texts intertwine, I think he has shown the opposite.

I doubt that Akenson has established that the destruction of the Temple forms for both religions a starting point, only an important motif. We cannot characterize New Testament Christianity as focused upon issues of 70, and while for Rabbinic Judaism, the destruction asked the generative question, it did not dictate the character of the final answer, only details thereof. I am not inclined to concur, therefore, that Rabbinic Judaism and Christianity of the formative age run along parallel lines; indeed, my colleague Bruce D. Chilton and I have argued just the opposite, in great detail showing that the histories of the two religions run along intersecting, not parallel lines, our key-language being "trading places," and that for essentially this-worldly and political reasons. Akenson has allowed a massive dose of good will and ecumenical affection to shape a study that, in its own terms, requires the sources to yield a picture that, in my view, they cannot be made to sustain.

But for all of the good will that animates this loving and pro-Judaic book, Akenson's account of "parallel histories" pays remarkably little attention to the single most powerful testimony against seeing Christianity and Judaism as somehow co-equal continuators of the religion and Scriptures of ancient Israel. The Rabbinic sages cherished every jot and tittle of the Torah and staked their entire claim to truth upon their capacity to build from the Scriptures of ancient Israel to the Oral Torah as they recorded it. By contrast, Christianity retrojected backward its own fabrications, not even pretending to take seriously, in its own terms, the claim of Sinai. As a matter of fact, Christianity in its formative history rejected its patrimony in, and as, "Israel." Despite the numerous points of continuity that attract attention, the New Testament is an anti-Semitic book, the source of a more formidable contribution than any other piece of writing in all of Western civilization to hatred of the Jews and contempt for Judaism. That anti-Semitism, moreover, is not episodic but endemic, marking not only Paul's dismissal of "the Law" (a.k.a., the Torah), but also Jesus's violent condemnation of the Pharisees in Matthew and Mark, and John's even more hate-filled caricature of "the Jews." Akenson points to the figure of Mary as somehow representing a break with the past. But the very essence of the New Testament embodies poisonous hatred of "Israel after the flesh," "the Jews," "the Torah," not to mention the dismissal of "Judaism," and all the rest. How, out of all this, we are supposed to fabricate "parallel histories" I cannot explain and Akenson does not address.

But we should not miss the true excellence of this remarkable work. It is a work that uses the results of scholarship in the investigation of issues of general sensibility and culture. Akenson is a historian, meaning, a reflective and learned intellectual engaged by the story of the past. He has brought his historical faculties to bear upon diverse and unconnected problems, the history of Ireland for example, and still has written sixteen non-fiction books and five novels. So what we have here is the result of profound learning on the part of a writer and an intellectual who also is a scholar. The study of the history of Judaism in ancient times in dialogue with the history of Christianity in that same period has rarely attracted the systematic reading of a first-class intellectual and writer, such as Akenson certainly is. The result is engaging, witty, insightful, and well worth the sustained and coherent reading that the writer demands for himself.

6.

Gabriele Boccaccini. *Middle Judaism. Jewish Thought. 300 B.C.E To 200 C.E.* With a Foreword by James. H. Charlesworth. Minneapolis: 1993: Fortress Press

Gabriele Boccaccini, an Italian scholar of the history of Judaism in late antiquity from the University of Torino and now at the University of Michigan, here takes up familiar problems and finds something new and interesting to say. Specifically, he wants to figure out how to relate the diverse writings deriving from ancient Judaic authors: "They make sense in relation to epochs and ideologies that formed, delimited, and reinterpreted them...The task of the historian of thought is to describe an age in its complexity and in the contradiction of its expressions, using all the material available, canceling and verifying every traditional division without confessional presupposition...to reconstruct as much as possible the chronological and ideological links among the sources. In sort, the focus of attention should be shifted from the corpora to the age in which the constituent writings were composed, thus freeing the documents from the cage of their respective corpora and placing them on the same level." If I grasp what Boccaccini proposes, his points of stress will hardly surprise his American readers. Who today defends a narrowly confessional reading of ancient religious documents? No one will object to describing an age "in all its complexity."

What compels attention is the term, "Middle Judaism." This he defines as follows: "'Judaism' properly denotes the genus, that is, the whole family of monotheistic systems that sprang forth from the same Middle Eastern roots as a multibranched tree. To denote the many species of which the genus Judaism is composed, we should use only more specific terms, such as Samaritan Judaism, Rabbinic Judaism, an Christian Judaism." No one today will find that point astonishing. What is left is the Middle. For the Judaism in the time period he has chosen, he rejects both "early" and "late" in favor of what is left, "middle." This he deems solely chronological, referring "not to an organic and homogeneous system of thought, much less a theology or a spiritual category...The object of a history of middle Jewish thought...is not the identification and synchronic study of a Judaism (a particular ideological system) but the identification and diachronic study of many Judaisms...active and in competition in that historically limited period." Since most, though not all, work on ancient Christianity and Judaism concurs, the proof of the value of Boccaccini's proposals lies in how he works them out. Alas, as we shall see, by the end he gives us little more than the synchronic account of a particular point of a single ideological system encompassing all the diverse data of Judaisms of his "Middle Judaism," which is to say, precisely that muddle that he promises to sort out.

The recapitulation of broadly held ideas — the notion of a single Judaism having lost all currency outside of narrow, Orthodox Judaic or Israeli-nationalist circles, the conception of Christianity securely situated within the framework of Judaism enjoying broad acceptance these days — can command a serious hearing only when we are shown how a broad and complex corpus of data is sorted out. So we ask: just what do we gain by a chronological definition that starts at 300 B.C.E.

and ends at 200 C.E.? For the study of Rabbinic Judaism, nothing at all, since 200 marks the conventional date of closure of the first document of that Judaism, not the last, and since the definitive characteristics of that Judaic system we call "Rabbinic" first made their appearance only in documents generally deemed to have reached closure after 400. So the terminal-date misleads. Boccaccini persistently refers to a Judaism — his "Rabbinism" — as "Middle" that has left not a single document in the time-period he has defined. To encompass the sources of Rabbinic Judaism within "Middle Judaism," his closing date much be 600, not 200. Whether starting with 300 BC, rather than with the formation of the Pentateuch in ca 450 BC, represents a net gain others will have to decide. It makes little sense to me, for the obvious starting point of all Judaisms is the Pentateuch; without Moses within the privileged Five Books, there is no Judaism. Then how Boccaccini will define an "early" or "earlier" Judaism, so as to allow for the middle of his sandwich, I cannot say.

But that set of problems must appear captious when we come to the purpose of this new taxonomy of Judaisms. For if by "Middle Judaism" Boccaccini claims to supply more than a chronological definition, intending to signify traits of other than mere synchronicity he holds to have been exhibited in common among the Judaic systems that flourished in the period he has delineated, then he has to explain what is at stake in his chronological taxonomy. But Boccaccini does not tell us what those more-than-chronologically coincident traits are supposed to have been. It follows that what we have is a definition that on the face of it represents little more than a rearrangement of pieces from a presently-familiar pattern to another pattern strikingly like the one we now know.

Surely the value of an allegedly fresh reading of familiar data emerges in that reading's power to shed new light on old facts. Since the announced time-frame contains little to attract interest, much depends on Boccaccini's unpacking of the conception, "Middle Judaism," and his systematic demonstration that the chronological proposal he makes materially improves our grasp of the diverse Judaisms of the time at hand. The traits common to all the Judaisms of Middle Judaism, the groupings among those Judaisms, the points of differentiation among them, the comparison and contrast of those same Judaisms — these define the intellectual task that the proposed account of "Jewish thought" over the half-millennium at hand should encompass. The least we should expect therefore is a systematic survey of the genus, with the exposition of how the species belong in the same genus but at the same time are to be speciated. Alas, Boccaccini does not oblige.

A brief account of the contents of the book, beyond the opening, theoretical chapter, will show the reason that this book disappoints. The chapter headings are these: [2] Toward a bibliography of Middle Judaism: An Annotated survey from Josephus to 1990; *Part Two:* A Cross Section, The Second Century B.C.E., covering [3] Ben Sira, Qohelet, and apocalyptic; [4] Daniel and the Dream Vision; [5] the letter of Aristeas; *Part Three:* Some Preparatory Sketches, dealing with [6] Philo of Alexandria: A Judaism in Philosophical categories; [7] James, Paul (and Jesus); [8] "Do This in Remembrance of Me:" The Memorial Value of Worship in Middle Judaism; [9] Flavius Joseph: The betrayed Memory; [10] Boundless salvation: Jews and Gentiles in Middle Judaism. In fact, all Boccaccini has done beyond announcing his new periodization is to go over this, that, and the other thing. The book contains no systematic account of its thesis, no careful demonstration of how the thesis works itself out in detail, no effort to place all bodies of evidence within the single framework of Middle Judaism. Boccaccini announces his thesis, but he does not argue it, let alone demonstrating its heuristic power in matters of detail. Disappointing us still more, the author does not even survey the diverse Judaisms that the author claims to encompass within "Middle Judaism," nor tell us how these compare and contrast. What we have is a mere potpourri of topical studies, not a sustained and coherent exposition at all.

Then we wonder whether through the detailed examples, an inductive argument is spun out. A subtle but stimulating mode of argument may be conducted by showing through a systematic shifting of details how large scale structures inhere in diverse bodies of data, so that these structures, once described through detail, may be compared and contrasted in the aggregate. But Boccaccini does not do that either. If Boccaccini had proposed that sort of inductive argument, we should find the evidence in the single analytical program brought to bear upon his topical chapters. But comparison of the outline he himself gives shows that he as followed no such program. The chapter on Ben Sira, Qohelet, and Apocalyptic deals with the problem of knowledge and the problem of salvation, running through a survey of what the several documents say about this and that. The treatment of Philo does not take up the problem of knowledge and the problem of salvation but rather "memory as a philosophical and religious concept" and "virginity as a religious ideal." I cannot find the issue of virginity elsewhere in the book, and "memory" is important in one chapter but absent in others. The chapter on "Do This in Remembrance of Me' talks about "the memorial value of worship in ancient Judaism," "worship as a memorial 'before God,'" "worship as a memorial' for future generations,'" "the memorial value of worship in Essenism," and "Do this as a sign that reminds you of me.'" These are not subjects that arise elsewhere. The chapter on Josephus then is wildly out of phase with most of the rest of the shank of the book. The chapters that fill up the shank of the book set forth free-standing expositions of various topics, heavily padded with long abstracts of sources; the topics rarely intersect, and the conclusions of one chapter are not brought into alignment with those of another, nor is any set advanced as evidence of ubiquitous and definitive traits of Middle Judaism; the term then subsides into a mere chronological convention.

The concluding chapter, "Boundless salvation: Jews an gentiles in Middle Judaism" simply abandons Boccaccini's announced insistence that the various bodies of evidence have to be described on their own and instead surveys what various documents contribute to a single doctrine in common. These are the cited sources for the "Middle Judaic" doctrine of Jews and gentiles: Philo, Josephus, Asenath, the letter of Aristeas, Pirqé Abot (the one Rabbinic document that plays any role here at all!), the Testament of Abraham, Jubilees, documents found at Qumran, 1 Enoch, others of the Testaments of the Twelve Patriarchs, and Paul's letter to the Romans. It would be difficult to fabricate a more devastating caricature of that very method that Boccaccini condemns in chapter one and then ignores through the shank of the book than this pastiche of opinions deriving from different times and unrelated writings; Middle Judaism emerges as just another fabrication, denouncing at the outset what is affirmed at the end.

Boccaccini seems therefore to have forgotten where he started. The concluding paragraph, briefly epitomized in his own words, captures the confusion that characterizes much of the book:

> ...if universalism means the capacity of attaching value to being different, then its opposite is not particularism or nationalism, but dogmatism and intolerance, namely, the pretense of possessing the whole truth or of having the only key to salvation. By this

definition, some Middle Judaisms were undoubtedly
sectarian and intolerant, others were able to develop
mature positions that were much more universalistic
than those of early Christianity...We have seen identical
universalistic conclusions emerging from diametrically
opposed starting points, with Jews and gentiles placed
on the same level for quite opposite reasons...This is
not a paradox or a surprise; whether the universalism
arises from mutual respect or from a confession of im-
potence, it is none other than a recognition of solidar-
ity, of a common commitment or a common suffering.

It is true that those middle Judaisms did not
succeed in surviving as distinct groups, while Christianity was even able to adopt the positions of these fellow
Judaisms to its own proselytic ends and forced Rabbinism to renounce any missionary activity. But thanks
to these forgotten voices the hope for a boundless salvation has been taken up by both of the main modern
Judaisms — Rabbinism and Christianity — and it re-
sounds today with its original force *from within these traditions* [his italics], the echo of an ancient and unforgotten
dream (p. 265).

I confess I have not got any idea what Boccaccini is driving at
in this statement; what is clear, however, is that, having in-
sisted that each Judaism must be described in its own terms,
he wants at the end to speak of all of them all together; when
he does, he finds everything and its opposite, solemnly
emerging with only stupefying banalities. That accounts for
the mystifying cloud of words in which he takes his leave of
his reader.

The upshot is that Boccaccini's intellectual ambition
yields an interesting idea, but not a very compelling or coherent book. What he has published is a set of essentially free-
standing chapters, not a well-crafted demonstration of his interesting proposition. He fails to make the case for his Middle
Judaism because the book loses its way beyond the opening
chapter — one possessed of genuine interest — and at the

end trails off into gibberish.

7.

MARKUS BOCKMUEHL, JEWISH LAW IN GENTILE CHURCHES. HALAKHAH AND THE BEGINNING OF CHRISTIAN PUBLIC ETHICS. *EDINBURGH, 2000: T&T CLARK LTD.*

This is a collection of essays in three parts, in general dealing with ethical teachings that transcend communal lines ("public ethics"). Part One: Christianity in the Land of Israel. [1] Halakhah and Ethics in the Jesus Tradition; [2] Matthew's Divorce Texts in the Light of Pre-Rabbinic Jewish Law; [3] "Let the Dead Bury their Dead:" Jesus and the Law Revisited; [4] James, Israel and Antioch. Part Two: [5] Natural Law in Second Temple Judaism; [6] Natural Law in the New Testament? [7] The Noachide Commandments and New Testament Ethics; Part Three: The development of Public Ethics. [8] The Beginning of Christian Public Ethics: From Luke to Aristides and Diognetus; [9] Jewish and Christian Public Ethics in the Early Roman Empire. The parts add up to less than the sum of the whole; the book works only in details, here and there, but never as a coherent statement. That is for several reasons.

First, the book is not coherent and does not set forth a proposition, clearly expounded, rigorously argued. Only the final essay, written fresh, addresses the issue head-on. Further, the work invokes category-formations that clearly are in the context of Rabbinic Judaism simply anachronistic, e.g., "natural law." Philo worked with that category, the rabbis of late antiquity did not.

Everything depends, second, on Bockmuehl's grasp of the Torah's theology of the gentiles, meaning, how the several Judaic religious systems framed a doctrine of Israel among the nations. But there is no systematic statement on that subject, and that is without regard to which Judaism's Torah is contemplated. The Rabbinic Judaic theology of the gentiles is expressed through details of the Halakhah, but to this Bockmuehl is oblivious.

Fundamental methodological problems on the use and construction of the sources, third, render dubious a variety of specific passages. The book treats "Halakhah" or law as uniform and "Jewish" or "Judaic" as simple, rather than allowing each Halakhic system to speak for its particular Judaism. So the complexity of the "Jewish" and "Judaic" is lost in these pages. It is as though Christian stood for Catholic and Gnostic. But everybody recognizes the diversity of "Christianity" and of "Judaism" in antiquity. The confusion is total, for "Jewish" stands for everything and its opposite. That is not the sole methodological problem. Then there is the problem of using sources to tell us about ideas held long before the redaction of those sources. Here, alas, Rabbinic sources of the third and later centuries are invited to clarify statements attributed to Jesus a long time earlier. Citing the Rabbinic sources in this way saves much work, but yields confusion and doubt.

Fourth, for a book on "Jewish law" or Halakhah, Bockmuehl is remarkably blithe: he cites a severely limited range of studies on the subject and knows very little of the field. The picture of the Rabbinic Halakhah is mechanical and never comprehensive and coherent. Its category-formations are never invoked, so we are asked to consider philosophical category-formations with no clear match in Rabbinic Judaism;

that is not only anachronistic, it is disproportionate and misleading.

Fifth, the book proposes to treat the Halakhah (of Rabbinic Judaism) outside of a systematic dialogue with the Aggadah (of Rabbinic Judaism), and that distorts everything, since the Halakhah and the Aggadah form a single, coherent theological statement. Hence the discussion on the Halakhah without attention to the corresponding, complementary Aggadah is seriously flawed. Take the opening composite of Bavli Abodah Zarah, for example, There, the correlation of the Rabbinic Halakhah with the Rabbinic Aggadah to frame a coherent doctrine of "the gentiles," is entirely missed. Bockmuehl has not done his homework here. He evidently has relied on people who themselves do not work on this period and its sources and cannot offer the help he requires. The upshot is, the account of the Rabbinic Halakhah on the critical issues of the book is uncomprehending.

Sixth, the scholarship at best is partial. For example, the only solution to the problem of anachronism in his principal category-formation — "natural law" in the Halakhic sources of late antiquity indeed! — lies through the demonstrated Aristotelianism of the Mishnah, therefore of the Halakhah. But Bockmuehl has missed entirely twenty years of research on the matter. So his discussions of Rabbinic Judaism ignore scholarship important to his problem. The upshot, once more, is that he rarely shows he knows how to read and understand in its own large systemic context a single passage of the Halakhah.

The work is superficial in other ways as well. It is noteworthy that the work of Wayne A. Meeks on the same issues is dismissed out of hand: "...'the origin of Christian morality' is for Meeks construed predominantly in social-anthropological terms, whereas the present study concentrates...on the question of the outworking and reappropriation of principles that were held to be divinely revealed" (p. 14, n. 30), the meaning of which is hardly self-evident in context. Meeks is owed a more dignified and respectful hearing than that!

For a book on Jewish law in Christian churches and on the Halakhah in that context, Bockmuehl has not mastered the literature of Jewish law and does not seem to grasp that it is the medium of theology for Rabbinic Judaism, the realization in concrete terms of a religious system and structure of coherence and cogency. His project asks an excellent question; the Rabbinic sources that are critical to his answer can help him answer that question. But not without more conscientious scholarship than these pages suggest. Knowing so little of context and ignoring massive, relevant research entirely, he has presented in this incoherent book merely a mass of details.

8.

DANIEL BOYARIN, *INTERTEXTUALITY AND THE READING OF MIDRASH.* INDIANA STUDIES IN BIBLICAL LITERATURE. BLOOMINGTON & INDIANAPOLIS: INDIANA UNIVERSITY PRESS

This rather thin, first book by the new Taubman Professor at University of California, Berkeley, proposes through examining a tiny segment of the anomalous and probably medieval exegetical text, Mekhilta, to clarify the nature of Midrash. The use of contemporary literary theory to explain Midrash is hardly news; the trend is more than a decade old. The results have proven trivial and dubious, as in Susan Handelman, *The Slayers of Moses: The Emergence of Rabbinic Interpretation in Modern Luiterary Theory* (Albany: SUNY Press, 1982). So Boyarin's is not a work of pioneering intellect, but of mere application and paraphrase. Unhappily, the application is not very compelling.

To be sure, using a medieval compilation for that purpose is exceedingly odd, and therefore certainly original, if perhaps ill-advised. Boyarin knows but dismisses B. Z. Wacholder, "The Date of the Mekilta de-Rabbi Ishmael," *Hebrew Union College Annual* 39 (1968), pp. 117-144. He maintains that Wacholder's view has been "decisively and definitively disproved by Menahem Kahana, 'The Editions of the Mekilta deRabbi Ishmael on Exodus in the Light of Geniza Fragments' *Tarbiz* 45, 1986, pp. 515-520." Indeed Boyarin goes on to state (p. 130, n. 3), "The Mekilta may be in the main, in fact, the earliest of rabbinic midrashic texts, although its final recension seems to have been a little later than some other early midrashim." This murky claim of his — what he means by "final recension" and how he knows what he says — is not spelled out but just tossed off.

Boyarin's ignorance of Mekhilta-scholarship, the very text to which he devotes his entire book, is genuinely alarming. First of all, Dr. Mireille Hadas-Lebel's major paper, on loan words from Greek and Latin in Mekhilta, has definitively demonstrated that these loanwords are terms that did not come into existence before the third or fourth century C.E. Borrowing these terms into Hebrew necessarily belongs to a subsequent date. That paper was written without reference to Wacholder's thesis but substantiated his views, point by point. Wacholder for his part has furthermore has dismissed Kahana's article (which was in Tarbiz 55, pp. 489-524, not the pages Boyarin cites!) as based on "insubstantial evidence." Boyarin also does not seem to know that Mekhilta attributed to R. Ishmael is asymmetrical in rhetoric and logic to the entire corpus of other, demonstrably-early Midrash-compilations, Sifra, and the two Sifrés, for example, as shown in my *Mekhilta Attributed to R. Ishmael. An Introduction to Judaism's First Scriptural Encyclopaedia.* Atlanta, 1988: Scholars Press for Brown Judaic Studies. How can a work that purports to describe Midrash on the basis of a few passages of a single, atypical text win our confidence when the author does not even know the scholarly literature on the document he claims to describe and interpret?

The book is written in a strange, turgid jargon, e.g., "...all of them [interpretations in Midrash-compilations] are more or less different from the commentary of the European traditions in that they do not seem to involve the privileged pairing of a signifier with a specific set of signifieds," and again, "I intend to articulate a theory of this text which will explain its hermeneutic moves as hermeneutic — i.e., without reducing them to some other species of discourse." At many points Boyarin seems to be talking mainly to himself. Without telling us why this is important, he identifies himself early on as an Orthodox Jew (p. ix); He calls himself a participant observer, so as to win credibility, I suppose; this confuses religious authenticity with intellectual accuracy. The apologetic point of the work is clear: "What in the Bible's text might have motivated this gloss on this verse?" He states at the end (p. 128), "Midrash is best understood as a continuation of the literary activity which engendered the Scriptures themselves." This sounds suspiciously like the familiar claim that Midrash says what Scripture really means, and that *is* Orthodox Judaism. In this book the literary critical frosting covers a stale but kosher cake.

Lest readers suppose that I exaggerate the oddity of his representation of Midrash, let me give a typical passage (p. 35) among the half-dozen or so that comprise the entire book. This shows us how Boyarin uses the language of literary criticism to tell us what a straight-forward reading of the text shows without literary criticism of this sort. First the reader must know that the passage we consider is not in the Mekhilta at all, but in the Talmud of Babylonia. So we are introduced to the Mekhilta by other-than-Midrash-texts, a fine instance of the intellectually vulgar Orthodoxy of this book: everything Jewish is the same as everything else Jewish, Midrash, Talmud, Bible — whatever. The reason he gives is that the names that occur in one document occur in another — and that's that. For Boyarin that gullibility does not pose a problem: "The Talmud preserves a story about the very rabbis of the Mekhilta which contains a nearly explicit commentary on midrashic intertextuality...."

> For this commandment which I command you today is not too difficult for you or too remote. *It is not in heaven* that one should say, Who will arise to heaven, take it and make it heard that we might do it. And it is not over the sea, that one might say, Who will cross to the other side of the sea and take it for us and make us hear it, that we might do it. Rather, the word [thing] is very close to you in your mouth and heart, to do it. [Deut. 30:11-14].

On this passage, Boyarin states the following:

> R. Yehoshua [to whom the passage is attributed (JN)] transforms the verse through his citation into meaning that the Torah is beyond the reach, as it were, of its divine author. The nature of R. Yehoshua's hermeneutic speech act here is vital to understand the text. If we do not perceive what he is doing with the verse from Deuteronomy, we could misunderstand him to be making precisely the opposite claim, namely, that the text is autonomous and sufficient in itself, not requiring the author to guarantee its true interpretation — a version of the New Criticism. By performing an act of tesseration of the language, however, the rabbi disables any such reading of his statement. Without fanfare, R. Yehoshua creates radical new meaning in this verse, simply by reinscribing it in a new context. "It is not in heaven" means not only that the Torah is not beyond human reach, but that it is beyond divine reach, as it were.

The "as it were"s do not help us much in figuring out what Boyarin wants to say here. "Not only that the Torah is not beyond human reach" should mean that the Torah is within human reach. "...but that it is beyond divine reach" means either, [1] "not only that it is not beyond human reach, but that it is [supply: not] beyond divine reach," or, [2] "it is within human reach but it is beyond divine reach." If we do not supply the *not* in version 1, we end up saying that Boyarin

thinks that the author of the passage is saying that human be-
ings can master the Torah, but God cannot. That strikes me
within the context of the text he purports to interpret as little
short of lunatic.

Adherents to the theory he expounds here will maintain that you can say pretty much anything you like about any
text, and in the next paragraph of the same passage, Boyarin
defends himself:

> This brings us squarely up against the di-
> lemma of any hermeneutic theory that does not allow
> appeal to author's intention as a curb on interpretation.
> Once that control is gone, it seems that any interpreta-
> tion is the same as any other, that anything at all can be
> said to be the meaning of the text. Such hermeneutic
> anarchy is clearly *not* the way that midrash presents it-
> self. Within our text both the dilemma and an answer
> to it are offered.

The sentence that follows, we have a right to expect, will
specify the dilemma and the answer. But here is Boyarin:

> Present within the narrative is a commentary on itself,
> namely: "What is 'it is not in heaven'? Said R. Yermia,
> Since the Torah has already been given from Mt. Sinai,
> we do not pay attention to heavenly voices, for You
> have written already at Mt. Sinai, 'Incline after the ma-
> jority.'"
> R. Yermia's rereading of R. Yehoshua solves
> the problem of what constrains interpretation. The an-
> swer is surprisingly modern: the majority of the com-
> munity which holds cultural hegemony controls inter-
> pretation. To put it another way: correctness of inter-
> pretation is a function of the ideology of the interpre-
> tive community.

Boyarin is saying that the message of the passage is: the
community controls the interpretation of the Torah. That is

quite so — but then, why write a whole book to say what we have always known Midrash to mean? If this is what intertextuality has to contribute to the reading of Midrash, it is not even trivial , but merely paraphrastic — just the *peshat.*

Much of the book walks over these same well-trodden paths; when we read his analysis of passage after passage, we know pretty much what we knew before we read his analysis. The publisher's blurb holds: "the best, most cogent and intelligent attempt to date to apply insights from modern literary criticism to the interpretation of midrash." But Indiana University Press appears to have forgotten its own publication of a far more original and compelling work, José Faur, *Golden Doves with Silver Dots* (Bloomington: Indiana University Press, 1986). Those who wish to gain whatever benefit a now-fading theory of literature may offer for the study of Midrash will do far better to dismiss Boyarin's vacuity and turn to Faur.

Boyarin has produced further research on other topics, but so far as I know, he has not returned to the problems so superficially and obscurely treated in this book. It is hard to blame him.

9.

ROBERT BRODY, *THE GEONIM OF BABYLONIA AND THE SHAPING OF MEDIEVAL JEWISH CULTURE.* NEW HAVEN AND LONDON, 1998: YALE UNIVERSITY PRESS

Professor of Talmud at the Hebrew University, Jerusalem, and well-known for his editions and study of Geonic writings, Dr. Brody here provides a systematic compendium on the literature of and concerning the Geonim, the Rabbinic authorities of ca. 500-1000 C.E., an age in the history of Judaism awaiting its systematic reconstruction. For what he has accomplished, Brody deserves only praise. He introduces the pertinent sources and points to the relevant scholarly treatment of them; no one will ignore this exceptionally useful work when taking up its subject.

But, as the contents show, it is not really a book, it is three monographs bound together in the same covers. Brody divides the book into three essentially unrelated parts: the historical setting, the classical Geonic period, and Se'adyah Gaon and after. And the three parts themselves cohere only loosely The historical setting deals with these topics in order: defining the Geonic period (Savoraim and Geonim); the primary sources (Epistle of Sherira Gaon, account of Nathan the Babylonian, the Genizah); the Geonic academies, continuity and change; the multifaceted role of the Gaon; the exilarchate; the struggle against heresy (Anan and the origins of Karaism, issues of contention between Karaites and Rabbanites, Rabbanite reactions); competition with the ites, Rabbanite reactions); competition with the Palestinian center; ties with the diaspora (the sphere of Babylonian hegemony, Palestine and Egypt, the Maghreb, Europe). The presentation of "the classical Geonic period" takes up the literary sources: the intellectual world of the Geonim (knowledge of languages, areas of interest, the supernatural, attitudes towards authority); the Talmudic sources (oral versus written Talmud, interpretation and application of the Talmud); extra-Talmudic oral traditions; the responsa literature; the She'iltot (the genre, form and structure, the She'iltot of R. Ahai, the sources of the She'iltot, the influence of the She'iltot); the earliest legal codes (Halakhot Pesuqot, Halakhot Gedolot). Finally comes a set of essays dealing with Se'adyah: Se'adyah Gaon, revolutionary champion of tradition (Se'adyah's career); the Halakhic monographs; Talmudic exegesis and methodology; theology; biblical exegesis; linguistics and poetry. Clearly, the classical, and correct, program of *Wissenschaft des Judenthums* governs; nothing can be done before these questions are answered.

Alas, as the survey of the contents shows, this is not so much a coherent book, with a cogent program, as a set of discrete research reports, a sequence of free-standing topical papers, encyclopaedia-articles really, some of them more, some less persuasive. The chapters tend to a certain (merciful) brevity and follow a simple formula: survey of sources, low-level paraphrase of their allegations or contents, and not much more than that, except where Brody has done original work. The best of the studies — the ones that draw on his own research — show confidence and mastery and historical imagination, the others summarize the work of third parties, encompassing, also, Brody's often captious outsider-opinions. What he knows first hand, he knows well; but his opinions outrun his knowledge in many areas. The treatment of Karaism is entirely a survey of secondary scholarship, and the presentation of Talmudic literature does not even survey scholarship beyond the most sectarian limits. Indeed, in not a few of the areas where he relies on secondary accounts, alas, Brody does not do a thorough job even of bibliography. Here he gives not so much an opinion as a mere local prejudice: the books omitted are the ones his crowd apparently will not read. That is why many of the treatments are not only incoherent but shallow; the wild incoherence of the presentation of Seʿadyah suffices to make the point that Brody does not do philosophy or history of ideas.

An account of "the shaping of medieval Jewish culture" certainly could have come forth. That is shown by Brody's conclusion, a perfunctory, three-page "epilogue," which can well serve as the opening lines of the coherent book, as distinct from collection of topical essays, demanded by Brody's misleading title, with its concern for Jewish culture: "One might say that this was the last formative age of a unified Rabbanite Jewish culture...Those who have written on this period have rightly emphasized two related phenomena: the transformation of the Babylonian Talmud from a literary corpus to a legal 'code,' which...could serve as an authoritative guide to religious practice...In addition, the Geonim...were engaged in a bitter and ultimately successful struggle against an even more fundamental challenge...to Rabbinic Judaism, mounted by a variety of sectarian movements..." These are tremendously provocative propositions. But none of this affects the logic of the book; it is tacked on, but ought to have stood at the head and dictated the program of the whole. And, it may be noted by the careful reader, the vitality of the prose of the epilogue contrasts with the lifeless prose characteristic of the shank of the book. Where things began to get interesting, Brody stopped work.

Consider then what Brody misses or treats in a superficial and trivial way. He writes about the most important period in the history of religion for monotheism (inclusive of dualism): Christianity in the Near and Middle East, Judaism, Zoroastrianism, and Islam. That is to say, in the same period as that of the Geonim of Babylonia, in the same place and within the same political framework, Islam confronted both Judaism and Christianity with a challenge at once political and intellectual; the regnant religion, Zoroastrianism, began its long, slow decline by perspicaciously writing down its heritage of religious classics; and the now-well-established Christianity of the eastern Roman Empire renewed itself in the crucible of the Muslim *défi*. In Brody's hands, Zoroastrian supplies no analogies (compare, on this same period, this writer's *Judaism and Zoroastrianism at the Dusk of Late Antiquity. How Two Ancient Faiths Wrote Down Their Great Traditions*), Islam scarcely made any profound difference to Judaism or more than an adventitious and practical impact upon it, and in Brody's mind Christianity rarely supplied analogies to clarify the situation of Judaism. It would be difficult to imagine a more complete failure of historical imagination, a more pedestrian recapitulation, in a more parochial manner, of writings that took shape in a time of enormous upheaval. Working within an intellectual ghetto, Brody has succeeded in making boring the single most interesting period in the history of Judaism from late antiquity to the nineteenth century.

But if the failures may characterize an entire academic community, the successes belong to the author himself. These are those of industry, erudition, and systematic inquiry into primary and some secondary sources. Whether the discussion is grounded in personal mastery of sources or merely superficial survey of secondary work, the book gathers a massive amount of information and organizes it accessibly. So, in the balance, Brody's book is definitive and opens many doors. Providing a survey of sources and learning on a variety of relevant subjects, Brody has written what will stand for a generation as the definitive account of the sources: thorough on the principal subjects, broad in scope, and accessible. Here is the starting point for all future research on its subject. Now others, with richer capacities for framing important questions and constructing a coherent historical account of culture can take over and turn the sources into the cultural history that eludes Brody's grasp.

So, as I said, Brody has also provided a research-tool of inestimable value, and no library of Judaism will miss this reference-work. In the balance, then, we must be glad for what we have been given. The philology in hand, others, with different gifts and capacities, may now turn to history and culture.

10.

MENACHEM ELON, *JEWISH LAW. HISTORY, SOURCES, PRINCIPLES*. TRANSLATED FROM THE HEBREW BY BERNARD AUERBACH AND MELVIN J. SYKES. PHILADELPHIA AND JERUSALEM, 1994: THE JEWISH PUBLICATION SOCIETY OF AMERICA. IN FOUR VOLUMES.

This huge work, running over 2200 pages in four volumes, richly subsidized by Philip and Muriel Berman, presents an English translation of the Hebrew *HaMishpat HaIvri*. Elon is an Israeli Supreme Court justice and has written widely on Judaic law, with special attention to the relationship between the law of Judaism and the law of the State of Israel. The work follows a clear outline, in these parts: the history and elements of Jewish law; the legal sources of Jewish law: exegesis and interpretation; the legal sources of Jewish law: legislation, custom, precedent, and legal reasoning; the literary sources of Jewish law; Jewish law in the state of Israel. The author's explicit intent is to present not merely an account of the law of Judaism as presented in Scripture, the Talmud, and medieval and modern codes and responsa, but "an insightful understanding of Judaism itself." The author presents the law, therefore, in the context of not jurisprudence alone but history. As is already clear, much of his discussion concerns the history of the law, not only its principles; the character of the historical literature, not just the inner structure of the law viewed phenomenologically. Here again, he discusses the literary sources, not only the law that they present.

Elon himself recognizes that history is not required for the presentation of law: "From the internal perspective, Jewish law is a seamless web in which elements from the earliest to the most recent are woven into an integrated analytical whole, for which history is... irrelevant." But he immediately proceeds to claim, "Full understanding of any area of Jewish law...requires an appreciation of the law's creative, vitalizing impulse, which can be attained only by careful study of the changes in that area over the course of time, the relationship of those changes to the general nature and circumstances of each historical period, and the particular characteristics of the various centers of Jewish population where Jewish law governed Jewish life." So Elon explicitly claims to give us not merely an account of a vast and encompassing legal system, that of Judaism, viewed whole, from the perspective of eternity. Rather, he wants us to receive his account as a history of the law, its context and its unfolding through time and circumstance.

Unhappily, Elon grasps nothing of historical scholarship in our century, and the work violates the most basic rules of historical inquiry. His knowledge of the literary-critical study of Rabbinic literature is equally selective and shallow, with the result that his presentation of the character of the legal documents is simply unreliable. Organizing the whole as an account of history and literature, Elon fails to give us what he promises, which is, a work on the law in itself. Only when he reaches our own day — Jewish law in the state of Israel — does he deserve a hearing within the framework of contemporary principles of learning. Otherwise the work is a curiosity: false as to history, uninformed as to literature.

As history, for ancient times — the times of Scripture and the Talmuds — the work is hopelessly ignorant and utterly uncritical, because Elon knows nothing at all about the critical historical work of the nineteenth and twentieth centuries that has reshaped our understanding of the history of ancient Israel, on the one side, and the period of the Mishnah and the Talmud, on the other. It is not as though he has read the modern critical literature and chosen to argue with it; Elon appears to have read almost nothing in modern biblical studies, and in the critical study of Rabbinic literature he is equally ignorant. All Elon does is paraphrase the sources, in the obvious conviction that if the source says something happened, that is what happened, in that way; if the source says something was said, that is what was said, in those words. But these premises of historical fundamentalism have long since lost all currency in academic scholarship, and they deny to Elon any serious hearing in the academy or among educated people.

His history of the law to the end of Talmudic times is simply uncritical nonsense, an embarrassment to Israeli scholarship, which outside of the yeshivas certainly knows better. I state very simply that not a single line of this work so far as it pertains to the history of biblical and talmudic times can be taken seriously. As to Elon's account of "the literary sources of Jewish law," the discussion of the biblical, Tannaite and Amoraic literature, to which much of volume III is devoted, is simply not up to date. Beyond the work of the early part of our own century, Elon has grasped nothing of scholarship on that subject; it is not that he knows and disagrees, it is that he simply has not read a vast literature on the very documents he purports to describe. He cites nothing that a modern Orthodox Jew has not written, and he grasps nothing of the issues of scholarship on Rabbinic literature — none of the debates, none of the issues. Alas, I may state very simply that while Elon knows a lot, he does not understand the character of the Talmudic literature, beginning to end; he can at best paraphrase, but he cannot analyze or explain it. That is because he has not done his homework in scholarship: he just does not know the territory, and from his footnotes, it is clear, he does not want to know it.

The pseudo-history around which Elon organizes the work impedes the presentation of the law itself, so he has gained nothing by his piety but lost all possibility of a cogent and systematic presentation of the law, which he surely must know. Readers who want an account of not the history of the law but the law itself will find most of the book confusing and disorganized. Because of his interest in what he conceives is "history," Elon has chosen to lay matters out not in a single coherent structure but in a pseudo-historical pattern. The result is that we do not have a systematic picture of Jewish law and its principles at all, history having taken the place of system. That accounts for the presentation of "legislation, custom, precedent, and legal reasoning" not as an account of a normative law but as a sequential picture of "legislation in the Tannaite period, Amoraic period, Geonic period...." Then comes in volume three another history, this time, the literary sources: Sinaitic revelation to the Tannaim, Tannaitic period, Amoraic period, and so on. If you want to know anything at all about the law of Judaism, not its history and literature, you will find frustrating the organization and exposition that Elon provides.

If most of the work on history and literature up to medieval times is simply worthless, one part of the book wins respect — but therefore stands in judgment upon the rest. It is Volume Four, which is devoted to Jewish law in the State of Israel. Here Elon turns from pseudo-history to a first-class exposition of law in its political context. His topics are these: Jewish law from the abrogation of Jewish juridical autonomy to the establishment of the State of Israel;" "Jewish law in the general legal system of the State of Israel;" "the law of personal status in the Rabbinical and general courts;" and the like. Here Elon knows that of which he speaks, and the entirety of volume IV demands a close and attentive reading. Now he clearly knows the critical literature and the issues, and here he presents matters in a well-structured and cogent manner — thus underscoring his intellectual failure in much of the first three volumes.

Because of the intelligence of Volume IV, Elon cannot be dismissed as just another uneducated yeshiva-type of true believer, the Judaic counterpart to the Bible-belt fundamentalist. But for obvious reasons, he also cannot be relied upon for a sound and informed account of a single historical or literary problem of ancient Israel or late antiquity that he claims to portray. What he gives us as "history" is gullible garbage, and his portrait of what he deems the law's "literature" is simply ignorant. The work is so confused and disorganized that I doubt it will make much of an impact upon other than Orthodox practitioners. But that is a pity, for, when he comes to the interplay of the law of Judaism and the State of Israel, Elon enters a realm in which he participates not as a by-stander, then passing his opinion on matters he does not control or even fully grasp, but as a major player. All the more pity that the larger part of the work, which purports to tell us how things really happened, is a stale rehash of untenable and discredited notions. What a waste! He could have been a contender. Predictably, for this tripe the Hebrew edition of the work in 1979 got an Israel Prize.

11.

MENACHEM FISCH, *RATIONAL RABBIS. SCIENCE AND TALMUDIC CULTURE.* BLOOMINGTON, IN, 1997: INDIANA UNIVERSITY PRESS

Fisch has written an intellectually ambitious book, and the high aspiration implicit on every page to make a considerable mark on Talmud studies in the academy deserves the response of serious and sustained attention. He has succeeded in establishing that the Talmud of Babylonia contains some sayings and stories that he classifies, quite persuasively, as traditional, and others, as anti-traditional. Not an experienced book-writer and scholar of Judaism, however, Fisch sets forth this perfectly good idea in an intellectually prolix and confused manner. His idea has merit, his execution thereof none. Fisch ends up flogging his observation to death.

His book is fundamentally flawed through errors of confusion of distinct modes of thought and analysis. Perfectly valid and, in the hands of others, well-formulated modes of description, analysis, and interpretation — theology, hermeneutics, and exegesis, not to say, historical and literary criticism — come and go in these pages, so that we never can be entirely certain where we stand in the argument, or what is at stake. Specifically a task in religious thought has been assigned to secular modes of inquiry. I think Fisch has made every mistake one can make in confusing theological hermeneutics with historical and literary analysis. He wants mere facts to prove religious convictions, but even if all his facts were factual — and many are not — he still should not have proved his theological proposition. And his presentation proves verbose, pretentious, prolix, and in the end, boring. A mathematician, physicist, historian and philosopher of science at Tel Aviv University and at the Shalom Hartman Institute, Jerusalem, Fisch claims to wish to address to the Talmud, broadly construed the ontological and epistemic questions of philosophy. He does so in response to two essays. The first is Harold Fisch's *Poetry with a Purpose*, where Qohelet ("Ecclesiastes") is read as irony, and the second is this writer's lecture at Tulane University, "Why No Science in Judaism?" (published in *The Making of the Mind of Judaism*. Atlanta, 1987: Scholars Press for Brown Judaic Studies). Professor Harold Fisch, Professor Menachem Fisch's father, reads Qohelet "as an ironic reductio ad absurdum of the very possibility of an anthropocentric, self-sufficient notion of rationality." I maintained that the modes of thought that produce coherent discourse in the Talmud make scientific learning improbable. Fisch proposes the following argument:

> Contrary to the claim attributed by my father to Qohelet, science...provides a living example of a self-sufficient, humanly attainable, rational undertaking that is well aware of its own shortcomings. And, contrary to Neusner, the Talmud's manner of Halakhic reasoning seemed to me to resemble quite closely the type of discourse I had learnt to associate with the scientific method of trial and error.

Here Fisch deals with scientific rationality, with a reconstruction of talmudic epistemology along those lines. That is what he tells us he is going to do.

But this book is not about philosophy of science and it does not deal with Harold Fisch's or my proposals at all. *Rational Rabbis* sets forth a theological argument about traditionalism and anti-traditionalism in the documents of the

Oral Torah as these trends are revealed in various talmudic stories and sayings. Affirmed on one page, denied on the next, Fisch's theory of the historical unfolding of these trends and the temporally determinate points of conflict between them then invokes historical "facts" to validate the presence of an anti-traditionalist "voice." Faced with a barrage of signals about the critical spirit that is supposed to animate the whole, we in the end are asked to accept as fact a mass of attributions of sayings to named masters and descriptions of events, temporal sequences of opinion, and all of the other panoply of the uncritical and gullible pseudo-history that with diminishing success Israeli scholarship asks the rest of the academic world to accept.

The source of energy in the arguments of Fisch's book makes manifest that he is engaged in an altogether different enterprise, one to which both his father's and my essays prove of only marginal interest and in which they play no important role. We provide not the reason but only the excuse for what we shall see is a rather clumsy, intellectually unrefined, demonstration, through naked historicism, of a theological proposition never argued in its own terms at all. Not only so, but while the prose in some of the sections — those involving philosophy of science — is spare, dynamic, and purposeful, when he comes to Talmudic subjects, Fisch turns verbose and prolix. Readers can test that proposition by counting the number of adjectives per page in the opening section, on philosophy of science, with the number on any page chosen at random in the shank of the book. The book then shows itself unfocused and uneconomical and amateurish because, as I shall explain, beyond the opening pages on philosophy of science, the writing only occasionally exhibits the rigor that philosophy of science is supposed to inculcate.

Something Fisch calls "Talmudic culture" (then not defined carefully) then is characterized along the specified lines. The work is in two unequal parts, about a fifth on philosophy of science, and the rest on Rabbinic Judaism. First comes Science as an exemplar of rational inquiry, and, second, the Jewish covenant of learning. This latter section, the bulk of the book, is in these parts and topics:

Chapter I. The great Tannaitic dispute: The Jabne Legends and their context: traditionalism and its discontents, the Jabne reforms, the testimony of Eduyyot, "It is Not in Heaven," Jabne's anti-traditionalist manifesto, a traditionalist response: Hillel and b'nai Beteira;

Chapter II. The changing of the guard: Amoraic texts and Tannaitic legacies: discerning the Bavli's point of view, a schematic overview; introducing the Bavli's paradigm: Berakhot 19b, the logic and rhetoric of transgenerational negotiation, Yerushalmi and Bavli compared, anti-traditionalism for the advanced, and giving away the game or the gentle art of inaudible instruction; and

III. Understanding the Bavli: problem one: explaining the Bavli's double-talk, problem two: discerning the rule of the Mishnah for the Bavli, the Mishnah as a formative code, rational rabbis, or the Mishnah as textbook, "Turn thee around" (Bavli Menahot 29b) or Back to the future."

If this summary of the chapters and their divisions leaves us wondering what has become of "rational rabbis," and their science, at the outset Fisch organizes his statement in response to my view, which he quotes,

> that the paramount of documents...inculcated a particular way f forming propositions and also a particular mode of joining these propositions together into sizable compositions of thought. The very means by which these modes of thought were transmitted and held together, the extraordinary power of analysis and argument characteristic of the normative documents — these explain also the incapacity of those same modes of thought to frame philosophy, including natural phi-

losophy.

Now my stress is on "*means by which these modes of thought were transmitted...*," since I emphasize on how the system formulated by the sages was put together and transmitted by the Talmud of Babylonia, which is a highly systematic mode of thought and argument set forth as commentary, that is, in traditional form. I characterized the Bavli as a system in the form of a tradition ("a traditional system," "a systematic tradition"), and that defined the center of my argument.

The refocusing of matters makes a difference. I have argued in subsequent works that the system itself took shape in profoundly philosophical ways and appealed to philosophical modes of argument. The method corresponded to that of the natural history in the manner of Aristotle, the modes of analysis to the dialectical analysis in the manner of Plato's Socrates. These propositions I show in *Judaism as Philosophy. The Method and Message of the Mishnah*. Columbia, 1991: University of South Carolina Press, and in *Jerusalem and Athens: The Congruity of Talmudic and Classical Philosophy*. Leiden, 1997: E. J. Brill. *Supplements to the Journal for the Study of Judaism,* respectively.[24]

To meet the challenge, Fisch maintains, "one must...compare the ontological and epistemological assumptions behind each of the two great intellectual endeavors, Torah study...and Western science." And that is what he proposes to do. The focus of his analysis is supposed to be, quite properly, the character of science. But Fisch can have formulated his argument in its own terms, for none of this plays any

---

[24]Fisch knew neither of these works when he wrote the book before us, the latter appearing simultaneously with his monograph; but if he kept up on the scholarly literature, he ought to have known the former. It is the fact that Israeli scholarship on Judaism simply does not read overseas work or pay much mind to it. Israeli mathematicians, physicists, historians and philosophers of science, certainly do.

role in his book; it is window-dressing. In fact, at stake in this book, prominent in nearly every discussion in Part II, approximately 80% of the whole, is an acutely contemporary issue pertaining to the politics of Israeli religious life.

It follows that Fisch has composed, in the guise of an academic work of history and hermeneutics, an actively theological polemic against Israeli Orthodox Judaism, which is traditional while he wishes it were otherwise. He wants to set aside the triumphalism — not to mention the obscurantism — of its traditionalism, and this he will do by explaining "the frequently tacit, meditative discourse about the nature of humanly possible intellectual achievement that shaped the thinking of the framers of the Talmudic canon." His main argument is "to substantiate...the presence in the Jewish texts of a major voice, or school of talmudic thought, whose views of human knowledge, learning, and intellectual accomplishment bear a striking resemblance to the latter-day theory of rationality argued for in Part One...anti-traditionalist by virtue of its commitment to the critical appraisal, rather than to the unquestioned reception of its inherited teachings." Part Two proposes to locate and retrieve this anti-traditionalist voice. And here is the theological charge:

> It is a voice that shares with the modern constructive skeptic the idea that no knowledge is set forever, that all knowledge needs to be questioned for its deficiencies, that former rulings and sensibilities have to be constantly reinterrogated. It is a voice that shares with this school of thought a fundamental skepticism towards all first-order knowledge claims, yet premises standards and criteria for deciding between rival conjectures...the view of rationality I argue for and the view of Torah-study I aspire to expose and analyze share a basic openness, an intellectual modesty and a genuine pluralism, that...render the retrieval of the latter especially timely.

Now this formulation on the face of it focuses Fisch's interest on an immediate and practical question facing the practice of Judaism in the state of Israel; it can have been formulated without introducing Harold Fisch's reading of Qohelet or my *Making of the Mind of Judaism.*

For Fisch has given us a theological thesis in the form of a philosophical analysis of a literary problem in historical terms — a massive and needless complication of an issue best argued in its own terms and by appeal to the authoritative documents themselves. He has turned a perfectly valid observation about diverse viewpoints in the Talmud into a problem of hermeneutics, beginning in theology and ending in exegesis, that he is engaged in solving. But he has framed matters in historical and literary terms. So as we move through the book, we can never be sure to whom he wishes to speak and for what purpose; that is what I mean when I term the work prolix and unfocussed, amateurish as book-writing goes. When he speaks of "a steadfast, reactionary traditionalism that preaches rigid and dogmatic adherence to a set of inherited norms for no more reason than that they are inherited," he has turned to a different audience from the one that an academic monograph comprises for the purpose of learning. He has made a tendentious theological argument (as he admitted in so many words)[25] but given it the form of mere secular scholarship. It is a theological argument constructed out of data he deems the mere this-worldly facts of cultural

---

[25]In so stating, he admits he paraphrases Daniel Boyarin. He says his work is consciously modeled after Boyarin's "constant intellectual self-reflection." What, in ordinary language, this can possibly mean — do we have Spinoza's God in academic garb? — I cannot say. But, as we shall see, the massive confusion between theological and historical and literary categories, the dismissal of standard critical considerations, the framing of matters in a self-indulgent way, the casual and capricious dismissal of massive components of the scholarly canon, such as characterize Boyarin's opus to date, also mar Fisch's.

precedent.[26] That confuses matters not only for readers but for the author himself, and it also marks the work within its own limits as political and in the end not pure in its academic vocation.

In fact Fisch implicitly comes to that same judgment when he centers the shank of the book on the texts that he deems pertinent. Since he wants to recover that "voice" that he wishes spoke for Judaism in his own country, in quest of his cultural precedent in the documents the other side values, he frames matters in literary terms: "Whatever second-order considerations informed these texts are to a large extent embedded in the editorial policies and narrative frameworks employed by their framers and redactors." He then thinks that we can take the texts apart "at their appropriate stratified seams" and "reconstruct...each subtext in relation to its proper place, time, and context...." These form on their very surface claims as to not hermeneutics and exegesis in the service of theology, but (mere) historical and literary fact. Those whom he criticizes rightly reject these critical considerations, reading the documents within an altogether different hermeneutics.

But then Fisch shifts ground. He promises only an account for "theories of knowledge...that directed and motivated those responsible for the texts in their finished form." When he speaks of Jabne (a.k.a. Yabneh, Jamnia) or the debates of the Houses of Hillel and Shammai, he means to use "short-hand for the talmudic redactor's views of these matters." In so stating he prays ritual obeisance to the critical program that I have advanced, as those familiar with that program will recognize in every sentence of his presentation.

---

[26]The role of "Talmudic culture" in this book is never explained and only occasionally active. My sense is that he has borrowed the category from the rather odd title of Daniel Boyarin's chair at University of California, Berkeley.

But as we shall see, it is only a formality. For Fisch does make numerous claims that are historical, not merely phenomenological, about the order in which ideas unfolded and the context in which they took shape. He uses the historical past tense; he thinks he is presenting precedents out of determinate time, embodied by great sages, and not merely stories that illustrate attitudes he wished would prevail. The methodological upshot is everything and its opposite: stories and history, descriptions of facts and normative judgments.

To prove his announced proposition about science in Judaism, Fisch did not have to make any judgments of a determinate, temporal and contextual character at all. But, as matters turn out, whether Fisch to accomplish his goal had to give us an account of science as we know it seems to me subject to doubt. The doubt is this: had he not responded to his father's essay and to one of my books that caught his eye, would the issue of science have been required at all for an essay on the two voices, traditionalist and anti-traditionalist, that he wishes to identify in the Talmudic writings? I think not. The history and philosophy of science that he lays out link up to Talmudic theology only because Fisch has so set forth his theological argument as to invoke them. That responds to his professional situation in those fields. Only a mathematician and physicist, of enlightened, integrationist Orthodox convictions, who has turned to philosophy and history of science would have found necessary this quite idiosyncratic framing of the theological question.[27] But one must

---

[27]At the end of this exposition, what emerges is, "The existence of theories of rationality...will not suffice to sustain rational discourse. What are needed are well-established institutions geared to value, stimulate, promote, and reward debate, criticism and reform." But that is the very point I thought I was making about the transformation of a system — Aristotelian method, neo-Platonic message, Socratic medium of analysis — into a tradition, namely, the Talmud's Judaism of the dual Torah, in *The Making of the Mind of Judaism,* which concludes on that very point: Bible

wonder why his publisher has denied him the advantage of a critical reading, and, further, one must find puzzling the professional qualifications of those with whom, at the Hartman Institute, Fisch engages in academic dialogue. Not experienced in book-writing, he has been poorly served by both referees and colleagues.

More to the point, the shank of the book can have been written, and now can be read, pretty much in its own terms. For the rest, "the same notion of rational action...is not only implicit in the modus operandi of the rabbis...but can be shown to have been explicitly and self-consciously adhered to by many of the framers of these documents." Had matters been packaged simply as "anti-traditionalism" and "traditionalism," the point would have been entirely clear. He wants to show that the texts "are framed...as long and sustained arguments against blindly following tradition...Anti-traditionalists take the teachings of their forebears in utmost seriousness, but do so...with a view not to following them indiscriminately so much as to seriously putting them to the test...to reason rationally about the content of their legacies in the same way open-minded and self doubting agents were shown [in the section on science] to act rationally when strivingly knowing to improve upon the systems on which they work."

Not only so, but despite his protestations about not doing history, Fisch thinks he has identified "in at least one major Tannaitic corpus" anti-traditionalism not as merely "one viable option among many" but the normative one. "The anti-traditionalist...is a voice that is central to any understanding of how the founder-fathers of Torah Judaism conceived of themselves and of their great intellectual undertaking." Now that statement unabashedly claims to speak of a

---

and Bavli, tradition in the form of a system, system in the form of a tradition.

determinate past, on the one side, and a specific "corpus," on the other — marks of historical and literary judgment. We no longer speak of what documents say but what the named fathers of Torah Judaism actually thought. So at stake in the end is not a viewpoint that the author wishes to espouse and sustain with appropriate proof-texts, but rather a specific judgment of a historical- and literary-critical character upon the texts that are studied. This work did not have to take the academic form that it did, but since it has, it must be read in the explicit context the author has invoked in judgment of his work: history.

This historical and literary critical claim — denied on one page, embodied in actual words on the next — too is (alas!) explicit: "it is at the Tannaitic level, where the question of the proper attitude towards the teachings of one's forebears hardly effects the redactory and narratory [sic!] level of the text, that the anti-traditionalist voice can be heard most audibly, while in Amoraic treatments of Tannaitic writings, where one would expect the anti-traditionalist approach to be felt most conspicuous, it is present, but curiously and vexingly muted, especially in the Bavli." But most (though not all) of the stories that Fisch labels "Tannaitic" receive the label because of the names in the stories — therefore assumed to have said what is assigned to them, at the time and place that the story-teller has determined — and not because of the point of origination, the document in which the story first appears. He devotes much attention to stories in the Talmud of Babylonia that bear the sign of Tannaite status but first occur only in the final document of the corpus. Indeed, most of his most explicit evidence in fact originates in the final document of the Oral Torah in its formative age, the Talmud of Babylonia, rather than in the first documents to reach closure. On that basis, one might form exactly the opposite hypothesis as to the history of traditionalism and anti-traditionalism in

Rabbinic Judaism in the formative age: the earliest documents were traditionalist, the final one the most sustainedly anti-traditionalist of all.

Fisch claims to characterize the "Amoraic" stratum as traditionalist. But that allegation is simply false in light of the persistent critical spirit toward received opinions exhibited by the Talmud and its authorities both named and anonymous; the regnant voice of the document is dialectical and critical of every factual allegation and proposed probative argument — it is what makes the Talmud talmudic.. The dialectical argument that imparts to the Bavli its dynamism and systemic character in no way gives comfort to what Fisch would call traditionalism. It is fundamental, negative, persistent, tough-minded, systematic, and fresh. Not only so, but the Amoraic materials encompass a vast range of stories about the indeterminacy of specific propositions, the priority of *Auseinandersetzungen* in the processes of learning, the determinative power of reason — all of the traits of Fisch's "anti-traditionalism."[28] So a vast corpus of Amoraic materials, which Fisch knows full well, contradicts his ordering of matters, and, readers may stipulate, a considerable corpus of Tannaitic materials bears the marks of deep traditionalism — beginning, after all, with the opening chapter of tractate Abot! At this point one is tempted to cry out in despair, *iqqar haser min hassefer* — the book misses its point.

So grand a mistake in the characterization of layers of writing ("Tannaitic" and "Amoraic" read as historical not-withstanding) is possible only because Fisch has at once denied the historicist hermeneutic and adopted it. That is, while

---

[28]The really interesting question is how such a sustainedly-critical mode of thought as the Talmud inculcates has produced so subservient and amiable a spirit of traditionalism as characterizes the yeshiva-world that Fisch denounces. That is a question of culture, of Talmudic culture, awaiting his attention.

Fisch repeatedly denies intending a historical account and means by "Tannaitic" "that which is presented by the rabbis as Tannaitic," that is mere dust in the eyes of the scholars. In fact he has a diachronic logic which should give him early anti-traditionalism and late traditionalism, and he says so in so many words; he cannot then take away what he has given with an open hand. Not only so, but when he wishes to explain the data, he invokes nothing less than historical *context,* — not philosophical *logic* — time and again. Fisch not only confuses theological with literary and historical discourse but simply ignores the boundaries between literary analysis and historical narrative.

A single, craftily worded formulation, suffices to show the confusion (I italicize the qualifying language to underscore its substantive irrelevance): "*It is possible that* the Halakhic discussions and the legends recorded by the talmudic literature attest to the fact that *at least some of the* rabbis *may have* regarded, *if even in retrospect,* the shifting of the prime focus of religious performance from the Temple to the academy, from the altar to the synagogue, as a welcome development, as a step forward more than as a necessary evil." With or without the italicized language, the statement concerns what happened, and that is history, not hermeneutics, let alone exegesis of texts. Fisch honestly believes that the texts tell him what was happening beyond their limits, at the time of which the speak, in the place of which they speak. But surely a viable alternative would direct our attention to the time in which the texts take shape, and the issues alive in that day and age and venue. It is possible that the Halakhic discussions attest to the fact that at least some of the rabbis who fabricated these discussions....

And again, in the same context, "...with the fall of Jerusalem Rabbinic Judaism...was in fact significantly transformed from a largely ritualistic religion dominated and regulated by the Temple rituals to a 'community of learners' whose religious life was both structured and informed by the talmudic academy." He cannot have written this sentence and many like it if he really thought that "Tannaitic" means merely, "that which is presented by the rabbis as Tannaitic." Within the very same context he has shaded over into an account of how things were, which (lest we misunderstand) he explains by reference to the historical circumstances that defined Rabbinic Judaism.

Lest readers doubt the inferences I draw, the following language is Fisch's, not mine, in the context of the sentences just now quoted:

> The high point of the talmudic revolu-
> tion...was undoubtedly the establishment of the Jabne
> center...by Rabban Yohanan b. Zakkai..

This, I maintain, is a blatantly historical statement in a diachronic context, not a mere synchronic and analytical characterization of what some stories allege about this and that; historical facts, e.g., the destruction of the Temple, are invoked to explain other facts, which, by consequence, cannot be represented as mere traits of writings but as things that really happened.[29] What Fisch does not realize is that merely alleging a critical position does not suffice; one has also to frame questions within the premises of criticism. That explains why Fisch formulates his presentation as essentially historical, temporally determinate, with the sources attesting to the period of which they speak, not of those for whom they speak,

---

[29]Not only so, but without explaining how late sources tell us what really happened four or five hundred years prior to their redaction, he takes as fact a variety of late allegations, e.., "This is...the widely accepted interpretation of the Talmuds account of Rabban Yohanan b Zakkai's decision to abandon and surrender the besieged Jerusalem on condition that Jabne...be saved."

even while claiming time and again that that is not what he thinks. The very framing of matters betrays him as a highly sophisticated fundamentalist. Once again, hear Fisch:

> We shall focus attention in the first instance on the rabbis' own description...of one crucial moment in the course of one crucial phase of the process. The crucial phase begins with the destruction of the Second Temple and the foundation of the new center of Jewish life and learning at Jabne...From this point on, according to talmudic lore, hampered no longer by the Sadducees and Boethusians, who had virtually vanished after losing their Jerusalem Temple-centered power base, the rabbis set about in earnest to define and deliberate the order of the day among themselves.

Now the qualifying language once more notwithstanding, Fisch has organized his discourse, has framed his questions, has formulated his dialectic, within the premise that he deals with historical facts.[30] Many times as I read his book I regretted he did not know or absorb the explicit lessons of my *Reading and Believing: Ancient Judaism and Contemporary Gullibility.* Atlanta, 1986: Scholars Press for Brown Judaic Studies, where I point to numerous cases in which the premise of the sources' historicity alone can explain the framing of historical questions to the sources.

Had he really believed that all we have is the claim of "talmudic lore," he would have placed this "revolution" of his not in the aftermath of the destruction of the Temple but at that point at which the Talmudic lore took shape and made

---

[30]Worse still, the footnotes for the section under discussion refer only to sources and to articles that take those sources at face value. Fisch really does not grasp how matters change when critical-historical issues of method register. It would be easy to cite note after note that cites a source to sustain a historical fact. But Fisch has promised us that that is not his view of matters.

its statement, in pseudo-historical terms of a determinate point in the past, of what amounted to its theology of the Torah and the proper way in which it should be studied. Narrative theology, after all, defines the mode of discourse of the written Torah; theology in the form of a story constituting the medium of the prophetic message in Genesis through Kings. But in the context in which Fisch wishes to formulate his thesis about traditionalism and anti-traditionalism, to the audience that he wishes to persuade, arguments from historical precedent as set forth in the holy books will carry weight and compel conviction. Not only so, but within integrationist, Western Orthodox Judaism, to be able to show a correspondence between theories of knowledge (epistemology) and a prestigious school in the philosophy of science marks a proposition as weighty and legitimate.

And, once more, Fisch himself supplies the evidence for what is at stake in his presenting his data in one way, rather than in some other:

> In the course of these revolutionary developments, the texts comprising the talmudic canon were written, collated, anthologized and edited.

But if he really believes that the texts are all we have and speak only for themselves, not for what lies beyond their margins, then how does he know that the texts were written at a determinate point, "in the course of revolutionary developments," of which, after all, we are informed only by the very texts that Fisch maintains took shape at that particular moment.

In light of these observations, the shank of the book, noted above, enjoys considerably less interest than at the outset one might have hoped. Once we perceive what actually is going on, we understand the reality. The work is a mass of fundamental contradictions between a critical and a fundamentally gullible spirit. He has given us Yabneh as the turning point, but then tells us "in the Bavli...the anti-traditionalist voice of talmudic Judaism receives its clearest articulation as well as its most effective stifling." These are simply not the same things, they are statements of two distinct orders. Quite what this reference to a metaphor of an anti-traditionalist voice" means is difficult to say. But let me try. I think Fisch means, the Bavli contains stories that convey both viewpoints. Then why not say matters in a clear and simple way and be done with it? And why spend the first fifth of the book on an account of philosophy of science, which then plays no weighty part in the exposition of the Talmudic stories?

But the book sometimes comes alive and overcomes the dread weight of dreary, pseudo-critical argument about pseudo-historical facts. Where Fisch really lives, there he transcends the empty pretense to which I have called attention and sets forth powerful arguments, and I think quite profound analysis. Here he shows what he could have done, had clear thinking and careful, analytical differentiation dictated his strategy of exposition and argument in behalf of his ideas. His discussion of "traditionalism and its discontents" — involving a systematic exposition of the realist position in hermeneutics — shows that of which Fisch is capable. Here he engages in no pseudo-historical reflection but undertakes a systematic argument, a clear and carefully crafted analysis of two contradictory *positions*. And, it pays to notice, when he reaches what he has mastered and knows well, he also writes in unadorned and vigorous prose, without all the heavy burden of prolixity and verbosity, needless and pointless qualification and an excess of wordage, that slows up the reader's progress in much of the rest of the book. Here he shines:

> one would expect thoroughly traditionalist centers of learning...to be [a] unflinchingly dogmatic in preserving

their legacies; [b[highly selective; [c] genuinely critical only of the credentials and authenticity of the bearers of tradition but never of the content of their teachings; and [d] to view themselves as fighting a hopelessly loosing battle to preserve and transmit an inevitably dwindling body of revealed truth. All four features are explicitly associated with the traditionalist opposition envisaged by the Jabne stories, and all four are reputed to have been markedly reversed by the triumphant anti-traditionalist Jabne reformers.

The elegant passage goes on for some pages, and here we do not have to wonder whether he is paid by the word.

Alas, from this point, we plunge back into the paraphrase as history of a variety of stories, deriving from a variety of documents of various periods and venues, and the old pseudo-history and paraphrase of fables take over and put an end to analytical discourse, such as Fisch shows himself entirely able to mount (if not to sustain). To address the remainder of the shank of the book would require saying the same thing about many things, and it suffices to say that the book as a whole suffers from the deep flaws indicated by this survey: a confusion of types of discourse, a claim to criticism that is denied in the very formulation of matters, and a profound misunderstanding of the requirements of theological discourse. Fisch is a victim of the historicism that he clearly hoped to sidestep. This is because he has evaded the critical issues — differentiating theological from historical discourse, devising an accurate and reliable way of characterizing "the Talmudic position(s)," and dealing with the whole and only then the parts.

Any serious worker, motivated by curiosity, will test his mode of explaining data by devising other explanations and asking whether his is the best, the most plausible, way of interpreting the facts. This Fisch does not commonly do, as even the snippets I have given show. That is why it is obvious that he undertook the work to make a point important in his circles of contemporary Orthodox Judaism, and he wants "Talmudic culture" to prove his point by providing a probative precedent. So he has set out to find precedents for the kind of Orthodox Judaism that he wishes would prevail in the state of Israel. He has found those demonstrative facts among the anti-traditionalists for whom his book forms a protracted cheer. That, and not "talmudic culture," is, sum and substance, is what this book is about.

How to explain this disappointing outcome of what is obviously a sincere effort? It is the enthusiasm of the autodidact, the specialist in one thing who wishes to invoke what he knows in the service of what he wants, in some other context altogether, to prove. Clearly, what Fisch knows in a professional, not an impressionistic or merely political, way is philosophy of science, his academic vocation. He also has the power to compose a beautiful treatise of abstract comparison and contrast, as I just showed. But he has worked much harder at philosophy of science than at study, in a professional way, through systematic reading of the academic literature, of the subject at hand. And he is surrounded by amateurs like himself. I state flatly that Fisch simply does not know most of the critical literature produced in the past three decades concerning the sources with which he purports to deal. It is a work, then, of surpassing ignorance of the field in which it claims its place. In his enthusiasm for his position Fisch does not formulate a null hypothesis, such as social and natural sciences routinely set forth; he does not attempt to produce diverse explanations of the same phenomenon and show why his explanation is the most plausible, he does not conduct a critical argument with himself. With lavish spreads of chirpy words he papers over enormous holes in his argument. Time and again he marks himself as a thorough-going amateur.

I do not think he would dare to present to philosophers of science a proposition set forth in the shoddy and ill-informed manner in which he sets forth that of the shank of the book: an effort not to analyze a problem but to prove a point by reading the evidence in one way only. And I do not think he would publish in philosophy of science a work that ignores a sizable sector of the literature on the problem of his monograph. I doubt that a professional monograph series in history and philosophy of science would have permitted so bald a disaster to take place in its pages: a failure simply to consult the pertinent academic literature and to conduct a systematic *Auseinandersetzung* therewith. As between his un-winning enthusiasm and his massive ignorance of much of the scholarly literature, which he has not read, and, worse still, the implications of which he has not absorbed into the fabric of his argument and its formulation, I am inclined to blame the failure of the book on the latter. Fisch really does not know the territory, he has not read the critical discussion of several decades, and that is why he could formulate his proposition — the theological one, I mean — in so goofy a manner.

So a good intention has come to poor execution. The failure of intellect that characterizes the very framing of matters here, I am inclined to think, finds its explanation in the difference between vocation and avocation. It is what must happen when a scholar of Jewish origin and commitment who has achieved distinction in a secular field of learning presents himself as a voice in the sacred sciences. There he decides to use what he has learned in secular learning for advancing a bright idea in the service of the sacred sciences of Judaism that he knows but has mastered only superficially. Scholars from the periphery bring to the center of those sacred sciences important learning only when those scholars at the margins of matters devote to the sacred sciences the same rigorous thought and disinterested learning that have distinguished them in their secular studies. And first of all they must do their homework in the same disinterested and conscientious way in the Judaic area that they do in the secular one. Absent that same seriousness about the Torah that the secular sciences demand, the result can only prove immature and enthusiastic: theology made easy, criticism evaded, only the immediate requirements of local theological politics well served.

12.

ISAIAH M. GAFNI. *LAND, CENTER AND DIASPORA. JEWISH CONSTRUCTS IN LATE ANTIQUITY.* SHEFFIELD, 1997: SHEFFIELD ACADEMIC PRESS. JOURNAL FOR THE STUDY OF THE PSEUDEPIGRAPHA SUPPLEMENT SERIES

Professor of Jewish History for Talmudic times at the Hebrew University, Isaiah Gafni here presents his Louis Jacobs Lectures in Rabbinic Thought of 1994, given at the Oxford Center for Hebrew and Jewish Studies. The lectures are on these subjects: [1] Jewish dispersion in the Second Temple and Talmudic Periods: punishment, blessing, or universal mission? [2] At home while abroad: expressions of local patriotism in the Jewish diaspora of late antiquity; [3] Between activism and passivity: rabbinic attitudes towards "the Land;" [4] Burial and reinterment in the Land of Israel: the best of both worlds; [5] Babylonia and the Land of Israel: the loyal opposition. The work focuses on problems of culture and religion, not the actualities of historical events. Gafni describes the project as follows:

> The first two chapters set out to examine two distinct psychological and behavioral components that nevertheless may have combined to establish a Jewish comprehension of the nation's continued dispersion...an introspective Jewish attempt to explain the ongoing Jewish dispersion in the light of the corpus of

sacred Jewish texts...From a totally different direction, Jews in the diaspora also found themselves addressed on the issue by their brethren living in the Land of Israel. For a number of reasons and within a particular historical context the sages of Palestine began to project voluntary diaspora life as something akin to national treason and abandonment

The second chapter...detect[s] the various ways in which a Jew might identify with his non-Jewish surroundings and evince a sense of...local patriotism

The third chapter of my study examines the crucial stages in the development of what might be considered in modern terms an active Zionist ideology, that is, a Palestinian demand for commitment to the Land that was accompanied...by an attempt to render all Jewish life outside the Land illegitimate

And so we find ourselves by the third century confronted by two rabbinic communities...that appear to be on a collision course which can only result in some sort of mutual excommunication. The fact that this did not take place suggests that religious as well as practical solutions were formulated...the fourth and fifth chapters of this study take up these solutions and examine the religious behavior as well as the rhetoric that enabled the major community of the Jewish diaspora in Late Antiquity to assert itself and assume an almost totally independent position vis-à-vis the Land of Israel, while at the same time evincing a loyalty to the Land not only as a hallowed religious concept but also as the historically sanctioned center of Jewish leadership.

The section, "Conclusions," yields the following main points:

The Jewish understanding of dispersion [involved] how different Jewish communities perceived their particular position within a range of contexts. Certain Jewish authors attempted to explain their community's role within the broad sweep of Jewish history...[there was] a major distinction between the sense of "belonging" evinced by Jews in the Graeco-Roman world and a totally different sort of familiarity with the local surroundings felt...by the Jews of Babylonia...These communal self-images...were influenced in no small way by events of the immediate past and...the destruction of the Temple...placed the general issue of dispersion...in a totally new context...For the first time we begin to encounter statements requiring a commitment to the Land that go far beyond the keeping of certain agricultural laws within its borders...it was precisely at this time that the Jewish community beyond the Euphrates river realized the enormous potential for its own development that was created by the sweeping redefinition of Jewish religious values...introduced by the sages of the Yavne period in their question to fill the void left by the destruction...the rabbinic literary corpora of Palestine and Babylonia reflect a growing tension between the communities, based on totally different concepts of how, and under whose guidance, the religious life of the Jewish people should be run...

The shank of the book focuses upon a sequence of research-problems, well articulated; the work is erudite and well-argued. The book is somewhat diffuse, but the fourth and fifth chapters hold together well and work out a single problem.

Issues of method and of substance clearly demand attention. As to the former, Gafni's utilization of stories as evidence for what was actually happening invokes critical considerations only inconsistently. At some points he thinks sayings represent the time and place of their author, in others, not. But he does not take for granted the historicity of attributions and narratives, and that represents a step forward. Not only so, but since he pursues problems of culture and religion, the uncertain theory of how to use Rabbinic sources for historical purposes does not weigh heavily throughout. At critical points, e.g., in chapter five, Talmudic stories bear a heavier weight of probative historical truth than they might

justifiably be asked to carry. But the real problem, start to finish, is that Gafni clearly asks the sources to tell us not only
the viewpoint of the authors but also, and especially, what
was going on in the world beyond the sources, as my summary indicates, and that remains to be demonstrated, not
merely assumed as methodological given. Since he has made
his own the critical agenda of academic Talmudic studies, he
will want to address that issue and its implications for the
framing of research problems. But in the present case, I think
his choice of a problem in the main matches the character of
the sources and his use of them.

     As to matters of substance: Gafni to begin with in-
vokes, but does not justify, analytical categories that are self-
evidently contemporary. These are not demonstrated to pertain to the period under discussion. This the author admits at
the outset. Then the problem of category-formation accounts
for the haphazard and not entirely cogent program of exposition. In his framing of the question of Land and Diaspora, I
think Gafni is right: it is not a, but *the* critical issue of ancient
Judaism from 70 onward. But that is not for his reasons —
his topical program, which, as I said, mixes quite distinct
communities of Judaism and discusses "the diaspora" as
though it were of one mind and one character. That requires
him to mix together a variety of distinct bodies of sources,
different from one another not only in origin but in character
and historical pertinence.

     Why do I insist that Gafni has identified a critical is-
sue then, not only now. Powerful arguments based on the
very character of the Judaism that was nascent in the very period at hand would have sustained his insistence upon the
centrality of the Land. The Mishnah and the Halakhic system
inaugurated there builds upon that very foundation, amplify-
ing the great themes of the Pentateuch — the loss by Israel of
the Land running parallel to the loss by Adam of Eden, the

restoration of the Israel to the Land as the goal of the entire structure. If I were interested in analyzing the categories under discussion here, I would have begun with the contrast between the two Talmuds' reception of the Halakhic system, the Yerushalmi's focus upon the laws pertinent to the Land, the Bavli's omission of reference to those category-formations altogether. I should then have framed the issue first of all as a Halakhic one, and only then as an aggadic one, e.g., the status of commandments that pertain to the Land alone and how these are to be negotiated abroad, the priority of the Land such that much of the halakhah bore no consequences for Jews overseas, e.g., the entire purity-system excluding only menstrual uncleanness. There is where Land/Diaspora relationships permeated the very fabric of the Rabbinic culture. The problem facing Babylonian Jewry derived from the very character of the Pentateuch: how can one practice the Torah of Moses beyond the Holy Land? The Halakhic system set forth by the Mishnah and the Tosefta — which is to say, *The* Halakhah — reinforced that question and made it urgent by actualizing the Pentateuchal narratives and norms into a systematic design for holy Israel's social order, cases transformed into laws, narratives into normative principles. Gafni has approached this problem from a trivial perspective, rather than at the heart of matters: Hananiah, Joshua's nephew's, intercalating the calendar outside of the Land defines his principal case in chapter five!

From the creation of the halakhah by the Mishnah to the twentieth century, the Land formed a ghostly presence for diaspora Israel, meaning nearly everybody — not to be ignored, but not to be admitted into the primary discourse either. It would be unfair to say Gafni's book misses the main point of its problem, but it does not hit the mark either. Nonetheless, as a work of erudition and learned imagination, the lectures fit the occasion and the honoree, and deserve respectful reading.

13.

MOSHE HALBERTAL, *PEOPLE OF THE BOOK. CANON, MEANING, AND AUTHORITY*. CAMBRIDGE, 1997: HARVARD UNIVERSITY PRESS

Halbertal, a professor of Jewish Thought and Philosophy at the Hebrew University, writes on "the canonical text and the text-centered community. In particular, I seek to understand the Jewish tradition as a text-centered tradition...as this centrality [sic!] affects life on earth...I have chosen to focus on the shared commitment to certain texts and their role in shaping many aspects of Jewish life and endowing the tradition with coherence." This, he claims, "takes the place of theological consistency." In this work of ignorance and self-indulgence, all he means is that various Judaic systems have diverse views: "These conceptions...have little in common and they are specifically Jewish only insofar as each is a genuine interpretation of Jewish canonical texts." But who is to determine what is a genuine interpretation and a wrong one? What we have is an exercise in theology in the form of description of how various documents have been read — that is to say, an abdication of intellectual responsibility. Halbertal meanders through this and that and in the end discovers nothing very special.

If the program of the work — Judaism through books — strikes readers as familiar, being the model that has governed intellectual history and theology from the formation of the Wissenschaft des Judenthums to the present, the execution will disappoint as well. The work is badly written, ignorant of most of the scholarship of the past half-century on many of the very writings treated here, and disorganized and free-associative — a mass of confusion and disconnection. The impoverished aspect of intellect finds its match in the poor quality of research.

Predictably, the book is sketchy and sustains no continuous account even of the announced subject. The work is organized "thematically," "different historical moments and...the various canons as they relate to the theme at hand." How much hard work Halbertal saves himself in the resort to "thematic" presentation of the topic (we can hardly say, the problem) he has chosen to address. He summarizes the work in this language:

> The first chapter discusses relationships between canon and meaning. The second treats tensions and competing ideas about the notion of authority of texts and interpreters, while the problem of the value of text and curriculum is discussed in the third chapter. Each chapter deals with a different canon within the Jewish tradition: the fist focuses on the canonization of the Bible [he means, Tanakh, he does not deal with the New Testament] and its effects on Jewish trends in its interpretation; the second analyzes the canonization of the Mishnah and subsequent codes in the Jewish tradition as they relate to the problem of authority and controversy; and the third deals with the struggle accompanying the rise of the Talmud as the main text in the Jewish curriculum from the Middle Ages onward. Although the intense production of different Jewish canons over such a long time does not receive a systematic historical treatment, the accumulated total does serve as a continuous resource for dealing with problems of canons in their relation to meaning, authority, and value within the Jewish tradition...

Anyone who has followed scholarship in the study of religions and their texts (not "canons"!) will find nothing surprising in an inquiry into how the continuous reading of authoritative writings over time provides a means of defining a religion in an other-than-theological way.

Covering so much ground, Halbertal depends upon secondary literature throughout, passing his opinion everywhere but contributing original scholarship nowhere. Then the value of the work — meaning, Halbertal's opinion on this and that — must rest in the end on the quality of research, and that is in two aspects.

First, does he bring fresh ideas or conduct stimulating analyses? No, he does not. What is truly remarkable in this book is how Halbertal solemnly and pretentiously states banalities and asks us to receive them as wonderful and new. Any standard religious studies textbook or encyclopaedia article (and Halbertal seems to know almost nothing of the study of religion) will greet this work with a huge ho-hum. For from square one ("Texts form a normative canon; they are obeyed and followed, as, for example, are Scriptures and legal codes") to the conclusion on "the Bible" instead of the Talmud in Israeli politics (the reversal of the curriculum from Talmud to Bible represents a major shift in political awareness and identity...."), what we have is an interminable parade of self-evident and (in context) vacuous observations, things that textbooks and encyclopaedias and handbooks have long recorded. What Halbertal contributes is a turgid way of saying the obvious. In defense of Jerusalem scholarship I hasten to add — that conception of what scholarship requires cannot be imputed to Hebrew University professors alone.

Second, does he at least provide a reliable account of the state of the various questions he raises? No, he does not. Alas, while most professors conduct a dialogue with scholarship, I state flatly that, when it comes to his treatment of the

Mishnah and of rabbinic literature, which I know, Halbertal presents himself as utterly ignorant; he simply has not read the scholarship outside of what he implicitly deems "canonical." But that marks Halbertal as a politician, not a scholar, for in scholarship the canon encompasses all learning, not only some of it. His narrow, selective reading of a vast corpus of work on the very subjects that he addresses marks the man as too ignorant of a vast range of scholarly discussion to deserve consideration. All we learn from Halbertal's second chapter is how things look to someone who does not choose to read the scholarship on his subject. (Not a specialist in the areas treated in the first and third chapters, I can only hope he does a better job there, but I doubt it.) The result is pseudo-scholarship of surpassing superficiality and sustained, conceptual confusion.

14.

GALIT HASAN-ROKEM, *WEB OF LIFE. FOLKLORE AND MIDRASH IN RABBINIC LITERATURE*. TRANSLATED BY BATYA STEIN. STANFORD, 2000: STANFORD UNIVERSITY PRESS

By "folklore," people generally mean, the expression of ordinary people, as distinct from the high culture of intellectuals and other educated persons. Professor Galit Hasan-Rokem, Hebrew University folklore scholar, here deals with "folk narratives" embedded within Lamentations Rabbati, a fifth or sixth century Rabbinic reading of the book of Lamentations. She defines her focus of interest in this language (p. 88):

"Folk narratives are a part of literature. A mutual relationship prevails between the written literature of a society and its folk literature, including its oral sources...Folklore refers to a range of creative modes performed through auditory, visual, and cognitive means."

This last refers to "popular beliefs and their concrete expression in customs and rituals. Common to all forms of creativity in folklore as a cultural phenomenon is that they are traditional and collective." Given the clarity of this definition, we should expect an equally well-composed program of inquiry, and we are not disappointed. But in fundamental ways the enterprise demands equally clear analytical exposition, which we shall have to seek elsewhere in Hasan-Rokem's corpus, because it is not here.

There are two principal issues that the work provokes, first, the classification of the data that are analyzed, second the promise to clarify a particular document of the Rabbinic canon. As I shall point out, the epistemological foundations of the field of folklore define as premises a set of judgments not necessarily subject to rational criticism. That is because no clear criterion of verification or falsification attaches to the judgments made as to what is, or is not, folklore. If, as we shall see, the learned rabbis produce "folklore," then what would not qualify as "folklore"? And why is this a useful category-formation in the analysis of Rabbinic culture and literature?

Second, while claiming to speak of "Midrash" in Rabbinic literature, Hasan-Rokem limits herself to some stories in a single document. She ignores the document viewed whole and does not compare and contrast that document to others of its classification and canon. So we have to ask whether she has defined a documentary context or explained the venue of the stories that she addresses: what validates her judgment that these stories represent "Midrash." The two questions, to which we return presently, are complementary, the first asking whether "Midrash" qualifies as "folklore" and second whether the venue of the stories has been properly described, analyzed, and interpreted. Much of the rigorous thought required to validate the enterprise has yet to be undertaken by Hasan-Rokem. She begins in the middle, not at the beginning, of her exposition.

Rather than focus solely on what she does not accomplish, let us turn to what she does contribute. Here is a brief summary of her program and proposition:

1.   "The study of folk narratives in Rabbinic literature:" "The concern of this book is with the presence of

folk literature and folk culture in Palestinian aggadic literature in Late Antiquity...The scholarly concern with aggadic literature is rich and manifold...All scholars of aggadic literature have acknowledged that folk literature was an aspect of the spiritual and cultural creativity of the rabbis..." Here I find much confusion, and for obvious reasons. If we take "the rabbis" to represent high culture, then how conceive of "folk literature" as a part of their creativity? There follows a potted survey of prior works on folklore of ancient Judaism, a lot of opinion-passing of no particular interest. This is the one chapter of the book that should have been dropped. That is because it is vacuous and pretentious — just a collection of commonplace opinions, lacking all critical acumen — and contributes nothing. The book is better than its beginning — by far. Each of the chapters of the shank of the book works on a particular story, but whether the story exemplifies something beyond itself, a trait of the document as a whole, is never established. The main contribution of the work is the acute and sensitive reading of these stories.

2. "The literary context of folk narratives in the Aggadic Midrash: interpreting narrative structure:" "the literary context...the most visible within the general framework encompassing the folk literature included in aggadic Midrash." Now we have Aggadah as a venue, but not as "folklore" by definition. But this is quite confusing, for the categories are not carefully delineated, with the result: "The novelistic folk narrative of a tragic human destiny at the time of the destruction of the Temple...unfolds in the Midrash, after its literary re-creation, as a masterful work of art." The story here concerns two children, taken captive in the fall of Jerusalem, and how in captivity they realized that they were brother and sister. The reading of the story, which occupies the greater part of the chapter, does little to validate its classification as "folklore," since the elements of high art are per-

suasively identified and interpreted. If Chagall qualifies as folklore, so does this story in Hasan-Rokem's subtle reading of it.

3.   "The genre context of folk narratives in the Aggadic Midrash: Riddles about the wise people of Jerusalem:" Here the argument of folklore is much more articulate and compelling: "One of the ways to identify a folk narrative within the Midrashic corpus is to place it under a specific genre rubric." I believe what she means (English is not her native language) is, there is a set of genres characteristic only or mainly of folklore. If we can classify a story of a Midrash-compilation within one of those established genres, we may fairly assign it to the category of folklore. Here she turns to a sequence of eleven riddle tales (p. 45). These she reproduces without attention to their formal traits, without noting the highly sophisticated rhetorical medium that conveys the stories. But she makes her case: "this collection of riddles is not only one of the clearest conceptualizations of generic coherence in Lamentations Rabbah, but one of the most cohesive such collections in the entire corpus of rabbinic literature." Not only so, but she concludes with a passage of surpassing eloquence: "The subject, then, is loss. Loss takes many forms, in the world and for humanity. Life could be said to go from loss to loss, transforming one into another. When the human being turns from the darkness of loss to the glare of loss, life becomes an attempt to understand one loss through another, an attempt to understand the God within loss and the loss within God. The nothingness" (p.63). At stake in this work is something far more profound than issues of folklore analysis. The dedication here is realized: "in memory of Amitai, my firstborn (1973-1990)." Here scholarship rises to the height of transcendence, aesthetics shades over into theology, and the stakes of learning enter into solemnity. Anyone who doubts that scholarship too verges on the sublime had best engage

with Hasan-Rokem. This chapter strikes me as the strongest in the book, and the best argument for folklore as a scholarly episteme in the analysis of culture.

4.   "The comparative context of folk narratives in the Aggadic Midrash: folk narrative as intercultural discourse:" "Folk narratives in aggadic Midrashim convey the immediate cultural context of the narrators…Yet folk narratives, recognized for their cultural and linguistic mobility, may also indicate links between their society of origin and other cultures" (p. 67), demonstrated through three of the eleven stories dealt with in the preceding chapter. India and Arabia yield parallels. Hasan-Rokem would like to link the Rabbinic stories to the Arabian counterparts, shading over into an implicit allegation of borrowing: "part of the communication between the cultures." This chapter carries forward the foregoing and is systematic and well-organized.

5.   "The folkloristic context of folk narratives in the Aggadic Midrash: tales of dream interpretation:" A passage of Lamentations Rabbati dealing with the interpretation of dreams is taken up: "On the one hand, this passage is a folk narrative describing events about dream interpretation; on the other, it sheds light on a characteristic folk practice, the endeavor of dream interpretation, providing us with detailed information about its participants, its underlying beliefs, and its spiritual assumptions." Here Hasan-Rokem does not exploit available methods of comparing and contrasting comparable or parallel stories as these occur in various Rabbinic documents. That is, she ignores the synoptic method, which is commonplace in literary study. While introducing comparable stories that occur in other documents, Hasan-Rokem does not systematically compare them. That leaves her open to the charge of being impressionistic and unsystematic. She concludes, "The interpretation of dreams is a powerful cultural tool that serves to regulate relationships between social

forces. The rabbinic context privileges scholars in the academy as legitimate dream interpreters. These scholars thus play
a central cognitive role in the...attempt to map out the twi-
light zones of uncertainty surrounding human life." What all
this has to do with folklore I cannot say, nor does she. She
concludes with what can have served as the starting point of
analysis, were the issues those of cultural interpretation as
they are in the academic study of religion: "It is not a mere
coincidence that stories of dream interpretation, like riddle
stories, have a central position in Lamentations Rabbah, a
Midrash about the destruction of the Temple, for they are intimately connected with the fundamental experience of this
text." Clearly, then, the document figures, and the issues of
documentary analysis circulate in Hasan-Rokem's mind. But
they are not realized in analysis and exposition, systematic or
even episodic. Here is a brilliant idea that goes to waste because it is not lucidly articulated and rigorously expounded.

6.   "The social context of folk narratives in the
Aggadic Midrash: the feminine power of laments, tales, and
love:" "We read folk literature in Lamentations Rabbah in its
social context...highlighting the perspective of women, both
as characters in the stories and as part of the society creating
the folk literature." Women emerge "as bearers of concrete
folk-literary traditions, especially in the genre of the lament."
This chapter seems to me to work well. But it is filled with
special pleading.

7.   "The religious context of folk narratives in the
Aggadic Midrash: the rhetoric of intimacy as a rhetoric of the
sacred:" Here is another spectacularly weak chapter. And it is
weak because of a simple failure of scholarship. Hasan-
Rokem is making judgments without knowing the territory,
and she does not know that she does not know; her bibliography lacks an entire category of sustained scholarship on the
very subject under discussion. Specifically, Hasan-Rokem be-

gins with the following heuristic given: "Rabbinic Midrashim do not formulate a systematic religious doctrine or philosophy. Rather they constitute a complex of more or less fixed associations, in which congruity is ensured through the links to the biblical text, established through frequent reference. Central experiences in the relationship between the people of Israel and God…take various forms in the Midrash which, constantly reilluminated, create a complex and multivalent system of meanings." How a "system of meanings" is different from "a systematic religious doctrine or philosophy" I cannot say. I can only state that, to deny the presence in the Midrash-compilations of a corpus of systematic religious doctrine is to miss the very center and soul of the Midrash-compilations. There certainly is such a doctrine in Lamentations Rabbati, and it is articulated, dominant, coherent. Hasan-Rokem does not perceive it, because, as I said, she simply does not know the scholarship on this very document — as on all of its companions — that demonstrates its presence and defines its details. That is why I state very simply, in this chapter, Hasan-Rokem does not know what she is talking about. Her mode of argument — always from example and episode — here betrays her. It precludes her knowing what she is talking about. Had she examined the document whole and complete, e.g., outlining it as it has been outlined and so identifying its principal propositions, secondary amplifications, amassing of evidence and argument, all in exegetical form, she would have known better. Further, had she compared and contrasted it with other documents, also read whole and complete, she could never have written the ignorant judgments that she here sets forth. There is simply a vast literature on this very problem, of the existence of which she is ignorant. Pity.

8.   "The historical context of folk narratives in the Aggadic Midrash: three tales on Messianism:" Here at is-

sue is "the historical context of folk narratives found within
Palestinian aggadic Midrashim…History, because it reflects
the self-perception of a society over a time reaching back
from the present to the past, is itself a conceptual and cultural
category meaningfully present in folk narratives. The historical context of Palestinian aggadic Midrashim is reflected in
them mainly as a plight of suffering, oppression, and loss.
Folk narratives in this literature bear the same mark. The literature of the period…also contains elements of deliverance
from the painful and humiliating historical present, a deliverance that may be characterized as utopian in its hints of a
complete reversal of the course of history." Quite what she
means by "historical context" clearly differs from the ordinary use of that language. She does not mean, things that
really happened. Here she means, "the legend and the myth,
two generic terms…The distinction between folktale and legend is based mainly on the way each represents the world,
which is manifest in differences of form, content, and style.
The legend represents a possible world, in terms of concepts
and beliefs current in the narrating society. Almost everything
that is true of the folktale is reversed in the legend…but genres, as ideal types or models in general, do not usually appear
in 'pure' form. Folk literature offers listeners…countless in-
termediate forms, and elements characteristic of the folktale
may appear in legends, and vice versa." My sense is, this "criterion" of differentiation between the one and the other is so
subjective that she might as well claim, "I know the difference when I see it." There is no replicating her method and
producing the same result. But the story of Yohanan ben
Zakkai's abandoning Jerusalem as told in Lamentations Rabbati certainly is to be classified as a claim to tell history, something that really happened, not legend or myth in the view of
the story-teller. Here Hasan-Rokem goes over quite familiar
ground: "the story about the fall of Jerusalem is also the story

about the creation of a new communal-cultural entity." How this qualifies — the story of the founding of Rabbinic Judaism's principal institutional expression, the master-disciple circle — as "folklore" I cannot say. It strikes me as the very opposite, and the sophistication of the narrative strengthens that judgment. Burt she insists, "The folk elements…are many and varied." Then, once more, we are left with a distinction that, in its realization, makes very little difference. And that judgment is validated by Hasan-Rokem herself: "The folk narratives discussed in this last chapter clearly convey the central assumption of this book in general, namely, that folk narratives in the literature of Palestinian amoraim are literary works devoted to the central issues concerning scholars and their society at the time." Who would have thought otherwise? Well, as a matter of fact, Hasan-Rokem thinks otherwise: "They are told within the generic context of folk literature, which includes the legend and the folktale as its main forms of prose, and they embody the dialectical interaction between those generic poles in the actual text. The comparative context of folk literature points to the links of these stories to the folk literatures of other contemporary cultural and ideological groups…and to types of stories found in other cultures and in other periods, on the other…" And so forth. All this adds up to very little: it's folklore, except when it's not folklore, and anyhow, what difference does it make?

The book contains many insights and aperçus of real value. This account of the parts does not do justice to the many valuable observations about this and that that Hasan-Rokem sets forth. But it does suggest that the whole adds up to less than the sum of the parts. There is no thesis, no proposition, no problem that is solved. I see three possibilities for a scholarly book of maturity and weight, ways of making a coherent statement, not just setting forth a mishmash of observations shading over into free association.

A scholar, first, can set forth a systematic state of the question, reviewing the literature — on method and substance alike — and so providing perspective on a subject. The opening chapter of this book does not accomplish that goal or even try; it is spotty and subjective and uncomprehending.

Second, a scholar can propose a proposition and systematically construct an argument — evidence, analysis — to sustain that proposition. I already pointed out one such massive and important proposal made by Hasan-Rokem herself: ": "It is not a mere coincidence that stories of dream interpretation, like riddle stories, have a central position in Lamentations Rabbah...for they are intimately connected with the fundamental experience of this text." I wish that I could point to the passage(s) where Hasan-Rokem defines what she means by "the fundamental experience of this text" and demonstrates that what she conceives to be that fundamental experience actually prevails in defining the generative problematic of the document. But she does not do so.

And, third, a scholar can define a problem that requires solution, spell out why the problem is important (what is at stake, why this not that?), how she proposes to solve the problem, why her proposed solution does solve the problem, and then, the matter having been defined, do the work systematically and thoroughly. This work of problem-solving, my account of the contents of the book shows, Hasan-Rokem does not address at all.

If further evidence of the incoherence of the work viewed whole is required, I offer the following mental experiment. Try reordering the chapters, putting No. 8 at No. 2 (omitting reference to Chapter One, the "state of the question" study). Would the sense of either chapter change? I think not. Clearly, chapters three and four go together. But if the chapters were set forth in some other order than the present one, each would make as much, or as little, sense as it does in its present position. That is a mark that the chapters are free-standing articles (except for chapters three and four, which are continuous). They do not take up and systematically spell out and demonstrate a particular proposition, they do not logically solve a problem, step by step, and they do not cohere, except because the author says they cohere, in their present, or in any other, order. What I take this failure to define a strategy of exposition to mean is, Hasan-Rokem is not working with any model of great scholarship in her mind, an ideal of what would mark true academic accomplishment. If I mention great works of problem-solving through analytical argument, such as Harry A. Wolfson's hypothetical reconstruction and systematization of Western philosophy from Philo to Spinoza, or great works of propositional demonstration, such as Gershom Scholem's *Major Trends in Jewish Mysticism*, I make myself readily understood. There are models of how the work should be done. I cannot point to the equivalent aspiration, the one that is replicated, even partially, in this work.

So much for the book in detail. Now let us turn to the two issues raised at the outset: does "folklore" pertain to Rabbinic literature? Second, can we really ignore the documentary context in which stories and sayings find their place in Rabbinic canonical compilations, and what do we lose when we do?

First comes the pertinence of the category, "folklore:" is this not merely a fabricated category-formation, yielding nothing of systematic, analytical interest? In the context of Rabbinic documents, once we have declared a story "folklore," what has we learned, what do we now know that we did not know prior to that declaration?

The main issue rises in the preface. It concerns the legitimacy of reading any passage of the Rabbinic corpus as the expression of anyone other than a learned sage: "Some approaches claim that patterns of study prevalent at the academies, reflecting the scholars'; intense exegetical concerns, had a decisive influence on the artistic form assumed by the texts. Other approaches emphasize the influence of the public sermon at the synagogue...My own approach is to show how both of these formative bodies — the academy and the synagogue — were also open to other socializing institutions...the family, rural and urban public spaces, and the political, commercial, and artistic discourse of the time. The voices expressed in the text represent both the elite and the broader layers of society" (pp. xi-xii). So by "folklore" a distinction is made between "elite" and "masses," the latter then constituting that "folk" that yields the "lore." Then how are we to know, other than a priori, what belongs and what does not belong?

Here the problem of the field of "Jewish folklore" presents itself: the venue of the data. Lamentations Rabbati is a highly formalized and disciplined text. It is a cogent statement and a coherent one. Included within it are stories that Hasan-Rokem classifies as "folklore." These she removes from their documentary context and analyzes in their own terms. But she does not undertake a reading of the document as a whole and position its folkloristic elements within the documentary context. But that context cannot be classified as ordinary; it is a highly sophisticated literary construction, part of a larger corpus of writings exhibiting acute religious sensibility. Everyone who has ever opened the document has recognized the presence of free-standing stories — the ones on which Hasan-Rokem concentrates. But do they represent the documents and suffice to classify the writing as "folklore." Or are they parachuted down into an elite piece of writing, for purposes that are readily surmised, e.g., supplement or illustration — or for no documentary purpose at all? These are questions that Hasan-Rokem does not raise, because for her, the matter is settled by definition. Synagogue-sermons (if that is what they were, and many doubt it, whom Hasan-Rokem does not know) or academic disquisitions define the main lines of structure and order of the documents that contain folktales (within her definition), but in focusing on those tales and subjecting them to acute analysis, Hasan-Rokem simply defines the document viewed whole.

This yields a complete misrepresentation of the character of Rabbinic compilations of Midrash Aggadah, which is disciplined, the product of sophisticated intellects and the work of high culture indeed (to remain within her categories). Indeed, she does not even acknowledge the working, in the document, of a theological system, the presence of a theological structure, which governs the selection and the ordering and exposition of most of the document. So we are asked to read "Midrash" as "folklore," but the character of the Midrash-document does not sustain the very taxonomic decision that defines the project. Folklore is "popular." But the aesthetics and theology of Lamentations Rabbati, as of most of the other Midrash-compilations of the formative canon, presuppose a high culture of sophistication, a level of knowledge of Scripture that renders the data into a ubiquitous presence, and the propositions spelled out as the outcome of profound and sustained, critical and rigorous thought. In this context, the Israeli religion professor, Ithamar Gruenwald of Tel Aviv University, writes, ""Folklore' accepts, even on academic grounds, a value judgment…it disguises an academic contempt for the 'local' that has no salon legitimization. If there is anything that Midrash is, it is not folklore. It makes no distinction between the upper and the lower, the central and the marginal, the learned and the intuitive" — so Gruenwald. In defense of Hasan-Rokem's book, I hasten to point out, she works within an established scholarly episteme, she is not obligated to define and justify her entire field. But Gruenfeld's critique of the entire field of folklore is not idiosyncratic but routine among academic scholars of the Rabbinic literature, and at some point, any ambitious exposition within that field is going to have to address the epistemological criticism that calls into question the entire enterprise.

Second, despite the promise of the title to deal with "Rabbinic literature," Hasan-Rokem addresses not the canon or even the complete document but only episodic passages in Lamentations Rabbati. She simply ignores the documentary context in which they appear, that is, the work itself that preserves those passages. The issue is not merely formal; it is substantive and critical to the hermeneutics. And she pays a heavy price for her insistence on examining the parts out of all relationship to the whole in which they participate. I have already pointed out the cost, to her presentation of Lamentations Rabbati, of her failure to see the document whole and complete, as a coherent and cogent piece of writing, with its own indicative, distinctive traits of rhetoric (form), logic of coherent discourse, and topical (theological) program. The net effect of her discussion of the document is to leave the impression of chaos where there is cogency and regnant order, of incoherence where there is a principal and unifying problematic that animates the document whole and accounts for the joining of its parts. Only ignorance of the context and of scholarship that has established that context explains how she can say, "Rabbinic Midrashim do not formulate a systematic religious doctrine or philosophy...." But they do. The problem is only, Hasan-Rokem doesn't know the books that demonstrate that fact.

My simply alleging the contrary — that context counts — hardly suffices. Let me spell the opposite view out in a brief way, and people may compare the traits of the document viewed whole with my as against her account of its theological system and structure in context. She claims there is no system. I claim there is. What is it?

The paramount theology of Rabbinic Judaism that animates the Midrash-compilations comes to realization, also, in Lamentations Rabbati, but, there, it is represented only in part. It is in that larger theological structure that the theological propositions dominant in Lamentations Rabbati find their context. On their own, their statement is insufficient and accorded disproportionate standing. The issue that pressed here finds its urgency in the occasion that is addressed, the events of the 9th of Ab as represented by Jeremiah and Lamentations, but its proper position only in that encompassing setting of coherent ideas. More to the point, the answer given here gains self-evidence only within that larger logic that renders coherent and sustains the system and structure of ideas of our document.

The Rabbinic documents of the formative age bear in common a single trait. Each of them finds many ways to say one important thing. And, but for secondary details, that one important statement recapitulates, and derives from, Scripture. As the survey in the first six chapters has shown, Lamentations Rabbati repeatedly registers just a handful of theological propositions. All of them derive from Deuteronomy and Jeremiah. They comprise a systematic instantiation of the theodicy implicit in Deuteronomy and Jeremiah, that what happens to Israel happens by God's plan and is meant to provoke the response of repentance for the sins of rebellion against the covenant that have brought on the present calamity. What our document does is patiently to repeat in concrete terms that governing principle, justifying God's actions in destroying the Temple in 586/70 and deriving from those events hope that Israel has the power to restore its relationship with God: as punishment followed sin, so surely will reconciliation follow repentance.

The theological statements of Lamentations Rabbati do not on their own constitute a complete and encompassing theological system. They deal with one important component of a system — the matter of theodicy, as I just said — but they do not address other, equally important ones, e.g., eschatology, anthropology, apologetics, theology of history, or cosmology. These are treated in other documents and surface here only marginally. So the Rabbinic theology seen whole takes up and systematically addresses all of these matters within a single cogent logic. Indeed, these chapters of theological thought and their companions represent necessary systemic components for the mythic monotheism set forth by Scripture. And, as a matter of fact, they are elaborately dealt with in other Midrash-compilations. But they are given slight attention, or entirely ignored, here. It follows that, to Rabbinic theology as system and structure, Lamentations Rabbati is necessary but not sufficient. Its critical contribution to the larger Rabbinic theology must find for itself its logical place within that sheltering system and structure.

That explains why two facts characterize the theological corpus that is set forth in the document. First, it does not form a complete systematic theological statement *on its own*. Second, it does make a coherent statement *of its own*. The former has to be spelled out, the second, demonstrated and made to stick.

The statement of the first of the two facts lays emphasis upon theological convictions integral to the theology of Rabbinic Judaism in its formative writings: God is both just and good and merciful. The second of the two facts, the one embodied in Lamentations Rabbati, is clear: Israel is responsible for its condition, which, through repentance, it can repair. Each statement is necessary, neither on its own is sufficient. The theodicy set forth here in the context of the calamities of 586/70 is crafted to deal with the enduring problem of monotheism: how can the all-powerful God permit such things to happen? Why does that self-revealed God permit those to whom he made himself known, Israel, to suffer degradation and subjugation to the idolaters? Only in the context of these convictions is the critical issue of Lamentations Rabbati self-evidently urgent, and only in that context is the response of Lamentations Rabbati compelling. Lamentations Rabbati identifies the occasion that makes the chronic issue, Israel's subordination to the idolaters, into the acute crisis that it is, Israel's suffering (out of all proportion to its sins, it would surely have seemed) and the destruction of the Temple and suspension of its medium of atonement. With its stress on sin as cause of suffering and repentance as medium of atonement, Lamentations Rabbati frames for itself a cogent response to the single most critical question confronting Israel, the holy people, then and now.

But if these standard issues of mythic monotheism dominate, then what about the equally critical convictions that are not recapitulated here at all, such as those suggested just a moment ago and prominent in other compilations but not this one? One example suffices. If by "gentiles" is meant "idolaters," then the subjugation, to the gentiles, of Israel, which is formed to serve and worship God and realize his dominion on earth, prove anomalous. That the victors are God's enemies defines the paramount question to begin with. If, by contrast, "the nations" formed a neutral category-formation, indifferent to God's interests, why should Israel's subjugation to the nations present a theological problem at all? That is one example of how the theological statement of the document is necessary but insufficient for the formulation of a coherent system and structure.

Lamentations Rabbati must be seen a critical component not only of a larger system of theological thought but also of a larger corpus of canonical documents. For of each document we may say what is clear of Lamentations Rabbati: even though what sages wished to say they could say best, perhaps only, here in response to the book of Lamentations, the document still forms a necessary but insufficient theological statement. That is why I insist: all the documents presuppose the questions and answers set forth by each in its own context. Viewed at the end, the canon of the Midrash-compilations is prior to its components, the system to the details of the system.

Indeed, we shall recognize the clear outlines of the theological construction set forth by the compilers of Lamentations Rabbati when we can explain, also, the points that other compilations of the Rabbinic canon register but that are omitted here. Within the theory set forth in this chapter, accordingly, we are able to explain not only what is covered but what is not covered: why this, not that? This I shall set forth in due course.

First comes the encompassing theological system, to which Lamentations Rabbati makes its particular contribution. Let me state the same matter in literary terms: *first comes the canon, and only then the document.* I have then to ask, if so, what of the Rabbinic theology not *of* but *in* Lamentations Rabbati (among all other canonical documents)? Let me spell out the main outline of the theological system that defines the context of all Rabbinic canonical documents, including this one. Hasan-Rokem explicitly denies the ubiquity and normative standing of what I shall now state as its governing theological system and structure.

Stated simply: the Rabbinic theology recapitulates the Scriptural theology of monotheism expressed through narrative, thus mythic monotheism. But while Scripture conveys the theology through its narratives, Rabbinic Judaism reflects upon the abstract principles that are conveyed in that narrative, systematizing them in law, exploring their implications in lore, alike. In Rabbinic Judaism monotheism, the belief that one, unique God created the world and governs what happens in it, takes not narrative but exegetical form, in the Midrash-compilations, and is embodied in the norms of the social order, in the Halakhic ones. But the story is Scripture's, and so, in proportion, is the law.

The story of mythic monotheism records that the one, unique, purposeful Creator of heaven and earth rules with justice and with mercy. According to the self-revelation of the one God in the Torah, oral and written, given to Moses at Sinai, God is not only God but also good. So monotheism by nature explains many things in a single way: whatever happens realizes God's will for justice and mercy, a single rationality. One God rules. Life is meant to be fair, and just rules are supposed to describe what is ordinary, all in the name of that one and only God. In monotheism a simple logic governs to limit ways of making sense of things. But that logic contains its own dialectics. If one true God has done everything, then, since he is God all-powerful and omniscient, all things are credited to, and blamed on, him. In that case he can be either good or bad, just or unjust — but not both.

How does this story come to recapitulation in the Rabbinic documents, and what form does the retelling take? In quite other-than-philosophical form, the Rabbinic sages think philosophically about the religious truths of Scripture and so produce theology. Through the documents of the Oral Torah read all together and all at once, we see with great clarity how the Rabbinic sages constructed a coherent theology, a cogent structure and logical system, resting on rigorous critical thought, the whole meant to expose the justice of God. In one way or another each of their principal documents rests upon the theological foundations of that system and structure. But none of them contains a full and systematic statement of it. Among the canonical documents Lamentations Rabbati participates in that theology and finds its natural context within it. Hence any account of the theological system and structure that imparts cogency to any particular document must begin with a picture of the whole.

The theology of the Oral Torah conveys the picture of world order based on God's justice and equity. The categorical structure of the Oral Torah encompasses the components, God and man; the Torah; Israel and the nations. The working-system of the Oral Torah finds its dynamic in the struggle between God's plan for creation —to create a perfect world of justice — and man's will. That dialectics embodies in a single paradigm the events contained in the sequences, rebellion, sin, punishment, repentance, and atonement; exile and return; or the disruption of world order and the restoration of world order. The great themes of Lamentations Rabbati, the recurrent points of emphasis — these find their context in that working-system and make sense only there. Never describing the document as a whole, but only in its parts, and ignoring systematic descriptions of the document read whole as though they did not exist, Hasan-Rokem has (predictably) missed the point of the document, bits and pieces of which she has brilliantly illuminated.

If her account of "folklore...in Rabbinic literature" emerges as chaotic and confused, subjective and idiosyncratic, that is because of work she has yet to undertake, not because of any frailties of intellect or intelligence exhibited in this study of hers, of which I find no evidence whatsoever. She is a gifted, serious scholar. Her achievements in this book are her own. Her limitations are those of the academic setting in which she does her work. Whatever is taken for granted derives from the academic culture in which she labors. Whatever is labored and intellectually rigorous derives from her own nature as a scholar and intellect. That is why I am confident we shall in time see not only better work, but quite good work, such as, if only episodically, presents itself even in this chaotic work, so rich in arbitrary and subjective judgments.

15.

CHRISTINE ELIZABETH HAYES, *BETWEEN THE BABY- LONIAN AND PALESTINIAN TALMUDS: ACCOUNTING FOR* HALAKHIC *DIFFERENCE IN SELECTED SUGYOT FROM TRACTATE AVODAH ZARAH.* ANN ARBOR, 1993: UNIVER- SITY MICROFILMS INTERNA- TIONAL

Without a theory of the whole, there is no comparing of parts. It follows that when Christine Hayes proposes to compare the two Talmuds, she implicitly affirms the theory of documentary autonomy that underlies the theory of documentary description, analysis, and interpretation. For hers is an exercise in documentary analysis, as comparison and contrast always entails. Here is how she describes her proposed study:

> The dissertation accounts for selected diver-
> gences between parallel passages of the two Talmuds
> dealing with laws governing relations between Jews and
> non-Jews. I proceed on a case by case basis and con-
> sider whether external influences (cultural, regional), in-
> ternal factors (textual, hermeneutical, dialectical) or

some intersection of the two best accounts for these legal divergences. While some legal differences reflect the differences between Jewish-Gentile relations in Hellenistic Palestine and Jewish-Gentile relations in Sassanid Persia, I critique a reductive brand of historical analysis that would posit external explanations for divergence between the two Talmuds without paying sufficient attention to internal factors. To avoid a reductive historicism, I focus on i) the character of the Talmuds as hermeneutic literatures employing specific strategies of interpretation, ii) the additional 300 years of analysis, debate and revision to which legal traditions were subjected in Babylonia, and iii) the way in which the later Babylonian sages transformed the nature of the Babylonian Talmud. Specifically, earlier layers — often resembling the Palestinian Talmud in style and substance — were incorporated into a dialectical superstructure moving the law in new directions.

Hayes produces results that prove inconclusive and representative only of themselves, and her own description underscores that fact. She could repeat the same experiment many times and produce no more definitive results than those before us, which consist in the end only of cases and examples of we know not what. Her generalization ends up in hermeneutics, not in the comparison she promises:

In regard to the specific issue of accounting for halakhic difference between the two Talmuds, I have argued that one must attend to a range of internal causes of halakhic difference — textual, hermeneutical, and dialectical — if one wishes to avoid a reductive brand of historical analysis. I have further argued that a sound knowledge of rabbinic canons of interpretation and strategies of reading are [sic] critical for reliable cultural-historical analysis of halakhic difference...I examined internal causes of halakhic difference between the two Talmuds in tractate Avodah Zarah. In other words, I examined the way in which halakhic difference might be traced to various aspects native to the exegetical enterprise to which the amoraim were devoted. I showed...that halakhic difference can result from the fact that the two communities of amoraim possessed divergent versions of the Mishnah itself...I demonstrated that syntactic oddities, gaps and semantic ambiguities in a mishnah could generate halakhic divergence between the gemaras as the amoraim struggle to interpret and analyze the mishnah in question......I turned to a discussion of the formal and actual halakhic differences that emerge from the Bavli's more systematic application of the hermeneutical assumption of verbal economy in the language of the Mishnah (an assumption shared by, but less fully developed in, the Yerushalmi). Chapter 4 explored the way in which the Bavli's more rigorous pursuit of dialectical strategies of interpretation and redaction led to halakhic difference between the Talmuds...I turned to a consideration of halakhic differences between the Bavli and Yerushalmi that lend themselves to a cultural-historical analysis. In each case, some unprecedented novelty or exegetical aberration signaled the possibility of an extra-textual pressure to modify the halakhah...pp. 387f..

These results prove diffuse, unfocused, and episodic; she finds no general principles, sees no patterns that account for differences beyond specific cases at hand; and if she pursued the same inquiry many times over, she still would not set forth an explanation of her data, but only, more facts. But the facts turn out to be not only episodic, but recapitulative, since she says in general terms pretty much what her cases indicate in concrete, specific ones. So it is an elaborate paraphrase of we know not what.

When we speak of making comparisons, we establish the premise that the things to be compared are both alike and not alike: sufficiently unlike to validate comparison and contrast, sufficiently alike so that the comparison will produce intelligible propositions.[31] Comparing things that are utterly unlike, e.g., belonging to distinct classifications, yields pseudo-scientific nonsense-statements, e.g., an apple has a stem, but a dog has a tail. Comparing things that are alike but different, however, requires that we find bases for the characterization of both things, so differentiating them as wholes as to warrant comparing and contrasting the parts. But, for reasons she spells out, Christine Hayes does not want to see the documents as a whole, only atomistically — and yet she does want to compare them. The result is inchoate; she pays a heavy price.

Denying integrity to that which is subjected to comparison, she can compare and contrast only bits and pieces, emerging with nothing much to say to anybody about anything at all; she ends with a reprise of her exercise and a mere paraphrase, in general terms, of the episodic results she has so labored to produce. Comparing I know not what to nothing in particular produces random and meaningless facts, nothing of consequence at all. That is the price she pays for declining to characterize that which she proposes to subject to compare — and insisting that characterization to begin with is impossible, leaving us to wonder why she bothered to do the work at all.

The problem is that Hayes denies that she is comparing documents, which she says we cannot describe, but wants to compare only episodic compositions or composites (*sugyot*). But how can we compare the parts of wholes we cannot describe? And, more to the point, why should we want to? If Hayes has no general theory of the characteristics of the Bavli and of the Yerushalmi, then she is left with data she cannot

---

[31]I spell out these matters, so far as they concern the study of Judaisms, in *Take Judaism, for Example. Studies toward the Comparison of Religions.* Chicago, 1983: University of Chicago Press. Second printing: Atlanta, 1992: Scholars Press for South Florida Studies in the History of Judaism.

explain at all, and, unable to generalize, she turns out to undertake an endless, thankless work of detail lacking all sense beyond itself. Clearly, she denies that we can describe the documents whole; but it turns out, she does not know my introduction to the Yerushalmi, my initial approach to the description of the Bavli, or my systematic theory of how the Bavli and the Yerushalmi compare.

It follows that Hayes shows herself imperfectly acquainted with the documentary method as I have defined it. Let me point to specific works that her dissertation does not take up, in her insistence that we cannot describe the Bavli and the Yerushalmi and compare them, whole to whole. Her bibliography does not include works of mine in print long before her publication: *The Talmud of the Land of Israel. A Preliminary Translation and Explanation.* Chicago: The University of Chicago Press: 1983. XXXV. *Introduction. Taxonomy*, or my first effort at the characterization of the Bavli whole, which was *Judaism: The Classical Statement. The Evidence of the Bavli.* Chicago, 1986: University of Chicago Press. More to the point, she does not cite works of mine that adduce evidence of the formal coherence of the Talmud, e.g., *The Bavli's One Voice: Types and Forms of Analytical Discourse and their Fixed Order of Appearance.* Atlanta, 1991: Scholars Press for South Florida Studies in the History of Judaism. She undertook her comparison of the Talmuds without making reference to *The Bavli's Unique Voice. A Systematic Comparison of the Talmud of Babylonia and the Talmud of the Land of Israel.*, in seven volumes (1993).

Her indifference to a careful reading of the works of others on the same subject explains how little she grasps of what is claimed and what is not alleged at all in the documentary method. For example, she misunderstands the notion of an "authorship," imagining that I refer to a single individual.

In several works employing this brand of re-

> daction criticism, Neusner feels justified in speaking of
> each rabbinic work, even the Talmud, as a single unit,
> as though authored by a single individual and giving
> testimony to a single community. Each rabbinic work is
> considered at the redacted level to be an authored text,
> shaped according to the ideology or philosophy of the
> final author/redactor(s) and bearing witness to the ide-
> ology of the period of redaction. Thus individual rab-
> binic texts can be arranged in a chronological sequence
> according to their dates of redaction and then analyzed
> so as to illuminate the diverse stages in the history of
> rabbinic Judaism... pp. 28-29

I am not sure I understand what she means by "redaction-
criticism," but she surely does not grasp the work of form-
analysis, which investigates the indicative traits of documents.
In formulating the results, I take for granted that we deal with
a textual community, a term that Hayes evidently does not
grasp. The rest of her description is, while merely approxi-
mate, acceptable. She further states:

> While it is certainly true that the very compo-
> sition and editing of rabbinic works exert an influence
> on the contents so that a rabbinic work is more than its
> sources, the privileging of the period of the text's reac-
> tion as the only period "represented" by the text, and
> thus the only period in any way (historically) retriev-
> able, is conceptually flawed. The documentarian posi-
> tions...are predicated on modern notions of authorship
> that simply do not apply to rabbinic texts, and b) ignore
> or violate the texts' own explicit markers of diachrony.
> p. 30

I concur with her insistence that a Rabbinic document contains compositions and even composites that antedate final
redaction, but how that is to be demonstrated in detail has
been investigated only in a primitive way. Since Hayes takes
attributions at face value, she does not understand the prob-

lem in a critical way. Her formulation is deeply uncomprehending:

> Late texts may cite early sources and thus provide evidence of an early period. How that sources is presented, contextualized, or treated in the later text may also tell us something about the later period, but that does not obviate the ability of the source to tell us something about the period in which it originated. p 34
>
> It is quite simply a fact, borne out time and again, that much material recorded in late texts reflects earlier traditions. Hence we find in the Babylonian Talmud material paralleled in tannaitic midrashim, we find in the Mishnah and Tosefta material paralleled in Qumran texts that date to the 2nd or 1st c. b.c.e.. It is therefore not uncritical, unscientific, unscholarly, or fundamentalist to remain open to the possibility that a given tradition may have a pre-history, or roots in an earlier oral tradition, when there is so much concrete evidence to support such a claim... pp. 36-37

I do not understand how she knows that "late texts may cite early sources," or the basis on which she finds certain that a statement originated in some period earlier than the certain one of redaction. That is the very problem subject to investigation even now.

Her second paragraph shows, once more, profound incomprehension of the critical program of the present century, for she posits a single, incremental Judaism, so that all Judaic sources, whatever the origin, attest, e.g., to a single, harmonious, unitary law, subject to development in diverse times and places but always one and the same. Only in that way can she make so silly a statement as to allege that what we find in the Mishnah and Tosefta that is paralleled in Qumran texts has to be "dated" to the second century. What she seems to mean is, we can show a given rule or conception to have circulated at some period prior to the formation and redaction of the Mishnah. No one denies that fact. But then, she wants us to conclude, the Mishnah or the Tosefta has derived that rule from a continuous process of tradition — from Qumran to our sages of blessed memory.

But on what basis does she posit that continuous, unbroken process of tradition? The happenstance that a datum circulated early, in one group, and circulated later, in some other, tells us that the datum is early, but it does not tell us that the document in which the item later on surfaces has gotten the item from the earlier one. Rabbinic writings cite a vast corpus of available books, inclusive (after all) of the Hebrew Scriptures. But no one assigns the Mishnah to the time of Ezra because the Mishnah's writers cite the Torah! Quite what Hayes is thinking here hardly proves clear, and much confusion obfuscates her meaning.

For the issue is not the antiquity of facts, but the determinate setting of the system that uses the facts in one way and not in some other. It is the system that imparts structure and order to the document, and it is the system that takes over data and shapes them all to accord with its purpose. Unless we suppose that the Dead Sea library circulated, also, among the framers of the system, we cannot know that what occurs in the one has reached the other in such a way as to attest to the continuity and harmony of the two bodies of writing. Hayes does not consider the problem of systemic selection out of a receive corpus of inert facts because she also imagines that a single Judaism unites all documents — and that is by decree. She has not contemplated the foundations for the contrary view, deriving from the study of archaeology as much as the diverse writings of various Judaisms. Only on that basis is she able to formulate the hypothetical process of formulation and tradition that sustains her picture of matters. That she introduces a process of "oral tradition"

In Hayes's defense, I have to say, most of the issues

she takes up in her "General Introduction," pp. 1-89, play no role whatsoever in the shank of her dissertation, which deals with "Internal causes of halakhic difference: textual issues; hermeneutical issues; and halakhah and history." She aims at using the sources for "history," and she can have reached all of the conclusions she does without discussing methodological issues that do not affect the way in which she chooses to reach her goal. She evidently deemed it necessary to explain why she does not do what she does not do; but the alternative approaches to the very same problem — the comparison of the two Talmuds — simply do not figure in that discussion, which turns out irrelevant to her work and useless to anybody else. The substantive remarks on the upshot of her comparison prove murky but not without interest, and when she proceeds to further work, she is likely to produce scholarship of clarity and compelling results.

16.

SUSANNAH HESCHEL, *ABRAHAM GEIGER AND THE JEWISH JESUS*. CHICAGO, 1998: UNIVERSITY OF CHICAGO PRESS. CHICAGO STUDIES IN THE HISTORY OF JUDAISM, EDITED BY WILLIAM SCOTT GREEN

Abraham Geiger stands out as the most interesting and original mind in critical scholarship on Judaism in the nineteenth century and a principal theologian of Reform Judaism. That is how he is represented in the definitive biography, Max Wiener, *Abraham Geiger and Liberal Judaism* (1962), from its publication the standard work in English on its subject—and in the aftermath of this dissertation, still—alas!—the standard work.

Here, in this much overcooked dissertation, pretentiously masquerading as culture-philosophy in a garment of dreary, sectarian jargon, we are asked to read Geiger not as a Reform theologian but as a post-modernist avatar:

> Geiger's work represents a revolt of the colonized, bringing the tools of historiography to bear against Christianity's intellectual hegemony... Intellectually, that hegemony began to end when the Wissenschaft des Judenthums [scholarship on Judaism started writing the history of Christianity as a branch of Jewish history...The Wissenschaft des Judenthums...is one of the earliest examples of postcolonialist writing...Postcolonial theory's recognition that minority literature is characterized by counter-discursive practices helps to illumine Geiger's work, inasmuch as

the logic of his historical arguments represented an inversion of accepted European self-understanding. Geiger's counterhistory constituted a transvaluation of Christian arguments against Judaism and functioned as a passionate defense of Judaism (p. 3).

Geiger represented the Pharisees, whom Christian scholarship portrayed in violently hostile terms, as the Reform Jews of their day: "liberal democratizers of Judaism.... Modern liberal Protestants who seek the faith of Jesus…can find it in Reform Judaism." Here Heschel finds "a form of counterhistory:" "Counterhistory is a form of polemic in which the sources of the adversary are exploited" and turned against the oppressor: "Geiger sought to defend Judaism by writing a counterhistory of Christian counterhistory:

> That is, he did not simply offer a straightforward rendition of the history of Jesus and Judaism but presented Jewish history in the context of his own, original counterhistory of Christianity (p. 14).

Heschel further calls on "gender theory" to clarify "some of the hidden motivations" for Jewish theologians intense interest in the origins of Christianity:

> The position of Jews entering the world of Christian theology is not unlike the position of women novelists entering the nineteenth-century literary world…women were required to 'kill the angel in the house,' the aesthetic ideal of the female promoted in male literature, before they could generate their own literature. Similarly, Jewish theologians initiated an effort to destroy the image of Judaism within Christian theology as part of their project of self-definition (p. 18).

Predictably, Heschel ends her post-modernist theory of Geiger with attention to Edward Said's *Orientalism*, where she finds nothing new: "The intimacy between knowledge and power may be better known to Jewish historians than anyone else."

This heavy dose of the regnant academic ideology, taken at the start, finds a match at the end, the story having been told, in a regurgitation of the same ideology. For Jews [Geiger] was "the ultimate overthrow of Christian hegemony. The extraordinary embrace of Geiger's position by modern Jewish thinkers is indicative of their deep satisfaction with their argument." There follows a survey of twentieth century response to Geiger's position that Jesus was a Jew and a Pharisee. Here Heschel passes her opinion on a great many issues she has not, herself, investigated, concluding with what must be simply the weirdest discussion of the historical Jesus of recent times. For the bizarre characterization Heschel fabricates, Jesus as a kind of "cross-dresser," only her own words suffice to convey the full idiocy of her interpretation of Geiger's oeuvre:

> The dispute over Jesus' religious identify that was set into motion by Geiger's identification of him as a Pharisee has never been resolved. Jews dress him as a Jew, Christians dress him as a Christian…. The theological situation lends itself to useful interpretation by means of poststructuralist critical theory. Read in postmodern categories, as cross-dressed, Jesus is at once both a signifier and that which signifies the undecidability of signification, pointing toward himself but also toward the place where he is not….The literary theorists…have argued that 'transvestism' is a category which reconfigures the relationship between male and female and places in question binary gender identities previously viewed as stable and known. For Judaism and Christianity Jesus functions as a kind of literary theological transvestite (p. 239).

Readers are asked to stipulate that I have copied her exact words and have not manufactured a malicious parody of post-modernism or grossly caricatured Heschel's take on Geiger. She writes with a permanently-straight face.

So much for the beginning and the end. But these are tacked on, fore and aft, and do not ruin the shank of the book at all. The dissertation-part of the book is written in workmanlike, professional prose and in no way invokes the phony "interpretative framework" promised at the beginning and invoked at the end. Mercifully, Heschel, once she tells her story of Geiger, forgets where she started, and at the end does not even pretend to refer to the nub of her narrative either. With rare lapses into post-modernist gibberish, what we find in the middle of the book, rather, are a series of professional, well-researched chapters on the life and work of Geiger, the raw material of a good, if tedious dissertation. Take away the gibberish and what is left is this systematic program of biography: the creation of a historical theology (early life and education), Judaism, Christianity, and Islam: prelude of revisionist configurations; reconceiving early Judaism; D. F. Strauss, the Tübingen School, and Albrecht Ritschl; the Jewish Jesus and the Protestant flight from the historical Jesus; from Jesus to Christianity: Geiger on the post-apostolic era; the reception of Geiger's work. All this is fairly standard and unexceptionable, if also unexceptional. The author shows herself industrious and competent, though whether she has improved on Wiener's prior biography is a judgment that only specialists in nineteenth century intellectual history of Reform Judaism can make.

Apart from this, Heschel, who taught at Case-Western Reserve and at Southern Methodist Universities and is now at Dartmouth College in the Department of Religion, has made her name as an editor of feminist works and left-wing academic ideology: *Insider/Outsider. Multiculturalism and American Jews and On Being a Jewish Feminist: a Reader*. She also edited an anthology *Moral Grandeur and Spiritual Audacity: Essays on Abraham Joshua Heschel*. I doubt that she is going to undertake any more intellectually exacting projects; editing and flip opinion-passing and ideologizing are a whole lot easier, and the words flow painlessly. But I hope she proves me wrong — for her father's sake.

17.

CATHERINE HEZSER, *FORM, FUNC-TION, AND HISTORICAL SIGNIFICANCE OF THE RABBINIC STORY IN YERUSHALMI NEZIQIN*. TEXTE UND STUDIEN ZUM ANTIKEN JUDENTUM, ED. MARTIN HENGEL AND PETER SCHÄFER, VOLUME 37. TÜBINGEN, 1993: J. C. B. MOHR (PAUL SIEBECK)

A revised dissertation (1992) at the Jewish Theological Seminary of America written under the direction of my student, the late Baruch M. Bokser (and in the model of his dissertation with me, *Samuel's Commentary on the Mishnah. Part One: Mishnayot in the Order of Zera'im* [1975] and his *Post-Mishnaic Judaism in Transition. Samuel on Berakhot and the Beginnings of Gemara* [1980]), this study of stories found in the Talmud of the Land of Israel tractates Baba Qamma, Baba Mesia, and Baba Batra ("Neziqin") is comprised by two unequal parts, "analysis of the traditions," (pp. 11-226), and "Evaluation (pp. 227-409). While the three Babas form a distinct subset of the Yerushalmi, as Y. I. Halevy, *Dorot Harishonim* (Vienna, 1923) first discovered, it is not equivalently clear that the utilization of stories in those tractates is to be distinguished from the way they are presented and exploited in others of the same Talmud.

It follows that the purpose of the dissertation — are

we testing a hypothesis about the Rabbinic Story in a particular sample of the canon? are we trying to find out how the Rabbinic Story in these tractates differs from the same elsewhere? does the particular character of the Rabbinic Story in these tractates tell us something more about those tractates? — hardly emerges, and diligent paraphrase, accompanied by massive compilations of diverse scholarly opinion, along with large doses of banalities, takes the place of a well-drafted thesis. Attaining laudable success in the parts, Dr. Hezser contributes little to our grasp of the whole — whether the Rabbinic Story, whether the three tractates she treats — because she has not asked, if I know this, what else do I know? And why does it matter?

That is not to suggest that Dr. Hezser contributes nothing to learning. Anyone who has occasion to consult the eighty stories she discusses will thank her for putting everything together in one place. Her discussions are uniformly painstaking, cautious, and informed. If many of her observations simply repeat in her words what the source under discussion has already yielded, still, her observations articulate interesting data. Each story is presented with notes on MSS variants, in a suitable English translation; she then discusses "redactional context," by which she means, the occasion and use of the story; "literary form;" and "historical significance." These latter investigations say much that is obvious and little that is interesting. Where a story occurs in more than one document, she sets up the versions in parallel columns and summarizes what she sees. The second part of the book then collects and arranges the information that has been laid out. Here she treats five topics: "the redactional uses of the stories in y. Neziqin;" "pre-redactional story-collections;" "the forms of the stories in y. Neziqin;" "parallels in the Yerushalmi, Babli, and Midrashim;" and "the historical significance of the stories in y. Neziqin."

She finds "a great amount of editorial work on the y. Bavot. The editors formulate narrative traditions as glosses on the Mishnah, Tosefta, and Amoraic statements and harmonize their wording with prior statements." Half of the stories appear in groups of two or more, and she plausibly argues that "y. Bavot editors drew material from various pre-existing collections of stories, supplementing this material with occasional stories that were circulating separately and were not part of any collection." But she does not then ask what these observations imply about the literary process that produced the collections as we have them (in writing? oral?), let alone the literary history of the Talmud as we know it. As elsewhere in the book, where her results prove determinate, she asks no important questions about them.

The chapter on the forms of the stories distinguishes among the following: case-stories; example stories; pronouncement stories; anecdotes; etiological tales; and legends. Since we deal with only a small segment of the Yerushalmi, and a still less weighty segment of the corpus of stories in the entire Rabbinic canon, quite what these categories mean and how they help us to read the stories in context and otherwise hardly emerge with clarity. Why classifying data matters, what these various categories imply for our reading of stories in other Rabbinic documents — these issues are not raised. Here failure to define a determinate context for inquiry proves fatal.

The section on parallels also suffers from the absence of a hypothesis on the character and relationships of various documents that share stories; the discussion ranges hither and yon and yields many opinions but mostly confusion. Hezser discusses only a small part of the literature in which various versions of the same story in diverse documents come under discussion, missing, inter alia, this writer's *The Peripatetic Saying: The Problem of the Thrice-Told Tale in Talmudic Literature.*

Chico, 1985: Scholars Press for Brown Judaic Studies, which is a reprise and reworking of materials in *Development of a Legend* (1971) and *Rabbinic Traditions about the Pharisees before 70* I-III (1973). But lacking a theory on the character of the documents, she reaches no interesting hypotheses on how to explain the way stories gain or lose weight as they move from one compilation to another — or why that is the fact. So what she provides is simply long sequences of parallel columns, followed by her own summary of what the columns display to the naked eye — but no explanation, let alone generalization.

Finally, the new consensus of learning outside of the State of Israel, that stories in the Rabbinic literature cannot be read as factual, historical accounts of things really said and done, finds confirmation in her discussion. Here Hezser goes over familiar ground of the critical bases for rejecting the theory of Saul Lieberman that these particular tractates originated in Caesarea in ca. 350 C.E.. She takes her place in line after the three others who — each for his own reasons — have dismissed Lieberman's theory in the past few years: Moshe Assis, in "On the Question of the Redaction of Yerushalmi Neziqin" (Hebrew), *Tarbiz* 1987, 56:147-170, Ya'aqob Sussman, in "Once again on Yerushalmi Neziqin" (Hebrew), *Mehqerei Talmud. Talmudic Studies*, ed by Y. Sussman and D. Rosenthal (Jerusalem, 1990) I:55-133, and this writer, in *Why There Never Was a "Talmud of Caesarea." Saul Lieberman's Mistakes*. Atlanta, 1994: Scholars Press for South Florida Studies in the History of Judaism. It is clear that Lieberman's theory no longer enjoys a serious hearing, and his methods are now universally rejected as well.

Clearly, in its parts, the dissertation undertakes numerous useful exercises. But the sum of the parts yields less than a cogent whole, for, read altogether, the diligent collection and arrangement of observations about one thing and another, together with a compilation of various opinions on this and that, serves no clear and determinate purpose. That is because Hezser comes to the data without a set of questions that define the intellectual context and so instruct her on why she wants to know one thing, rather than some other — or what urgent questions sustain her detailed labor. By contrast, Lieberman read the same tractates to prove a point. So too, the great Rabbinic exegetes of the Yeshiva-world knew precisely what they wished to learn in these compilations, as in all others. Anyone who has worked through the commentary of Pené Moshe to the Yerushalmi knows how a master-intellect can frame a coherent exegetical program and execute it with panache. By contrast, Dr. Hezser does not tell us what is at stake in her research; the indeterminate and often platitudinous character of her comments suggests that she cannot explain why her results make a difference. That failure explains the often aimless (and sometimes inane) result. Collecting and arranging information hardly constitutes an inductive argument concerning a proposition; the game of show and tell in the end leaves us puzzled.

18.

HAYIM LAPIN, *EARLY RABBINIC CIVIL LAW AND THE SOCIAL HISTORY OF ROMAN GALILEE. A STUDY OF MISHNAH TRACTATE BABA' MESI'A'.* BROWN JUDAIC STUDIES VOLUME 307. ATLANTA, 1996: SCHOLARS PRESS

This revision of a doctoral dissertation accepted at Columbia University covers these topics: the social study of the Mishnah (definitions and historical background, methodology: the Mishnah as a literary artifact, the Mishnah as a historical document); Mishnah Tractate *Baba' Mesi'a': literary and redactional problems* (sources in the Mishnah, the shape of sources, traces of the redactional process, the problem of attributions, the Mishnah as a literary artifact); institutions and relationships in Mishnah tractate *Baba' Mesi'a'* (economic institutions: money, markets, banks; economic and social relationships: finder and loser, deposits, buyer and seller, lender and borrower, laborer and employer, lessor and lessee); conclusions: Rabbinic civil law and the social history of Roman Galilee. There are two appendices: a text, translation, and annotation of the tractate, and Mishnah Tractate *Baba' Mesi'a'* and other Tannaitic corpora. Before is a rather elaborate work, but in fact, two problems, one literary, the other historical, define the focus; unfortunately, the two do not intersect, and the result is confusion.

Lapin does not promise "a narrative history in the

conventional sense," and he concedes that "Rabbinic legal texts cannot be taken in any simple way to describe what people did." He maintains that "in order to understand Rabbinic texts in the context of their social and historical background in a way that elucidates that context...it is crucial to come to terms with those texts as literature." He repeatedly assigns to me the origin of these and kindred views, which he endorses. Colleagues familiar with the history of scholarship over the past three decades will concur in my characterization of the work (like that David Kraemer in his splendid study of suffering in Rabbinic Judaism) as part of the second generation, building upon, but moving beyond my *oeuvre*.

Lapin so states in so many words: "These questions inform the conception and organization of Chapter II, which bears a distinct methodological debt to the procedure that Neusner worked out in his *History of Mishnaic law* series. On the assumption that different tractates may have different histories that may be obscured if analysis centers on specific topic.., this study centers on one tractate...I attempt to deal seriously with the Mishnah as a literary artifact of late second- and early third-century Roman Galilee. What is important is not only the broad programmatic purpose of the Mishnah...but also what the Mishnah betrays about its own composition. This attention to redaction, too, follows Neusner's earlier procedure, but is entirely ignored in his work on the order of Neziqin." Lapin is quite correct, since I had already presented my main methodological results in Volumes XXI *The Redaction and Formulation of the Order of Purities in the Mishnah and Tosefta,* and XXII *The Mishnaic System of Uncleanness. Its Context and History* in my *History of the Mishnaic Law of Purities* (1977). I saw no reason whatsoever to repeat the same operations for the other divisions, regarding the results as essentially repetitive and self-evident.

Lapin follows my views not only on literature but also

on history. But here he moves out on his own. As to the Mishnah as a historical document, Lapin states, "Where this study clearly breaks with the approach laid out by Neusner is in the attempt to deal seriously with the Mishnah as a document shaped by and reflective of a history." Instead, "The present study attempts to root the Mishnah's civil law in smaller-scale interactions in the agrarian world of Roman Galilee. Thus the primary focus is not 'law' as a coherent system of discourse but rather how individuals deeply interested in legal questions construct and respond to the environment in which they live through their exposition of legal materials. In framing the study in this way...I am not denying the fictional character of the Mishnah in general...The goal of the present study is rather to explore the horizons of this fictional world."

The subject-matter of the tractate, a sequence of rules on questions of economic interest, brings Lapin into the circle of my specific work on that subject as well. Where Lapin differs from my *Economics of the Mishnah* (1990) is as follows: "Although I agree with Neusner on many issues..., I take it as my starting point that any description of an economic system, however utopian, is fundamentally influenced by the economic notions of its authors, and indeed reflects upon the social and economic world of these authors." Here Lapin parts company from me, since he wants the Mishnah to be read in the context of other data of a legal or economic order, and I seek but have yet to find solid evidence that permits us to move from the text to the world beyond the text. By contrast, Lapin states, "In order to understand the Mishnah we must be willing to attempt to ask about the world outside of its mental and descriptive boundaries."

Clearly, the issues are accurately and intelligently drawn, and a work that draws so heavily upon my own is bound to win a close and careful reading from me. My main point of interest must be, how does Lapin propose to move from the text to the world, and what does he claim to learn from the text about the world, or from the world about the text? To answer those questions, alas, Chapter II, literary and redactional problems, may simply be ignored (pp. 35-118). Even if he were right on every point, the results bear only slight relevance to the announced program of the book. True, Lapin accepts my methods (of that period) for evaluating attributions: "It is easy to see why Neusner concluded that this tractate is largely the product of this generation...I have made much the same argument." His conclusion, after a long and tedious discussion, is simple: "there is frustratingly little that can be used to reconstruct the immediate social and institutional frameworks in which this first literary artifact of the Rabbinic movement was produced...the redaction of the Mishnah was...an effort to increase the centralization and institutionalization of the Rabbinic movement." No one can differ with so general a conclusion, for which intricate literary analysis is hardly required proof. But in this chapter mighty labor brings forth inconsequential results, most of them not even relevant to the announced program of the book. His Doktorvater, Professor David Halivni, here owed him the service of a few tough questions on how his dissertation was to cohere.

That is why Chapter III (pp. 119-235) forms the only part of the book to address the announced topic of the work as a whole. Here Lapin wants to know "the extent to which the Mishnah's civil laws can be used as a source or map for the social history of Roman Galilee...One dimension of this problem is the relationship between Mishnaic material and other, non-Jewish, evidence for economic practices and relationships...I have attempted...to give attention both to the broad commonalities and the differences between the way the same institutions and relationships are reflected in our tractate and in Roman juristic texts and papyri from Egypt, Dura Europus, and the Judean Desert...What is significant...is that despite important differences [the tractate] presents a battery of economic institutions and relationships that would be wholly familiar to the authors of the non-Rabbinic texts...This means that the Mishnah, however utopian its ultimate picture, responds to economic structures (fundamentally, an agrarian economy) and works with assumptions about those structures that were common throughout the Roman world."

Here in alleging that the document "responds" to the world beyond, Lapin wanders beyond the limits of the evidence that he himself sets in the prior chapters, since he claims not only parallels but points of intersection. He thus confuses verisimilitude with authenticity. Parallel lines do not meet, and interpreting parallels requires harder work than Lapin has invested. But perhaps he saw no urgency in unpacking the exact consequence of parallels, e.g., in law, for the stakes in this work are rather low.

That is because the points that he makes, while beyond exception, prove not very remarkable: "Money functions...as a general medium of transaction and exchange...Markets involve the meeting of people for the exchange of goods and services...the Mishnah...provide[s] little information on these matters. An examination of the tractate, asking how the people who produced it perceived markets and how they wanted them to be run, shows essentially three things: first, that the Rabbis who produced the Mishnah treated agricultural produce as the basic stuff of the marketplace; second, that trade was carried out at least in part by specialists; third, that markets are assumed to have a 'market price...'" And so on and so forth — so what else is new? Given the rather commonplace character of these and similar propositions, we cannot find surprising that the book of the chapter is made up of long footnotes and digressions; when the main burden of the chapter proves so light, there is plenty of space left for filler. In Lapin's defense, I hasten to add, no one who consults these sources will want to miss his discussion of them; if they do not yield the social history that he seeks, they do form a first-rate account of the specific passages he takes up.

The book exhibits two profound and pervasive flaws. Where Lapin goes awry is in confusing a document (a Mishnah-tractate) with a topic (the social history of Roman Galilee). That is to say why the book is incoherent. Half of the book is on the traits of the Mishnah-tractate, the other half, on the topical program of that tractate.

The book's second quite formidable flaw emerges here. The treatment of the topical program is necessarily truncated, when only, or mainly, the Mishnah's presentation of that topic is taken into account. Our sages of blessed memory set forth their ideas about the subjects treated in this Mishnah-tractate in four distinct bodies of writing, [1] the Mishnah-tractate, [2] the corresponding Tosefta-tractate, [3] the systematic exegetical commentaries upon the portions of Scripture that yield topical materials pertinent to the Mishnah-tractate, and [4] an indeterminate portion of the baraita-sayings of the two Talmuds devoted to the same topical program. Swallowed up in his painstaking review of the contents of the Mishnah-tractate, Lapin loses sight of even the nearest horizons beyond the document he has privileged. He in no way exploits the contents of other sources of law on the same topics besides the Mishnah, even though most people would expect to find in them at least some material relevant to the period of the Mishnah's composition.

The result of Lapin's confusion of the document with the topic is that we do not have a systematic and thorough account of the law of the place and time of the Mishnah, but only the law of the Mishnah (with some attention to intersecting passages of the Tosefta). No one would argue that the entirety of the Tosefta, Midrash-compilations, and baraita-sayings assigned to second century authorities belong to them or to their period; an iron consensus today maintains the opposite. But who would remove from the second century the bulk of the baraita-sayings, and who would concur that we may now ignore, in our study of the Mishnah, the Midrash-compilations (Sifra, the two Sifrés) that address the same topical program and find nourishment in the same intellectual world as the Mishnah?

I fear that in insisting we may read the Mishnah in its own terms and framework, I have mislead the coming generation. For when we speak of the Mishnah, we address *its* law, but not *the* law. An account of not the Mishnah-tractate alone but the whole Rabbinic civil law in the context of the social history of Roman Galilee, on the one side, and in the setting of the comparison of our sages' law with laws occurring in other Judaic as well as gentile sources, requires a quite different setting from the one that Lapin has chosen for his work. Lapin has paid either too little or too much attention to the other compilations that contain laws that belong together with those in the Mishnah. If his work is on the Mishnah-tractate, then it is too much, for the other materials should not appear at all; if it is on the early Rabbinic civil law and the social history of Roman Galilee, then it is much too little, for the materials deriving from other venues are not intensively examined at all. Given the proportion of the book devoted to the Mishnah (the first hundred pages of or approximately 40% of the whole), I think it is the former. But then Lapin has it all wrong: he speaks of the Mishnah sometimes, the law sometimes, and the world beyond the Mishnah and its law sometimes.

In this context Lapin's conclusions deserve close attention, since they illustrate the confused focus of his vision of matters:

> The Mishnah...do[es] not simply describe the way in which Palestinian...Jews lived their economic lives. The stories...in which Rabbinic luminaries carry out these laws certainly suggest that in at least some strata within the Mishnah these laws were expected to be practicable. In addition, the similarities between the Rabbinic conceptions of how particular kinds of contracts were to be constructed and their counterparts in non-Rabbinic and non-Jewish sources suggest that a substantial portion of Rabbinic civil law does mirror social practice. Nevertheless, Rabbis do not appear to have had institutional authority in Galilee beyond their own adherents in the second or third centuries. Moreover, the legal program that the Mishnah outlines is ultimately an ideal one, in which the Temple still stands and in which high priest and king still function. Thus it is never clear to what extent people who might have followed rules corresponding to those of the Mishnah will have done so because Rabbis or their tradition require it.

As is clear, Lapin moves back and forth across the frontier between a thoroughly critical attitude and a desire to reach some positive, historical conclusions. On the one side, the law is sufficiently like law we know elsewhere as to suggest that the Rabbinic law mirrors social practice. So we have history. On the other side, the document is utopian. So we do not have history. The confusion derives in the end — so I think — from Lapin's somewhat obscure conception of the meaning that parallels are supposed to yield.

That is not to suggest Lapin produces no interesting propositions for further thought. But Lapin's further point of insistence, that the tractate addresses the interests of the landholding town dwellers, is left essentially undeveloped; it is one of the most interesting points of the work. Here he would have learned from the Marxist reading of matters that I published a quarter-century ago, *Soviet Views of Talmudic Judaism. Five Papers by Yu. A. Solodukho*. Leiden, 1973: Brill. Lapin's homework is, alas, incomplete, and, it goes without saying, his reading of the work of his predecessors is not only ungenerous and captious but also uncomprehending. Perhaps he was so eager to show himself superior to those on whose work he depends that he did not trouble to ask whether he really understood that work as well as his often-spurious "criticisms" would purport.

A variety of questions flow from Lapin's conclusions, but these are drawn in a four-page conclusion that ought to have marked the beginning of the book. Still, since Lapin replicates my conclusions, it is surely captious to ask for more. For my part I could not have stated matters better than he does when he says: "It is in the wake of a period of 'pacification' and integration into the Roman empire that the Mishnah emerged, with its imagined world in which the Temple still stood. Mishnaic civil law is not best seen as a codification in the late second century of laws that by that time were of treat antiquity." Here he footnotes an article of his, alone, as though his conclusion is supposed to surprise an entire generation of scholars who have worked on the same documents and reached the same position But he moves into his own territory in his concluding remarks: "The Rabbinic movement was one of wealthy intellectuals attempting to redefine who Israel was, its proper relationship with its God, and how that relationship should manifest itself in nearly every facet of human life, including economic practices. In doing so, the Rabbis...articulated an egalitarian ethic that incorporated all (male) Jews into 'Israel' without regard to social status." Now here is a proposition worth debating! But first it is to be unpacked and carefully explained — something Lapin does not do. As usual in the current spate of not-fully-baked dissertations that Brown Judaic Studies is publishing under its new management, the most interesting ideas come in the final paragraph and bear no relationship to anything that has gone before.

But we must not see the work only on its own. In context it emerges as a distinct step forward for its area of study. If we compare the work to its competition, what do we see? Lapin takes first place in a line of recent works on the same subject, ahead of Goodman, Safrai, Levine, and S. J. D. Cohen, among others. Read side-by-side with Martin Goodman's *State and Society in Roman Galilee* (1983) and *The Ruling Class of Judaea* (1987), it is far more mature, better researched, and learned and scholarly. Read along with Ze'ev Safrai, *The Economy of Roman Palestine* (1994), Lapin's work compares as does day against night: his book is critical and enlightened, Safrai's is gullible, dull, and essentially paraphrastic. The critical thinking uniformly characteristic of Lapin's book shows up the shoddy and uncritical character of the recent titles by Lee I. Levine, The *Rabbinic Class of Roman Palestine* (1989), and *Galilee in Late Antiquity* (1992). Compared with S. J. D. Cohen's "The Place of the Rabbi in Jewish Society of the Second Century" (1992) and other occasional, light-weight articles on the same general problems, Lapin's thorough, systematic book compares as does authentic weighty scholarship to episodic passing of opinion on this and that. So, in all, despite its formidable flaws of confusion as to focus and purpose, Lapin's dissertation wins high praise for intelligence, careful and interesting thought, and exceedingly close reading of both sources and secondary literature, and the book, as I said, augurs well for the next generation, as it now takes up and builds upon the challenge that my work has laid down.

19.

LEE I. LEVINE, *THE RABBINIC CLASS OF ROMAN PALESTINE IN LATE ANTIQUITY*. JERUSALEM: YAD ISHAK BEN-ZVI; NEW YORK: JEWISH THEOLOGICAL SEMINARY OF AMERICA, 1989

Dean of the Jewish Theological Seminary's Jerusalem center, Levine treats these subjects: first, "the challenges of the third century," with attention to the sages during the first centuries C. E., urbanization, institutionalization, and a new attitude towards the People, the role of Judah I in shaping the rabbinic class, the sages in a new historic context: The Galilee, the urban aristocracy, and the patriarch; second, "the status of the rabbinic class," with attention to the ideal of Torah-study, the uniqueness of the sages, special privileges of the sages, the social support system of the rabbis, the size of the rabbinic class, the economic support system, stratification within the rabbinic class, was there a Sanhedrin in Palestine during the Talmudic era, and pluralism and tension among the sages; third, "the sages within Jewish society," the sages and Galilean Jewry, the image of the sages, the responsiveness of the sages to the needs of the community, the sages and *ammei haaretz*, friction between the sages and the people, the place of the sages in Jewish society; and fourth, "the sages, the patriarch, and community life," the dominant position of the patriarch in late antiquity, sages at the time of various patriarchs, the sages as parnasim, the sages and the urban aristocracy, the patriarchate and the urban aristocracy, rabbinic attitudes towards communal involvement, the sages and the patriarch: tension and cooperation. The book ends with "the status of the sages in late antiquity: an assessment."

This account of the contents shows us that Levine surveys evidence in a thematic way, rather than arguing a coherent proposition. His difficulty in sustaining a coherent argument affects not only the book as a whole, but even the chapters, subdivisions, and paragraphs, which tend to shade over from one thing to something else. Indeed, the book looks like an anthology, with lots of sources and some free-associative remarks tacked on. But three problems render the volume a mere curiosity, of no scholarly value whatsoever.

First, Levine's theoretical framework, involving the Marxist term, "class," proves jerrybuilt and sustains no solid structure of inquiry. That is not surprising, since, in his ignorance, Levine seems unaware, in invoking the metaphor of "class," that his use of so Marxist a category will puzzle an entire generation of scholarship in Greco-Roman antiquity, which finds many problems in a category Levine invokes so innocently. In his defense, it must be said that he uses the word "class" in a very private way. By "class" he means merely "a group for whom social and religious issues are of prime importance, yet it differs from a 'party' primarily with respect to its political involvements or, more precisely, the lack thereof. This does not mean that a 'class' is devoid of all political aspirations....Rather it sees itself first and foremost as a religious elite and functions primarily as such. By this definition...the rabbis...resembled a 'class.'" I suspect that so idiosyncratic a definition of so common and problem-laden a term will startle people with a firmer grasp of problems of social metaphors than Levine evidently has. I should have thought he would want to have learned from scholars of class-status and class-structure in antiquity, beginning, after all, with M. I. Finley, *The Ancient Economy* (1985), *Studies in Ancient Society* (1974), and the like. They will have taught him that invoking the category "class" for antiquity presents difficult problems of social-economic theory, starting with the difficulty of identifying pertinent data to justify the economic analysis of society to begin with. But, alas, Levine seems oblivious to the fact that his generative category, "class," derives from a very specific theory of political economy; not a single line of his book suggests he grasps the implications of his choice of "class." By his own definition, he can have used any number of other analogies, with equal lack of discernment. "Class" means more or less what he wants it to mean, which is everything and its opposite, depending on the context.

Second, Levine's use of archaeological evidence, in the judgment of qualified scholars, is simply incompetent. Here I defer to Fergus Millar (*Journal of Theological Studies* 1991, 42:275-6), who points out that "the most important single piece of recent archaeological evidence bearing on this topic..is treated in very cursory fashion. Indeed it is not even translated precisely." In a few sharp words, Millar has dismissed Levine's use of evidence that, as "professor of Jewish History and Archeology at the Hebrew University since 1971," he should be assumed to have mastered decades ago.

Third, Levine's use of the literary evidence, bearing the veneer of a critical method, proves gullible and everywhere uncritical. There is scarcely a line of analysis of the documents he quotes on every page; he never characterizes his literary sources or explains their traits or tendencies; they are just a mass of reliable information, so far as he is concerned. To be sure, as is the custom, he acknowledges that there are critical problems in using ancient literary sources (pp. 16ff.). But, without a trace of demonstration or analysis, he simply alleges, "Our sources are most abundant for Palestine of the third and fourth centuries, and the increase in quantity is paralleled by a greater degree of historical credibility." This is because the writings were redacted near the time of events they describe or masters they cite. But why that fact (if it is a fact) makes the documents more credible he does not explain.

More to the point, even though general considerations may point toward greater plausibility, we still have to analyze, point by point, each piece of literary evidence and assess in its own terms whether it tells us about something that really happened or something someone thought happened, and, if the latter, who thought so and why. Levine evades this question, which is critical to the enterprise, by a series of mere assertions: "Undoubtedly, reports of particular incidents are often a reliable type of evidence. Contrastingly, when a sage expresses his opinion about a matter or his hope for a certain situation, it is unclear whether his words accord with reality, whether they had any effect on it, or whether these were merely pious hopes." Why the former is the case Levine does not tell us. Levine seems to think that if he merely says something, that makes it so. Rather, he hastens to assure us that "the problem of historical reality is somewhat less acute," because, in this book, his concern is "with the rabbis themselves, their position in the community, attitudes toward others, involvement in the life of the community....their opinions and desires are no less significant than incidents and events; it is our task to understand them and place them in some sort of historical perspective."

What these pieties add up to is simply nothing. For when it comes to actual use of sources, we have the same old rabbinic-fundamentalism, e.g., "On one occasion R. Abbahu was even approached by a gentile woman for the same purpose." Footnote: J. Nazir 9, l, 57c. On the release from vows in the second century, see T Pesahim 2, 16, ed. Lieberman, p.

147; M Nedarim 5, 6; 9, 5; M Gittin 4, 7." Now what this adds up to (and I choose at random among thousands of candidates) is simply [1] X (really) did so and so, because [2] the source says so; and then, as further evidence, come [3] references to (also uncriticized sources) pertaining to a period two centuries earlier: temporal categories do not apply to Levine's "torah," any more than in the theology of Judaism they do to the Torah of Moses. Millar's judgment on Levine's misuse or uncritical use of literary sources is simply, "Although the normal expressions of caution appear, no such serious analysis is carried out." Levine is a fine example of the "pseudorthodoxy" — a critical veneer covering a core of pure credulity — Morton Smith ridiculed two decades ago.

Invoking a Marxist category he simply has not taken the trouble to master and explain, claiming to use archaeological evidence he does not competently use, alleging to consult in a critical manner literary sources he cites with perfect faith but absolutely no critical judgment, Levine exhibits contempt for scholarship as it is practiced in the academy. No wonder the publisher, Jewish Theological Seminary, by way of up-front prophylaxis, has given the book its own review, in a Foreword by Ismar Schorsch, Chancellor of the Jewish Theological Seminary, who is also the publisher of the book. Schorsch praises the book: "Never has the rabbinic elite of the third and fourth centuries been so fully drawn as to yield a portrait graced by the majestic blend of all available sources — primary and secondary, literary and archaeological, Jewish and non-Jewish. The simplicity and incisiveness of the text conceal the endless process of distillation. This blend will undoubtedly become the reference point for the generation of scholars to come." Many having read the book will find that judgment bizarre.

Discounting the usual hyperbole of a blurb, coming from one's own college president no less, one can account for the disparity between the hopelessly uncritical, indeed incompetent character of the book and its publisher's accompanying blurb only by the theory that, the chancellor either has not read the book and is saying what he thinks politic, or has read the book but has not actually understood its disgraceful ignorance. But quite plausibly, Schorsch calls Levine "vintage Seminary," pointing to his studies with Saul Lieberman there; with that judgment no one can disagree. This is precisely the quality of scholarship to be anticipated from a "vintage Seminary" product, now professor.

20.

JEFFREY L. RUBENSTEIN, *THE HISTORY OF SUKKOT IN THE SECOND TEMPLE AND RABBINIC PERIODS.* ATLANTA, 1995: SCHOLARS PRESS. BROWN JUDAIC STUDIES EDITED BY ERNEST SUNLEY FRERICHS, SHAYE J. D. COHEN, AND CALVIN GOLDSCHEIDER

What Professor Jeffrey L. Rubenstein, New York University, set out to prove in this extravagantly-researched but incoherent Columbia-Union Ph. D. dissertation I cannot say. Announcing that he will tell us "the history of Sukkot," what he has shown is, first, that the festival of Tabernacles (Sukkot) has no unitary, incremental, coherent history at all, and, second, that industrious research without a measure of intelligent reflection yields little of consequence.

His book has everything but a point. And that failure of intellect — the failure to ask, so what? if I know this, what else do I know? — deprives the book of any interest except as a collection of incoherent information. For had Rubenstein gone on to reflect upon the consequence of his findings, episodic and random as he (unwittingly) shows they are, he would have asked himself, if not history, then what? And the obvious answer, written across the surface of his findings, is, *systemic context*. But his conclusions, chapter by chapter, turn out merely to recapitulate in a few words what he has already said in a great many words, and the banalities and platitudes that substitute for rigorous thought mark the book as the result of first-class research but third-rate intellection.

The reason is that Rubenstein pays attention only to text, never to context. He conducts analysis of a topic that wanders from one document to another and appears in quite diverse ways in the several documents, without asking whether, beyond a few obvious traits set forth nearly at the outset (e.g., in the Torah), the topic coheres at all. My documentary approach has shown time and again that data on a given discrete topic set forth in a coherent statement, e.g., a document or its material equivalent, acquire sense and consequence only in the context of the system that utilizes those data (among others) to make its statement. But while Rubenstein uses the systemic documentary method that I have defined, he does so without understanding it. As a result, he collects his data correctly — book by book — but fails to interpret them in accord with his chosen method. Rather he looks for connections and continuities of data from one book to the next, without recognizing and interpreting the systemic and contextual setting in which those data make their appearance,. But then he has no interpretative framework in which to explain or endow with meaning the factual results of his research, as I shall show. And he says explicitly that he examines discrete documents, "in order to consider how the celebration of a festival developed over the course of time. The method is eclectic, but closer to history-of-religions and not simply history-of-traditions or theology." Quite what Rubenstein means by "history-of-religions" hardly emerges at all — but then why he rejects what he calls "history-of-traditions" or "theology" proves equally murky. But then "eclectic" joined to "method" surely represents a risible oxymoron.

Imagining a single, continuous Judaism, represented here by the festival, he chooses to treat everything outside the framework of its synchronic, that is, systemic (literary) context, asking documents to tell us what lies beyond, but not what lies within, themselves.[32] But, by contrast to what he proposed to do, what Rubenstein, a good researcher, has demonstrated is how data on a given theme take on meaning only in the context in which those data take their place. But because he has utilized a good method the purpose of which he did not grasp, he also did not see the point of his data. Publishing his results in the very series that I founded, and using my documentary method — the reading of data document by document in systemic context — Rubenstein simply has not then grasped that that reading serves to illuminate the document and its system in here, not some linear and continuous "Judaism" out there. The documentary method that he uses simply does not and cannot produce what he promises, which is, "the history of Sukkot," that is, the unitary, incremental, coherent history of the data collected from a great many documents. That is to say, he has followed a method he

---

[32]I have expanded on this matter in the following: *The Judaism Behind the Texts. The Generative Premises of Rabbinic Literature.* Atlanta, 1993: Scholars Press for South Florida Studies in the History of Judaism. I. *The Mishnah. A. The Division of Agriculture.* I. *The Mishnah. B. The Divisions of Appointed Times, Women, and Damages (through Sanhedrin).* I. *The Mishnah. C. The Divisions of Damages (from Makkot), Holy Things and Purities.* II. *The Tosefta, Tractate Abot, and the Earlier Midrash-Compilations: Sifra, Sifré to Numbers, and Sifré to Deuteronomy.* III. *The Later Midrash-Compilations: Genesis Rabbah, Leviticus Rabbah and Pesiqta deRab Kahana.* IV. *The Latest Midrash-Compilations: Song of Songs Rabbah, Ruth Rabbah, Esther Rabbah I, and Lamentations Rabbati. And The Fathers According to Rabbi Nathan.* V. *The Talmuds of the Land of Israel and Babylonia,* and *The Judaism the Rabbis Take for Granted.* Atlanta, 1995: Scholars Press for South Florida Studies in the History of Judaism.

does not grasp and cannot exploit, and the result, as I said, is a massive compilation of facts lacking all coherent meaning. To state matters simply, the documentary method yields synchronic phenomenology and not diachronic history. Used for diachrony, synchrony yields inanity.

Written in careful prose and industriously, if not comprehensively, researched, the dissertation claims to trace "the development of the festival over the course of a millennium." He begins with the ancient Israelite traditions, legal, narrative, and the like, discussing the origins of the Sukkah and the lulab. Then he systematically works his way through the diverse and incoherent data deriving from the Second Temple period, his subheads being documentary: Ezra-Nehemiah, Zechariah 14, Jubilees, 1-2 Maccabees, Qumran scrolls, Philo, Pseudo-Philo, Josephus, "Christian Scriptures" (!), Plutarch, numismatics and iconography. What we have here is a kind of concordance-research, spread over hundreds of pages. Concordance-results prove not very fascinating.

Then, from 70 forward, Rubenstein shifts from concordance-work to thematic compilation of data deriving from a great many documents, in general treating the Rabbinic documents in two contradictory ways simultaneously: [1] as uniform and one-dimensional, but sometimes ("eclectically") also [2] as free-standing and internally cogent. In the main, though, when he comes to the Rabbinic writings, he turns totally topical: the willow-procession, the water libation, the cultic background of the libation, rejoicing at the place of the water drawing, the same in the light of Hellenistic religions, extra Rabbinic evidence of the same, the lulab and the Hallel; then come the following: Sukkot and rain in Tannaitic sources; history of Tannaitic halakhah; Tannaitic midrashim: the clouds of glory; Sukkot in the Amoraic Midrashim. At no point does Rubenstein ask how what a given document tells us forms an integral part of the message of said document; at

every point he asks how a document attests to a datum beyond its limits. So he sees no Sukkot within a document and
its system, but asks a document to testify to Sukkot beyond
its own limits. Yet at each point, his evidence underscores the
intimate relationship between a document's representation of
Sukkot and that same document's larger polemical program.
The result is an enormous collection of essentially uninterpreted data, just as before.

A single example of the intellectual vacuity that results
must suffice to capture the bland flavor of the whole:

> The relationship of Sukkot to rain illustrates
> the adaptation of ancient components of the festival.
> Rabbinic Judaism inherited from ancient Israelite tradi-
> tion the idea that the divine judgment of rain takes
> place on Sukkot. Where the cult performed water liba-
> tions, willow-processions, and other rain making rites,
> the tannaim incorporated prayers for rain into the lit-
> urgy. The mechanism to ensure the continued fertility
> of the earth changed from cultic ritual to communal
> prayer, the conception of Sukkot as the determinative
> time endured...The persistence of Sukkot's connection
> to rain is related to the endurance of the mythic temple
> worldview in rabbinic times. The destruction of the
> Temple abolished sacrifices, the altar and other cultic
> rituals, but did not undermine their mythic underpin-
> nings...When we ponder the fate of a temple festival af-
> ter the temple is destroyed, we must be aware of the
> fact that the temple lived on in myth. In such a case a
> temple festival retains much of its original charac-
> ter...The endurance of the mythic worldview is of con-
> siderable significance. If this is not an idiosyncratic
> rabbinic phenomenon but reflects a widespread charac-
> teristic of religion, then we have evidence of the power
> of myth and symbol to sustain itself despite the de-
> struction of their original context...Destruction of place
> need not undermine the related religious practices and
> beliefs because the place endures in myth (pp. 321-
> 322).

Who is supposed to find illuminating these predictable and unexceptional results — results we could as well hang upon any other ancient rite in the context at hand? And since the same results characterize so much else, besides Sukkot, all of this adds up to very little, and certainly nothing that required more than 300 pages of research to produce. Rubenstein's "eclectic" method raises the question, why Sukkot is so much like all the "history" of most other rites, rather than what is special, in context, about Sukkot? But even though he claims to do something akin to history-of-religions, even very minimal work of comparison and contrast — the very essence of history of religions — does not find its way into this dissertation.

Why have the results proved incommensurate to the effort, that is, so much yielding rather little? Even Rubenstein concedes he has produced a mere research report, when he says, "The development of Sukkot during second temple and rabbinic times does not lend itself to neat summaries or hard and fast generalizations. Sukkot was a complex, multifaceted festival that underwent a complex, multifaceted development." But before doing the research, Rubenstein along with the rest of us must have known that fact.

What Rubenstein missed out of the data he has assembled emerges in another way of making the same observation. That is simply to note, Sukkot, like other enduring practices, served in a variety of contexts to make in its way the general statement that those who defined the context wished to make. Then what makes the work interesting is to investigate not continuity but discontinuity, not diachrony but synchrony. What is required is not merely to collect masses of discrete and contradictory data treated as uniform but to analyze them. And this, Rubenstein announces at the very outset, he refuses to do.

As I said, Rubenstein's attempt to produce a continuous history only proves that here continuous, incremental history contradicts the character of the discrete evidence, diachrony giving way to synchrony. Rubenstein has not asked himself the hard questions and shows only the ability to collect, arrange, and pass his opinion about, masses of discrete data. But then, his teachers also did not ask him those same tough questions. The upshot is, American doctoral education in the field of the study of religion within the specialization of Judaism hardly wins our confidence in incoherent work such as this.

21.

ZE'EV SAFRAI, *THE ECONOMY OF ROMAN PALESTINE.* LONDON AND NEW YORK, 1994: ROUTLEDGE

Safrai's discussion of the economy of Roman Palestine combines archaeological with Talmudic and some Classical sources in a survey of various topics, as follows: settlement patterns (classification of settlements); modes of production (agriculture, crafts & industry, services); trade in the land of Israel in the Roman period; the organizational framework of farming; open or closed economy in the Land of Israel during the Roman period (self-sufficiency vs. specialization); demographic multiplication and economic growth. Safrai does not set forth his goals, or why he thinks an account of an "economy" is either possible or consequential in this context. What else we know, if we know, e.g., that people raised sheep, he does not suggest. The result is a huge compilation of what Safrai claims are facts, but a considerable failure of intellect: information without purpose.

The intellectual vacuity of the whole does not exhaust the work's failure, since Safrai's completely uncritical reading of the Rabbinic writings casts doubt on the facticity of his alleged facts. Specifically, whether Safrai has intelligently and accurately utilized the archaeological reports in a critical and intelligent manner I cannot say. But his use of Rabbinic evidence is retrograde and ignorant. He allows Babylonian sources to tell us all about Palestine. Worse still, he quotes with equal confidence documents concluded in the third century and in the seventh century and in medieval times, all to tell us how things were long before the redaction of those documents, and he believes pretty much everything he reads in the Rabbinic literature. The result is a pathetic pastiche: a gullible reading of Talmudic texts covered by a veneer of pseudo-critical verbiage. Among five hundred dreary pages of examples, the following gives the flavor of the whole:

> A number of other sources tell of the great number of sheep in Judea. Thus, for example, the Tosefta states regarding the Temple that "calves were brought from the Sharon and sheep from the desert" (T. Menahot 9:13). BT Menahot 87a (=BT Sotah 34b) explains that the "calves came from the Sharon and the sheep from Hebron" and adds that Absalom, the son of David, had gone to Hebron in order to bring sheep from there. A midrash on the blessing of Jacob to Judah states in a similar vein that "all the valleys will turn white from the fields of wheat and the flocks of sheep" (Bereshit Rabbati 49:12) All this would seem to prove that the raising of sheep in the Hebron mountains was quite prevalent. Thus it appears that sheep gracing was rather limited in the Galilee and a rather widespread phenomenon in Judea.... (p. 169)..

Quite how the literary sources yield the economic facts that Safrai imputes is not clear. The Tosefta is a document that reached closure around two centuries after the destruction of the Temple; why, then, we should take as fact its information about prior practices (of limited pertinence to the larger question he proposes to answer!) Safrai does not tell us. The Talmud of Babylonia, redacted in ca. 600 C.E., then imputes to Absalom, son of Scripture's king David, in ca. 900 B.C.E., fifteen hundred years earlier, the intent of bringing sheep from Hebron. By Bereshit Rabbati I am not sure whether Safrai refers to Bereshit Rabbah (Genesis Rabbah) of ca. 450 C.E., or the much later, medieval compilation, but it makes little difference. All of this "evidence" proves nothing much, and "would seem to prove" cannot obscure Safrai's grossly uncritical use of literary sources in the reconstruction of economic facts.

Readers will certainly have noted, also, the rather awkward prose; reading Safrai is not always easy and is rarely enjoyable, since he writes a clumsy, uncertain, and alien English. He would have done better to write the book in Hebrew and have a native speaker translate it. But his style accurately captures the clumsy and wooden thought processes that have yielded this enormous collection of dubious facts, set forth in a dull way to yield propositions of little weight or consequence for the study of either economics or Judaism.

22.

Rabbinic Sources for Historical Study: A Debate with Ze'ev Safrai

Israeli scholarship in what is called there "the history of the Jewish people in the period of the Mishnah and the Talmud" defines a special chapter in the larger debate on critical utilization of Rabbinic sources for historical study. The reason is that an iron consensus operates, fully articulated, institutionally enforced, that, in general, all sources serve, except for the ones that do not serve. This is stated in so many words by Ze'ev Safrai, when he says, "Almost all Talmudic texts that meet the examination outlined in (a) should be accepted. However, each text should also be examined in the light of related historical sources to establish whether the picture portrayed makes sense according to all other available information."[33] He further alleges, "...we confidently follow a path that has been paved by many students of Jewish history, such as Büchler, Alon, Epstein, and others.." And, further, "With all due respect, this is just one of dozens of similar projects, an extensive discussion of the issue of methodology is beyond our scope." So Safrai may serve as a reliable witness to the methods that dictate how historical study of Talmudic and Rabbinic writings is carried on in the State of Israel and its universities. It may be characterized very simple: it is simply intellectually primitive and historically uncritical. Its questions are trivial, and its results, incoherent. No important insight into the character of the Juda-

---

[33]Ze'ev Safrai, *The Economy of Roman Palestine*. London and New York, 1994: Routledge, p. 4.

ism of the age emerges, and compelling answers to urgent questions do not emerge from work that believes whatever the sources allege but, out of that credulity, produces neither consequential facts nor provocative hypothesis. For, as we shall see in a moment, Safrai (confidently) utilizes "almost all" Rabbinic texts pertinent to his subject and deems everyone of them to present us with hard facts on economic life and behavior.

To show how accurately Safrai in his fundamental allegation concerning the historicity of "most" of what the Talmud and related writings say represents the methods of Israeli university scholarship on Talmudic history, let me point to the journal *Zion,* published by the Israel Historical Society, and focus upon the character of the articles in the field that that journal has printed. When people practice talmudic history in *Zion,* they limit their discussion to talmudic history in particular. The field does not encompass its period, but only one set of sources emergent from its period. And this explains the triviality of the results: while many of the scholars represented in *Zion* draw upon *sources* outside the Talmud, none of the articles deals with a *problem* outside the Talmud. Accordingly, talmudic history in the Israeli journal at hand finds definition as the study of historical problems pertinent to a given *source,* rather than to a chronological *period* to which that source attests.[34] It follows that talmudic history severely limits itself, in *Zion,* to literary evidence. While, once again, we may find allusion to archaeological data, no article in the past half-century has entered the category of inquiry in which archeology, as much as literature, defines the problem or contributes to its solution.

The methodology of reading the literary sources, which are the only ones to define the problems and solutions

---

[34]I return to this matter below.

of talmudic history in *Zion,* begins in an assumption universally adopted by the scholars of the journal: whatever the
Talmud says happened happened. If the Talmud attributes
something to a rabbi, he really said it. If the Talmud maintains that a rabbi did something, he really did it. If the Talmud tells a story, that stands for an actual event, controlling
for implausible miracles. So among the twenty-one articles
under discussion, I find not a single one that asks the basic
critical questions with which historical study normally commences: how does the writer of this source know what he
tells me? How do I know that he is right? On the contrary,
the two Talmuds serve, as much in fifty years of the journal
Zion as much in Safrai's latter-day book, as encyclopedias of
facts about rabbis and other Jews in the Land of Israel and
Babylonia. The task of the historian is to mine the encyclopedias and come up with important observations on the basis of
the facts at hand. The work of the historian, then, is just what
Safrai shows he thinks it is: solely the collection and arrangement of facts, the analysis of facts, the synthesis of facts. It is
not in the inquiry into the source and character of the facts at
hand. It does not require inquiry into penetrating questions
concerning culture, ideas, or intellect. Just as, for the literary
scholar, the text constitutes the starting point of inquiry, so
for the historian, the text at hand defines the facts and dictates the character of inquiry upon them. This is the case, beginning and end, from Alon to Kimelman (an American, as a
matter of fact). Whether it is Alon, telling us what Yohanan
ben Zakkai meant in his conversation with Vespasian in August 70, on the assumption that Vespasian and Yohanan were
attended by secretaries who wrote down their every word, or
whether it is Kimelman, telling us about the politics of the
priesthood and exilarchate as reported by a story in
Yerushalmi Shabbat 12:3, the method is the same: believe it
all, paraphrase it all, regurgitate it all, and call the result "his-

tory."

Safrai himself confirms my judgment that the fifty years of Talmudic history in *Zion* just now summarized and his own method correspond exactly. That Safrai stands for the generality of mainstream Israeli scholarship, and that the same rules of evidence, which we shall examine, govern throughout, furthermore is indicated by Safrai's confident statement that, in general, Israeli work follows the lines he summarizes and that in no way does he innovate in the use of evidence. He points, in particular, to another contemporary, younger Israeli scholar, Y. Gafni, who has written a book in accord with the same rules; speaking of the use of the Babylonian Talmud as a historical source, Safrai says, "In this area we have also followed numerous scholars, and have not sought any methodological innovations. Our position on this subject is summarized by Gafni in his discussion of the Babylonian texts in general, and the Jewish community in Babylon in particular."[35] The community of scholarship in the State of Israel[36] has established a firm consensus on these matters,

---

[35]He refers to Y. M. Gafni, *The Jews of Babylonia in the Talmudic Era* (Jerusalem, 1991) in Hebrew. Gafni's work was supposed to have been published in English translation by Yale University Press, but, as of this writing, five years after the Israeli edition in Hebrew, no word on the date of publication in English has been received.

[36]Scholarship in Europe concerning the history of the Jews and Judaism in late antiquity ("the Talmudic period") responds to the critical agenda of biblical studies and attempts a more critical stance toward the sources. But the results prove only marginally less gullible than the Israeli ones. Rather facile solutions to complex problems produce a veneer of criticism covering a foundation of credulity, that is, pseudo-criticism; see for example Martin Goodman, *State and Society in Roman Galilee, AD 132-212* (Totowa, 1983). Goodman's work is exemplary of what is not uncritical but pseudocritical. In the USA, by contrast, only a few scholars manufacture facts by simply alluding to a page of the Talmud, though retrograde work does appear from time to time. These, in general, are employed in Jewish-sponsored centers of learning and not in secular universities. But retrograde work does come from the academy too, as in

which, as we see, Safrai confidently claims to represent in his work. Hence in the use of Rabbinic writings in the composition of Safrai's Economy of Roman Palestine we gain a reliable picture of the established methods there, and, because matters are thoroughly articulated, it follows, we may compose a systematic critique of that position as well.

Publication of Safrai's *Economy of Roman Palestine* therefore defines the occasion, so a brief preliminary word about the quality of his book is appropriate. Safrai's discussion of the economy of Roman Palestine combines archaeological with Talmudic and some Classical sources in a survey of various topics, as follows: settlement patterns (classification of settlements); modes of production (agriculture, crafts and industry, services); trade in the land of Israel in the Roman period; the organizational framework of farming; open or closed economy in the Land of Israel during the Roman period (self-sufficiency vs. specialization); demographic multiplication and economic growth. Safrai does not set forth his goals, or why he thinks an account of an "economy" is either possible or consequential in this context. What else we know, if we know, e.g., that people raised sheep, he does not suggest. The result is a huge compilation of what Safrai claims are facts, but a considerable failure of intellect: information without purpose. He provides no account of a working economy, only a repertoire of data, some plausible, some dubious, out of which such an account might be constructed by an

---

sities. But retrograde work does come from the academy too, as in the deplorable book, *The Monarchic Principle. Studies in Jewish Self-Government in Antiquity,* by David Goodblatt (University of California at San Diego), Tübingen, 1994: J.C.B. Mohr (Paul Siebeck). *Texte und Studien zum Antiken Judentum* 38. Goodblatt's entire program of questions rests on the premise that answers on what named persons really said and did are to be found in the Rabbinic documents; absent that premise, he could not have framed the issues as he did.

economic historian of antiquity.

But — and here is the point subject to the fabricated debate I undertake in this chapter — Safrai's completely uncritical reading of the Rabbinic writings casts doubt on the facticity of his alleged facts. Specifically, whether Safrai has intelligently and accurately utilized the archaeological reports in a critical and intelligent manner I cannot say. But his use of Rabbinic evidence is retrograde and ignorant. He allows Babylonian sources to tell us all about Palestine. Worse still, he quotes with equal confidence documents concluded in the third century and in the seventh century and in medieval times, all to tell us how things were long before the redaction of those documents, and he believes pretty much everything he reads in the Rabbinic literature. The result is a pathetic pastiche: a gullible reading of Talmudic texts covered by a veneer of pseudo-critical verbiage. Among five hundred dreary pages of examples, the following gives the flavor of the whole:

> A number of other sources tell of the great number of sheep in Judea. Thus, for example, the Tosefta states regarding the Temple that "calves were brought from the Sharon and sheep from the desert" (T. Menahot 9:13). BT Menahot 87a (=BT Sotah 34b) explains that the "calves came from the Sharon and the sheep from Hebron" and adds that Absalom, the son of David, had gone to Hebron in order to bring sheep from there. A midrash on the blessing of Jacob to Judah states in a similar vein that "all the valleys will turn white from the fields of wheat and the flocks of sheep" (Bereshit Rabbati 49:12) All this would seem to prove that the raising of sheep in the Hebron mountains was quite prevalent. Thus it appears that sheep gracing was rather limited in the Galilee and a rather widespread phenomenon in Judea.... (p. 169)..

Quite how the literary sources yield the economic facts that

Safrai imputes is not clear. The Tosefta is a document that reached closure around two centuries after the destruction of the Temple; why, then, we should take as fact its information about prior practices (of limited pertinence to the larger question he proposes to answer!) Safrai does not tell us. The Talmud of Babylonia, redacted in ca. 600 C.E., then imputes to Absalom, son of Scripture's king David, in ca. 900 B.C.E., fifteen hundred years earlier [!], the intent of bringing sheep from Hebron. So sheep come from Hebron. By Bereshit Rabbati I am not sure whether Safrai refers to Bereshit Rabbah (Genesis Rabbah) of ca. 450 C.E., or to a much later, medieval compilation, but it makes little difference. Whatever Safrai finds in a rabbinic document, he believes as fact, within the most trivial and lenient strictures of what he imagines is "criticism." But the pseudo-critical character of the whole cannot be missed, since all of this "evidence" proves nothing much, and "would seem to prove" cannot obscure Safrai's grossly uncritical use of literary sources in the reconstruction of economic facts.

Lest the cited passage that illustrates Safrai's method of finding his facts in the literary evidence be thought exceptional, let me cite one more. This should serve to establish that characterizing Safrai's method as a simple opening of a document and believing pretty much everything he finds there is no caricature. The following is Safrai's account of Lod:

> Talmudic traditions from the Tannaitic period, and particularly from the end of the Second Temple and Javneh period, describe many rich landowners. R. Eliezer b. Hyrcanus was a resident of this city [Lod]. His family owned many lands as is clear from the Talmudic tradition describing his early years (Genesis Rabbah 41...). His father, at the end of the Second Temple period, had rather extensive holdings. R. Eliezer himself had a field at Kefar Tov, a site as yet

unidentified. A rich landowner living in the city and owning lands in the hinterland was a common phenomenon in the Roman world.

Another rich sage describing from an important family and living in Lod was R. Eleazar b. Azariah. R. Eleazar is basically associated with the Javneh period, and, apparently, also with Lod. Talmudic traditions do not mention his lands, but he must have had such possessions, since that is what would have made him and his family wealthy. He did have flocks of sheep , however (BT Shabbat 54b; PT Shabbat V, 7c, and parallels). Another rich sage of the Javneh period in Lod was R. Tarfon. R. Tarfon is described as a landowner (see for example PT Sheviit IV, 25b; BT Nedarim 62a...). One tradition relates that R. Tarfon gave R. Akiva money in order to buy an estate for the two of them (Leviticus Rabbah 34:16). These three sages were priests and came from important families. None of this is coincidence, but this is not the correct forum in which to discuss the matter (Safrai, pp. 93-4).

Genesis Rabbah reached closure at ca. 450 C.E.; the story that Safrai cites involves a long account of how some four hundred years earlier Eliezer left his father's fields to go and study the Torah with Yohanan ben Zakkai. How all this makes him a "rich landowner" is not clear; I wonder how many rich landowners had their sons working in the fields, as Eliezer is supposed to have been when he got the call to study the Torah. The treatment of Eleazar is equally bizarre; surely in Palestine at that time not everyone who was thought wealthy invested in real estate, though the Roman aristocracy and the Judaic sages alike deemed real estate the only form of worldly wealth. Tarfon is described as wealthy in two fifth and one seventh century documents — long after he lived; how these documents got the information they set forth Safrai does not say.

The story he cites in Leviticus Rabbah concerns the equation of wealth and Torah-learning, the latter deemed superior to real estate, and idea that otherwise does not occur in the mouths of first century sages at all, let alone in documents redacted prior to the fifth century.[37] Nor were all priests wealthy, nor did all priests own real estate of consequence, nor were all priests from important families, nor were all important families wealthy in real estate. But why go on? For none of these considerations affects Safrai's reading of the evidence, or his use thereof. It suffices to say that his work yields many hundreds of equally uncritical readings of the Rabbinic documents, which are taken at face value as sources of historical facts of the kind Safrai requires for his work.

To his credit, Safrai systematically sets forth his views on why it is proper to read the documents in the way that he does. I cite the entirety of his discussion and then comment on it, before setting forth in a more systematic way my own view of the problem at hand. This is what he says; note my underlining at (b)

THE RABBINIC SOURCES

On the question of the reliability of the Talmudic texts as historical sources.

The Talmudic texts are the main basis of our study and the source of information for most of the questions, answers and hypotheses put forward. In terms of the utilization of such sources, we have added nothing new, and we confidently follow a path that has been paved by many students of Jewish history, such as Büchler, Alon, Epstein, and others. This approach can be summarized as follows:

(a) Every source must be thoroughly checked, examining the original version against manuscripts

---

[37] I demonstrate that fact in my *The Transformation of Judaism. From Philosophy to Religion.* Champaign, 1992: University of Illinois Press, which Safrai does not cite, though the work contains two chapters devoted to the economics of Rabbinic Judaism.

and quotations of the 'Rishonim' (interpreters of the early Middle Ages) as well as additional evidence. After this, parallel sources are used to determine that this is really the original version of the law. Is the text different or distorted? What can be learned from the differences between the sources and from the ensuing questions and investigations?

(b) <u>Almost all Talmudic texts that meet the examination outlined in (a) should be accepted.</u> However, each text should also be examined in the light of related historical sources to establish whether the picture portrayed makes sense according to all other available information.

(c) Naturally, one should suspect texts of exaggeration and excessiveness, and of changes made to correspond with the esthetic and theoretical framework of the story and anachronistic descriptions (mainly of the Biblical period). Such exaggeration is, of course, more common in legends than in halacha, and the latter can be expected to be much more accurate. The researcher must identify the historical core in the text; it is this information that can serve as a source of knowledge.

(d) After the authenticity of the source has been established, the researcher must study it and determine its significance and the conclusions that can be drawn. In this context, a number of questions will be asked, and related options will be examined. For example, does the text represent something customary or something exceptional: Is the story an exceptional example that tells us about a general occurrence, or does it refer to an isolated incident or episode? Was the decision of the beit midrash actually carried out? What period does the source represent? What does it incorporate from earlier times and what new elements did the rabbis of the period add? The answers to such questions, in turn, lead to further investigation.

(e) All these tests apply to the Palestinian texts. We treated the Babylonian texts differently, as discussed below.

(f) This method of study based on deduction and analogy serves as an alternative to two other main methods. On the one hand, there is the traditional method, which is based on absolute belief in every source. Accordingly, the research focuses on application of the information. In addition, since all sources are considered indisputable truth, it is necessary to explain the discrepancies between them. These explanations generally ignore the constraints of reason and logic and require a willingness to reject some other sources such as manuscripts, texts from the Geniza..., some of the midrashim, and the like.

In contrast, another method challenges the belief in the rabbinic literature and its use as a historical source. We discuss this below.

In the context of the present research, it is not necessary to discuss the methodological assumptions presented. After all, this is not the first study of the history of the people of Israel and of Palestine. With all due respect, this is just one of dozens of similar projects, an an extensive discussion of the issue of methodology is beyond our scope.

Nevertheless, this does not excuse us altogether from the need to address the question of method. The main conclusion that arises from this essay is likely (or liable) to seem utopian. The summary seems too neat, and therefore it is not credible. Thus we must defend the way in which we utilized the sources, in general and in principle.

For this purpose we consider an alternative method of studying ancient sources. Using this method, numerous respected researchers...have presented arguments that question the validity of using rabbinic texts as a source of social history. The major arguments are as follows.

(1) In the Mishnah and Talmud periods, the rabbis headed isolated batei midrash. The laws that they developed emerged in these detached, isolated 'islands' of study. Thus the rabbis neither understood nor knew the reality of their times; it was not the background to their decisions, their attitudes nor even the legends told in the batei midrash. Sometimes this argument is presented in an even more extreme manner. The Talmudic literature is depicted not as a summary of opinions of a group of rabbis, but as personal literary creations. Accordingly, the Mishnah is not a public text, but the work of a single editor or group of editors. Consequently, each book or part of a book has a different social background, which must be discussed separately. Obviously, this type of research does not require the knowledge of all Talmudic texts, and such study becomes simple, one-dimensional, and unequivocal.

Applying this theory to our study, the image that emerges of the economy, the community and the settlement would not be true history but 'literary history,' or 'economics of the beit midrash.'

(2) The public at large did not obey the rabbis. Among the Jews, only a minority followed the rabbis, obeyed their decisions and was influenced by their sermons and moral teachings. It was also this small group that influence the outlook of the beit midrash; its customs and attitudes constitute the social and historical background for the decisions made in the beit midrash. According to this perspective, then, the texts do not provide a true image of the community, but that of a small group, a social stratum whose ties with the wider public were few and problematic...

As noted, although we will not discuss these broad methodological issues, brief discussion of those subjects directly related to our field of research seems warranted. Some of the following comments are restricted to this area, and some also have more general theoretical significance. Prior to the discussion, another aspect, more psychological than scientific, should be considered. The Talmudic texts pose an extremely difficult challenge to the scholar. The archaic Hebrew and

Aramaic integrated with Hebrew are a primary hardship. Moreover, the texts are written in a sort of inner code, the code of the beit midrash (school). All the interpretive and traditional Mishnaic texts assume that this code is known to the reader, so instead of interpreting it they use it. Thus the first sentence in the Mishnah Brachot 1,1 would be translated literally as, 'From when they call: listen!' when it actually means, 'From when people have to pray the Prayer of Shema.' In addition, the corresponding scripture for many of the passages is not clear; sometimes the textual basis for whole chapters is not explicitly mentioned. The material is not organized by subjects and the same issue appears in numerous sources. Conflicts between the sources, errors in a version and later editing of some of the texts all create additional difficulties. Furthermore, until recently there was no lexicon...and most of the essays have not yet been published in scientific, or even semi-scientific, editions.

It is no wonder, then, that many scholars have erred in their understanding of the texts and made mistakes in using them. Someone who does not know the Talmudic texts intimately will have difficulty making full use of all the rabbinic literature.

Needless to say, in this respect, graduates of the Jewish religious institutions have a distinct advantage. In modern institutions of this type, two to five hours a day are devoted to studying the Talmud...

These 'technical' difficulties must not influence our position regarding the reliability of the rabbinic sources. After all, difficulty in reading an inscription does not dissuade researchers, but actually stimulates them to make greater efforts to utilize the hidden information and to determine its implications.

For our purposes, a distinction should be made between three types of conclusions that may arise from the study of rabbinic texts.
(a) Did the rabbis succeed in changing or influence the social environment through their teachings? For example, did the prohibition against charging interest have an impact on lenders

and borrowers? Did the rabbis' utopian position (and their opposition to trade and urban lifestyles) affect the public? Did their moralistic policy and their desire to help the poor and the weak influence the economic structure? ...These questions actually apply to only a small group of subjects, as the rabbis generally did not try to mold economic life or to pronounce utopian commands;[38] they did not consider it their role to decide what to grow, how to produce, how to sell or to interfere in other purely economic matters.

(b) In the course of their writings, the rabbis refer to a certain religious-social background as though it were real. Thus, for instance, the rabbis assume that the entire public observes kashrut, keeps the Sabbath and attends synagogue. These assumptions relate to matters that were important to the rabbis. They considered these aspects of life as their realm, and in this respect the distance between themselves, their students, and the general public was prominent. After all, the whole community could not be holy. Regarding these matters, the rabbis' writings reflect the customs only of those who were accepted in the stratum of rabbis. Accordingly, one might expect that the background described in the text applies to the society of the beit midrash (school) alone....

---

[38] Safrai's statements here are simply astonishing; it appears he has not opened the pages of Mishnah-tractate Shebi"it, which legislates for the sabbatical year in a utopian spirit, among many tractates that deal with economic and political matters without attending to actualities. I challenge him, for instance, to demonstrate how Mishnah-tractate Sanhedrin is other than utopian, with its government in the hands of a king, high priest, and sages' court set forth in an age in which there was no king of Judea and no Temple high priesthood either. Much that follows in these paragraphs is pure gibberish. Perhaps in Hebrew the discussion in the next paragraph (b) is intelligible, but in English it is simply beyond deciphering.

(c) In the course of their discussions, the rabbis relate
by the way to the situation outside the beit
midrash. Thus, for instance, when they discuss the obligation of tithing, they assume that
in some places most of the produce is sent to
market...Perhaps the laws of tithing were
theoretical, and most of the public paid no attention to them at all, but is there any reason
to doubt that there were places where most of
the harvest was sent to the market? In this
case it might still be argued that the description is theoretical and is presented as a dialectic possibility alone. even more notable an example is the rabbis' description of the sale of a
house, in which they assume that it includes a
cooker and stove...We still do not know how
common the sale of houses was, but there is
no reason to doubt that the cooker and stove
were an integral part of a residential dwelling,
and it is also clear that they were considered
the most characteristic components of such a
house.

The decisive majority of subjects with which this work
deals belong to the latter type and resemble the last example presented here. A small portion are similar to the
previous example of tithing laws. In these cases we
must clarify whether the background to the text is real-
istic, or whether it was presented for the purpose of a
theoretical dialectic discussion.

Only very few of the references in this book
belong to type (a) or (b) above. In general, the rabbis
did not deal with formation of the economic structure
but with personal behavior and lifestyle within the economic structure of their time.[39] The rabbis were inter-

---

[39]A study of the cases reported in the pages of the Talmud of
Babylonia will show that the rabbis of that satrapy most certainly did deal
with conduct in the market place and claimed to decide cases about concrete matters of all kinds, fixing pricing, settling real estate disputes, imposing the law of the Mishnah on a variety of conflicts. This matter is dis-

ested in questions of ritual, ceremony, morals and social justice, and economic circumstances only served as
a framework, a setting for them. It is actually because
the economic, technological and agricultural subjects
were not generally the focus of the rabbinic literature
that it can be used as a source for the study of the
economy [Safrai, pp. 3-8).

At this point Safrai wishes to explain why "the historical description that emerges from rabbinic literature" is not "sup-
ported, echoed and confirmed by parallel external sources of
information, such as Roman and Christian documents..." He
points out that Roman literature represents "the imperial and
urban establishment," and Christian literature for its part contains little information. He proceeds with statements that
must astound scholars of Syriac literature, from Aphrahat
forward, which assuredly represented no "establishment,"
whether Iranian or Roman, but a group as humble as the Judaic one:

> The rabbinic literature reflects a completely
> different social stratum...This is the only literature from
> that period that represents the native residents and not
> the establishment, which was saturated in Greek and
> Roman culture. The Talmudic literature emerged
> mostly in the rural community, out of a struggle against
> the imperial culture, literature, and religion.
> ...Nevertheless, in the course of this work we do occa-
> sionally refer to evidence derived from external
> sources. In general, the comparisons and parallels with

cussed extensively in my *History of the Jews in Babylonia* (Leiden, 1965-1970:
E. J. Brill) I-V, which Safrai does not appear to know. Safrai's treatment
of the sages' range of interest as mainly personal, having to do with what
he calls "lifestyle," contradicts virtually every page of both Talmuds, as
well as every line of the Mishnah in every division. But these claims of his
play so inconsequential a role in the hundreds of pages of dreary narrative
that it hardly suffices to pursue the matter. We focus only on issues of historical epistemology.

> non-Jewish evidence are extremely limited and cast no
> doubt on our conclusions...(Safrai, pp. 8-9).

But as to archaeological evidence:

> In general, the archaeological findings confirm
> and validate the rabbinic texts and the use of these
> sources in our work.

We may leave it to archaeologists to judge whether Safrai's
characterization of matters accurately portrays the facts, and
to Classicists and Historians of early Christianity to evaluate
his reasons for excluding pertinent evidence in those bodies
of writings.

He excludes, also, the whole of extra-rabbinic Judaic
literature, on grounds that it is too early to attest to the period
of which he wishes to speak, but that clearly does not lead
him to omit, also, the documents of Rabbinic Judaism that
come long after the times that he claims to portray. So Philo
and Josephus are too early, but medieval compilations of
Rabbinic sayings (many of the Midrash-compilations he cites
for facts) are not too late — not to mention the Talmud of
Babylonia, ca. 600, two hundred years after Safrai closes his
gate. Since his systematic account supposedly pertains to
"Roman Palestine," I should not have thought he would wish
to exclude pertinent evidence concerning Greek- and Latin-
speaking residents, on the one side, or the Aramaic-speaking
Christians, on the other. I should have imagined that an account of an economy by definition must encompass all play-
ers in that economy, not only one group and the evidence of
its activities. But in this debate we are not concerned with issues of economic history, nor for that matter, for most of his
slogging journey through nearly a hundred pages on grains,
wine, pigeons, olives, is he; the realia of economic activity do
not form an account of an economy, they only contribute to

such an account, which, in the end, Safrai cannot be said to have set forth.

Safrai articulates a method. Let us now take him at his word and address each of its components, then set forth in more general terms what, in the framework of what he wishes to do, I propose is a valid scholarly program. Let us work our way through his arguments point by point, then generalize.

(a) All parties concur that every source must be thoroughly checked. I cannot point to a single instance in his book in which the procedure he prescribes has materially affected his presentation. This point, on which no one differs, must form part of the background of discourse. It supplies a veneer of pseudo-criticism alone. But the premise contained within it that if we have "the original version," then we have a reliable fact, is obviously fundamental to Safrai's view of matters. We may call this "philological fundamentalism:" a reliable text-version, properly understood word for word, constitutes a historical fact, not merely a textual one.

(b) Here is the crux of matters. What we have here is an argument from content, which is to say, if an ancient source makes an allegation, we must accept that allegation unless we find grounds on the basis of which to reject it. That same position was outlined to me in so many words in a conversation with the late E. E. Urbach in 1976, and I have heard the same apophthegm set forth time and again on those occasions, admittedly not very many, on which Israeli colleagues have engaged in discussion with me. Arguments from content rapidly deteriorate into allegations concerning [1] the ring of truth, [2] why our holy rabbis would not lie, and [3] the kernel of historical truth that is contained within the legend. On that basis, it goes without saying, a paraphrase of the biblical books from Genesis through Kings, with a few omissions of obviously implausible miracles ("related sources...makes sense..."), supplies us with a reliable, critical history of pre-exilic Israel: if it sounds true ("makes sense according to all other available information"), it is true.

Arguments from content such as these simply ignore the critical issues, how does a given fact reach written form (or other permanent formulation), and how does the written form of the fact then reach us? Without answers to those questions, we find ourselves in the position of believing everything (except what we choose not to believe) in documents that reached closure long after the period of which they speak. Such stout faith may afford access to Heaven, but it cannot today dictate the shape of critical, historical knowledge, any more than it has, for academic learning in all other fields of history, for two centuries and more. Why Safrai finds unnecessary an *Auseinandersetzung* with the entirety of Biblical scholarship, on the one side, and the whole of critical historical literature, on the other, baffles me. Outside of the little world in which he works, scholars who deal with sources of comparable character treat as urgent questions matters that he regards as bearing no consequence whatsoever. He states with blithe innocence positions deemed uncritical, indeed credulous and gullible, in every other field of academic learning but his own, and in whole continents in which his own field of learning is carried on, except his own.

(c) No one will dispute this point, which is necessary, but not sufficient, for any critical method.

(d) Quite what Safrai intends in this rather lugubrious formulation eludes me. The reason is that Safrai does not spell out the alternatives or tell us the consequences that he draws from the theoretical answers to his theoretical questions. Customary or exceptional? Then what is at stake? Are we to believe in what is routine but not episodic? Then what has happened to point (b)? When Safrai introduces the matter of "period," "what period does the source represent?" he assumes an answer to that question. But throughout his book, all facts are classified as to period by appeal to the authority to whom sayings are attributed. Then periodization of sayings and the facts they contain for him entirely depends upon the attribution of a saying to a sage. But these attributions are notoriously unreliable, for everyone knows that what is assigned to one authority here is given to someone else in another passage; sages themselves readily exchanged names and opinions as logic required; an entire document, the Tosefta, systematically reconfigures what is assigned to a set of sages; and the entire matter of attributions awaits systematic, critical investigation in its own terms. It is the simple fact that, at this time, we have no universal method of falsifying attributions, therefore, also, no method of validating them. Methods that may serve for some specific documents (my own for the Mishnah and the Tosefta) prove suggestive but not probative, and no others have been proposed within the framework of critical discourse.

(f) Safrai here proposes to distinguish himself from the yeshiva-world on the far horizon of the integrationist-Orthodoxy of Bar Ilan University, a world where everybody believes everything, not just nearly everything. But this "traditional" method, yielding the task of harmonizing what Safrai calls "discrepancies," and Safrai's gullible method, only marginally differ, for the reasons already spelled out.

Now to the second part of his argument, alternative approaches. I have reproduced Safrai's picture of contrary methods, but I find no reason to debate with him about them. A few remarks serve.

(1) It suffices to say that Safrai simply does not show a grasp of the methods he rejects, but only caricatures them. A single case suffices. Safrai alludes, at this paragraph, to my

The Economics of the Mishnah.[40] That book addresses the questions, why does the Mishnah set forth an economics, and what systemic message is conveyed through economics and only could have been conveyed through economics? Safrai's account of the matter shows no comprehension of that simple fact. The larger problematics of the documentary hypothesis lies beyond Safrai's horizon. The history of economic thought in antiquity plays no role in his picture of the economy of Roman Palestine.

(2) Safrai's characterization of the results of scholarship produced by those who have not studied in yeshivas can only be dismissed as bizarre. His language, as readers will have observed, is characteristically murky, but his intention is obvious: people who have not studied in yeshivas cannot study Rabbinic literature, just as those who (like Safrai himself) have not abandoned the intellectual premises of the yeshivas about the inerrancy of the holy books also cannot study history. But his example proves little less than risible. I cannot point to any translation of the Mishnah-passage he cites, in any language, that makes the stupid mistake Safrai admonishes us not to make. And his translation is simply ludicrous, since it does not portray the Hebrew at all, which yields not his preferred, rather exotic, "From when people have to pray the Prayer of Shema," but "From what time may they recite the Shema in the evening? From the hour that the priests enter [their homes] to eat their heave offering...." One does not have to study in a yeshiva and then leave to master a line of the Rabbinic literature of late antiquity, and a strong case can be made against yeshiva-study for those who wish to focus upon that literature. But one does have to study in a ye-

---

[40]Chicago, 1989: The University of Chicago Press. Safrai has the date wrong, but his gross inattention to detail throughout proves disheartening.

shiva to master the entirety of the halakhah of Judaism, which is a different matter; indeed, yeshiva-learning neglects a great many of the texts that Safrai himself cites or studies those texts superficially and at odd intervals, not in a systematic and sustained way.

For all his insistence that yeshiva-training is necessary for an understanding of the Talmud in its own terms and the rest of the Rabbinic documents of ancient times in their own terms, Safrai's own grasp of the Talmudic literature proves impressionistic, alas, infirm at best. That is because in yeshivas people study line by line but rarely aim at a grasp of the whole of a document. For example, his allegation that material is not organized by subjects is simply false for the Mishnah and mostly false for most of the rest of the Rabbinic literature organized around the Mishnah; and it is equally false for the Midrash-compilations, properly set forth.[41] He probably means, it is not organized by abstract principles, which is true. No one will argue with Safrai that someone who does not know the texts "intimately" will have difficulty using them; but nothing in his account of matters shows how that "intimate" knowledge, gained in yeshiva-learning and only there, has given him a deeper grasp of matters than the less "intimate" knowledge that is afford to those who have studied only in seminaries and universities. What advantage alumni of the schools he favors enjoy hardly emerges in the pages of his book, or in any other cited in his bibliography. In the end, this claim that only one approach to learning affords

---

[41]See my *The Components of the Rabbinic Documents: From the Whole to the Parts* (Atlanta, 1996ff.: Scholars Press for South Florida Studies in the History of Judaism), in twelve volumes. This work provides a complete outline of the twelve Midrash-compilations of late antiquity and shows that the documents are cogent and very carefully organized. Safrai seems to have formed the impression in his yeshiva-studies that the Rabbinic literature is simply chaotic, and that is the result of the exegetical studies that dominate in yeshivas.

access to the documents emerges as self-serving and spurious
and ad hominem. It will persuade only the believers, but they
are unlikely to read writings that rest on premises other than
their own. It suffices to say that this entire mode of argument
is contemptible. The rest of Safrai's discussion of method
need not detain us, since involved are questions of not
method but historical fact. I include the discussion because
he presents it within the stated rubric.

Let me now generalize from the examples of Safrai.[42]
I focus discussion on the concrete errors that render useless
for historical purposes nearly all work on the Talmud as history carried on in the state of Israel, whether at the secular
Hebrew University or at the Orthodox-Judaic Bar Ilan University. The articles in *Zion*, as well as elsewhere, like Safrai's
book, have taken for granted that the numerous specific stories concerning what given rabbis and other Jews actually said
and did under specific circumstances — on a given day, at a
given place, in a given setting — tell us *exactly the way things
were*. I speak, then, of a species of the genus, fundamentalism.
Safrai has provided a solid example, now let us generalize on
the basis of the example.

The philological fundamentalists have generally supposed that once we have established a correct text of a rabbinic work and properly interpreted its language, we then
know a set of historical facts. Safrai is explicit on this matter

---

[42]This part of my contribution to the debate draws upon, in extensive revision, my lecture written for the Historical Society of Israel but
cancelled by the Historical Society. Conference in celebration of its journal, *Zion*, on the occasion of its fiftieth volume. Jerusalem, Israel. Scheduled for July 2, 1984. This paper was mailed to Jerusalem on January 27,
1984, and the invitation to present it was withdrawn in a letter dated
March 5, 1984. Israeli scholarship does not give a hearing to viewpoints
contrary to those currently regnant there. That accounts for (among other
failures of learning) Safrai's strikingly limited knowledge of the work of
those he criticizes, as noted above.

at his point (a). The facticity will be proportionately greater the earlier the manuscript and the better its condition. These suppositions are correct. But these facts will concern *only* what the compiler of the text wished to tell us. Whether or not the original text was veracious is to be settled neither by textual criticism nor by philological research, valuable though both of these ancillary sciences are for the historical inquiry.

The fundamentalists further suppose that any story, whether occurring early or late in the corpus of rabbinic literature, may well contain valuable information, handed on orally from generation to generation, until it was finally written down. It is no caricature to impute to the Israelis the conviction that all rabbinical material was somehow sent floating into the air, if not by Moses, then by someone in remote antiquity (the Men of the Great Assembly, the generation of Yabneh); that it then remained universally available until some authority snatched it down from on high, placed his name on it, and so made it a named tradition and introduced it into the perilous processes of transmission. By this thesis nothing is older than anything else: "there is neither earlier nor later in the Torah." But Safrai does not even enter into the question of how sayings reach their final resting place in documents, or how the framers of documents acquired the information concerning long-ago times that they purpose to transmit. His certainty that all attributions are reliable forms a corollary to that prior conviction.

That documents' framers make choices and revise received materials is an established fact. Let me give one example of work Safrai does not appear to have read, or if he read them, understood. Synoptic studies of the traditions of Yohanan b. Zakkai and of the Pharisees before 70[43] indicate that

---

[43]*Development of a Legend. Studies on the Traditions Concerning Yohanan ben Zakkai* (Leiden, 1970: E.J. Brill) and *The Rabbinic Traditions about the Pharisees Before 70* (Leiden, 1971: E. J. Brill) I-III.

versions of a story or saying appearing in later documents
normally are demonstrably later than, and literarily dependent
upon, versions of the same story or saying appearing in earlier
documents. This is important, for it shows that what comes
late is apt to be late, and what comes in an early compilation
is apt to be early. Admittedly, these are no more than probabilities — extrapolations from a small number of demonstrable cases to a large number in which no demonstration is
possible. But at least there are grounds for such extrapolation.

The primary conviction of this Talmudic fundamentalism is that the story supplies an accurate account of what
actually happened. It is difficult to argue with that conviction.
A study of rabbinic sources will provide little, if any, evidence
that we have eyewitness accounts of great events or stenographic records of what people actually said. On the contrary,
it is anachronistic to suppose the talmudic rabbis cared to
supply such information to begin with. Since they did not,
and since they asserted that people had said things of which
they had no sure knowledge, we are led to wonder about the
pseudepigraphic mentality. By the time we hear about a
speech or an event, it has already been reshaped for the purpose of transmission in the traditions. It is rarely possible to
know just what, if anything, originally was said or done.
Sometimes we have an obvious gloss, which tells us the tradition originated before the time the glossator made his addition. But knowing that a tradition was shaped within half a
century of the life of the man to whom it was attributed helps
only a little bit. It is very difficult to build a bridge from the
tradition to the event, still more difficult to cross that bridge.
The fact is that the entire Rabbinic canon is a completely accurate record of the viewpoint of those who are responsible
for it. But the specification of those people, the recognition
of the viewpoint of a particular group, place, and time to
which the Talmud's various facts pertain — these remain the

fundamental task still facing us.

In all, as Safrai himself rightly emphasizes, talmudic history cannot be said to deal with great affairs, vast territories, movements of men and nations, much that really mattered then. Even the bulk of Israel, the Jewish nation, in the time of the composition of the canonical writings at hand, by the testimony of the authors themselves falls outside of the frame of reference. Most Jews appeared to the sages at hand to ignore — in the active sense of willfully *not knowing* — exactly those teachings that seemed to the authors critical. To use the mythic language, when God revealed the Torah to Moses at Mount Sinai, he wrote down one part, which we now have in the Hebrew Scripture ("the Old Testament"), and he repeated the other part in oral form, so that Moses memorized it and handed it on to Joshua, and then, generation by generation, to the contemporary sages. Now, to the point, the contemporaries of the sages at hand did not know this oral half of the Torah, only sages did, and that by definition. Only sages knew the whole of the Torah of Moses. So, it follows, the talmudic corpus preserves the perspective of a rather modest component of the nation under discussion.

How could we define a subject less likely to attract broad interest than the opinions of a tiny minority of a nation about the affairs of an unimportant national group living in two frontier provinces on either side of a contested frontier? Apart from learning, from the modest folk at hand, some facts about life on the contested frontier of the ancient world — and that was only the one that separated Rome from Iran, the others being scarcely frontiers in any political sense — what is to be learned here that anyone would want to know must seem puzzling.

Self-evidently, no one can expect to find stories of great events, a continuous narrative of things that happened to a nation in war and in politics. The Jews, as it happens, both constituted a nation and sustained a vigorous political life. But the documents of the age under discussion treat these matters only tangentially and as part of the periphery of a vision of quite other things. But if manifest history scarcely passes before us, a rich and complex world of latent history — the long-term trends and issues of a society and its life in imagination and emotion — does lie ready at hand. For the talmudic canon reports to us a great deal about what a distinctive group of people were thinking about issues that turn out to prove perennial and universal, and, still more inviting, the documents tell us not only what people thought but how they reasoned.

That is something to which few historians gain access, I mean, the philosophical processes behind political and social and religious policy, class struggle and popular contention. For people do think things out and reach conclusions, and for the most part, long after the fact, we know only the decisions they made. Here, by contrast, we hear extended discussions, of a most rigorous and philosophical character, on issues of theory and of thought. In these same discussions, at the end, we discover how people decided what to do and why. That sort of history — the history of how people made up their minds — proves particularly interesting, when we consider the substance of the story. The Jews in the provinces and age at hand adopted the policies put forward by the sages who wrote the sources we consider. The entire subsequent world history of the Jews — their politics, social and religious world, the character of the inner life and struggle of their community-nation — refers back to the decisions made at just this time and recorded in the Talmud. The stakes are very high. That explains why Safrai's (and other Israelis') failure exacts so heavy a cost of the common culture of their own country, which, after all, should find nourishment in exactly the documents under study here.

A further aspect of the character of the principal sources for Talmudic history, moreover, will attract attention even among people not especially concerned with how a weak and scattered nation explained how to endure its condition. The talmudic canon bears the mark of no individual authorship. It is collective, official, authoritative. Now were it to hand on decisions but no discussion, that collective character would not mark the literature as special. We have, from diverse places and times, extensive records of what legislative or ecclesiastical bodies decided. But if these same bodies had recorded in detail how they reached their decisions, including a rich portrait of their modes of thought, then we should have something like what the Talmud gives us.

But the points of interest scarcely end there. The talmudic corpus stands in a long continuum of thought and culture, stretching back, through the biblical literature, for well over a thousand years. Seeing how a collegium of active intellectuals mediated between their own age and its problems and the authority and legacy of a vivid past teaches lessons about continuities of culture and society not readily available elsewhere. For their culture had endured, prior to their own day, for a longer span of time than separates us in the West from the Magna Cart, on the one side, and Beowulf, on the other. If these revered documents of our politics and culture enjoyed power to define politics and culture today, we should grasp the sort of problem confronting the Talmud's sages. For, after all, the Talmud imagined as normative a society having little in common with that confronting the sages — isolated, independent, free-standing, and not — as the sages' Israel was — assimilated in a vast world-empire, autonomous yet subordinate, and dependent upon others near and far.

The principal fault of Safrai's representation of matters is not its fundamentalism but its triviality. The work is simply dull, and even if he were right about every fact, he still has given us no plausible and consequential account of the economy of Roman Palestine, only a massive collection of bits and pieces of unintegrated information. If this is what one learns in those many years in yeshivas, then the world must conclude that those years are mostly wasted on unimportant matters. It is beyond the walls of the yeshivas, Rabbinical schools, and Orthodox universities, US and Israeli alike, that the Talmuds and other Rabbinic writings are read for reasons of intellectual and cultural consequence.

23.

MICHAEL L. SATLOW, *TASTING THE DISH. RABBINIC RHETORICS OF SEXUALITY.* BROWN JUDAIC STUDIES, ED. BY ERNEST SUNLEY FRERICHS, SHAYE J. D. COHEN, AND CALVIN GOLDSCHEIDER. VOLUME 303. ATLANTA, 1995: SCHOLARS PRESS FOR BROWN JUDAIC STUDIES

When a field of learning has run its course, a newcomer to the field — a young doctorand — will replicate its intellectual bankruptcy by empty imitation of a tired paradigm. That involves substituting for the work of problem-solving a huge labor of industry and vacant erudition. Historicistic study of Rabbinic literature has now shown itself aimless, the results yielding no insight beyond themselves; it has become a labor of paraphrase and recapitulation, not question-asking and problem-solving. The first creation of Reform Judaism, die Wissenschaft des Judenthums has run out of ideas, and learning has now bypassed that field. But no other episteme has taken shape in some of the more prominent centers of the field, Rabbinical seminaries of Reform and Conservative sponsorship, some Israeli and all the German seminaries and universities, for instance, so in place of problem-solving within a generative paradigm, we are offered surveys of information on modish topics. Before us is definitive evidence of the progress to oblivion of a once-vital intellectual field, Judaic Studies in the classical texts framed as historical and cultural statements. A paradigm has lost its power, and, where it yet governs, no other has come to the fore. New places therefore will in time have to replace the old ones.

Before us is a fine instance of the larger trend to intellectual oblivion. Dr. Michael Satlow's doctoral dissertation out of the Jewish Theological Seminary of America under the supervision of Professor Shaye J. D. Cohen, now my successor at Brown University, in the name of a twin project of historical and "rhetorical" study of the stated topic, simply collects and arranges a great many passages of part of Rabbinic literature on the subject of sexuality. Out of the mass of material Satlow presents no interesting theses and raises no penetrating questions of comparison and contrast and solves no urgent problems. He comes with no theory and leaves with no insight. Worse still, the dissertation makes a series of promises that in the end the author never even attempts to keep. And yet the industrious author shows himself a good researcher and a careful (though amateurish) writer. That is why this dissertation — bad, on the whole pointless, work by an intelligent beginner — points toward the demise of a scholarly episteme, the historicistic-cultural one that has animated the field, *die Wissenschaft des Judenthums,* for nearly two hundred years: it has run out of questions to ask and problems to solve.

The main contribution of the work is its systematic outline of the topic, that is to say, the table of contents. Satlow treats six topics: incest, sex between Jews and gentiles, non-marital sex, homoeroticism, non-procreative sex, and marital sexuality. For each rubric, he subdivides in the same way, typified by "the treatment of homoeroticism: "rhetoric of definition," "rhetoric of categorization" "rhetoric of liability," "rhetoric of association," "rhetoric of the Other," "rhetoric of divine retribution," rhetoric of temptation," and so on. All of this is done in an impressively systematic manner, with first-rate bibliographical footnotes (but alas, also, amazing lacunae, entire areas of pertinent knowledge not ignored but declared not to exist, as we shall see).

The key to the project obviously is Satlow's claim to conduct an analysis of "rhetoric," but, as we shall see, the claim proves spurious. By "rhetoric," Aristotle meant, "the faculty of discovering the possible means of persuasion in reference to any subject whatever" (Satlow, p. 7). Satlow maintains that "any linguistic attempt to persuade a listener/reader can be termed rhetorical." None need take exception to that broadening of matters. But how the definition connects to the *actual* work at hand becomes progressively more obscure as Satlow proceeds, "The importance of persuasion in the 'enforcement' of norms and mores becomes paramount both in private zones and in societies that lack the power of coercion....The primary goal of this study is to examine the rhetoric used by the rabbis to discuss sexual norms. These rhetorical strategies are of two distinct types, which I will refer to as legal and persuasive. By 'legal rhetorics' I refer to Rabbinic discussions of the law, their attempts to define transgression them, and establish issues of liability" (p. 8). Everything depends, therefore, on what Satlow means by "rhetoric," and what emerges is, nothing very much.

How Satlow leaps from "persuasion" to "Rabbinic discussions of the law..." simply eludes my understanding. Here is a point at which his *Doktorvater* ought to have asked some tough questions concerning his precise meaning and intention. When Satlow consulted me about the work, having read the introduction and the conclusion, I raised exactly the questions I shall now present. He thanks me in his preface for my "trenchant" questions. But this is purely political. He does not appear to me to have grasped their weight. He certainly found no answers nor did his Doktorvater, whose intellectually shoddy *From the Maccabees to the Mishnah* exhibits the same failures of method and theory.

Satlow attempts to build the bridge from the conventional definition of "rhetoric" to what he promises as analysis of rhetoric when he gives a clear example of what he means: "Rabbinic rhetoric for example, defines the transgression called 'adultery...'" puts this transgression into a category based on prescribed punishments; and elaborates both circumstances that mitigate this transgression...and the liability occurred when an act of adultery also involves other transgressions...." But how "rhetoric" is distinguished as a medium of analysis (at the level of merely identifying pertinent data!) from "topic" is hardly specified, and how the predicate of the sentence pertains to "rhetoric" at all is not self-evident.

Let me spell this out in a simple way: what if we used the language, "Rabbinic *law*....defines...," or merely, "Rabbinic *literature*...defines..." or even "the rabbis define"? The functional meaning would be the same, and consequently the category "rhetoric" at the subject in no way dictates the character or contents of the predicate. For "rhetoric" bears no exclusionary sense — nor any inclusionary meaning either. We do not know what we must consider, or dismiss from consideration, in the rubric "rhetoric," nor how "rhetorical analysis" will in any aspect differ from a mere topical compilation. The upshot is, "rhetoric" here is interchangeable with a number of other categories, so it forms no category on its own. The sentence would be changed in no way; the predicate would amply complete the thought of the subject.

Satlow proceeds to explain "persuasive rhetorics,"

which are "those arguments that seek to promote sexual norms by other than strictly legal means...threats of human and divine retribution...all of these rhetorics are intended to dissuade people from engaging in certain sexual activities." Here, again, we are led to expect analysis of arguments, strategies of exposition, systematic inquiry into the use of language, perhaps even an effort at the form-analysis of Rabbinic texts that I have devised. He promises exactly that. But forthwith we are told the truth, which is, all Satlow honestly intends is a topical organization of the matter, once more with the now-dubious promise to tell us something about "differences between the rhetorical strategies employed by the rabbis in their discussions of 'who' one should or should not have sex with, and 'how' one should sexually conduct oneself." This is empty rhetoric; the vacuity of these sentences should not be missed, but the reader will discover that Satlow himself rapidly forgets his promises when he turns to the actual work.

Satlow's methodological failure exposes a deeper intellectual flaw in the entire project. Specifically, as a matter of fact, Satlow misses the critical problem of his dissertation, by never asking the obvious question: is there a rhetoric that is particular to this topic, such as would justify a dissertation on "the rhetoric" of said topic? If there is not, then the very project loses all cogency and purpose. And before us is the consequence. In fact, Satlow takes a position against an entire scholarly tradition, which he seems not to realize! For while the rhetoric of the Rabbinic literature forms a considerable problem, to which many have contributed, no one until now has suggested that that rhetoric when pertinent to a given topic requires analysis in its own terms, or will differ in quality or character from the rhetoric in Rabbinic literature that pertains to another topic. In fact, rhetorical variations occur by document — as everybody knows! — but not by topic or subject-matter considered either within a given document (e.g., sex in Sifra and sacrifice in Sifra are treated in precisely the same formal and analytical-rhetorical patters) all together within a sequence of documents.

Satlow's results prove that very point. That is in two aspects. First, as we follow the forms of discourse, we see differences between one document and another, but none between one of his subjects and another. For example, homoeroticism and incest are discussed within the same formal repertoire, and rightly so; but then there is no "rhetoric" of homoeroticism that is to be distinguished from the "rhetoric" of incest. Then why anticipate that "Rabbinic rhetorics of sexuality" will differ, by reason of subject matter, from "Rabbinic rhetorics" of civil law?. Second, in consequence, Satlow simply has not demonstrated that a specific rhetoric of sexuality is to be located within the corpus he treats (which, inexplicably, by no means covers the whole of the Rabbinic canon but only selected portions thereof, some Halakhic, some aggadic). But then he promises what he himself shows he cannot deliver. Here is a thesis that proves its own antithesis, and the author does not even notice.

So much for the possibilities of *Kulturforschung* in *die Wissenschaft des Judenthums*. As to "history," where that glorious episteme sparkled in its day, Satlow makes occasional remarks about how the various documents treat a given subtopic differently, e.g., "Palestinian and Babylonian rabbis appear to have held differing assumptions about sexuality" (P. 315). But that observation is random and undeveloped, yielding only the following utterly inane conclusion: "Despite contact between these Rabbinic communities, they were separated geographically, were dominated by different super-powers, and were part of vastly different cultural milieus. Palestinian assumptions and attitudes are close paralleled in contemporary Western non-Jewish sources. We know far less about Babylo-

nia, and the non-Jewish milieu in which the Jewish...community lived, and the interaction between this milieu
and the Babylonian rabbis." This allegation of "our" ignorance, alas, is arrant nonsense. *We* know a great deal about
Iranian culture in Sasanian times; a vast literature, program-
matically coherent with the Rabbinic literature,[44] touching on
topics Satlow treats, records Zoroastrian mores. Satlow has
not done the research; the "we" should be "I know far
less...." Here again, his *Doktorvater* owed more than he gave.

Not only does history in a more than episodic sense
not emerge, but in the end Satlow confesses he cannot limn
even general outlines of a coherent narrative: "This study is
not a history of the Rabbinic constructions of sexuality.
Rather, it is a preliminary step toward the investigation of
these constructions. Throughout this study I have gathered,
rhetorically classified, and analyzed the data upon which any
such sexual history will be based" (p. 315). Precisely! Here he
reviews his own book, as positively as he dares. In a moment
we shall see just what this "rhetorical classification" attempts.
But the main point is not to be missed: Satlow provides neither history nor cultural analysis, only a collection of information, classified logically, with informative footnotes about
this, that, and the other thing.

Over and over again Satlow says as much, even from
his opening pages, when he humbly confesses that all he has
done is to collect and arrange information out of a limited selection of ancient Rabbinic documents: "I hope that simply
through my collection, organization, and analysis of Rabbinic
texts on sexuality this study will contribute to, and continue
to stimulate, the developing dialogue on Rabbinic sexuality. I
will be happy if this study also makes some modest contribu-

---

[44]As I showed in my *Judaism and Zoroastrianism at the Dusk of Late
Antiquity. How Two Ancient Faiths Wrote Down Their Great Traditions.* Atlanta,
1993: Scholars Press for South Florida Studies in the History of Judaism.

tions to those areas with which it intersects." Another self-composed review! But we must wonder on what basis, then, he received a doctoral degree for what in all humility he confesses is a labor of collecting, organizing, and (what he regards as) analyzing, texts on sexuality. That is to say, Satlow shows in the end his awareness that all he has done is collect and arrange sayings on a given topic. He also hopes that people who collect and arrange sayings on the same topic as it occurs in other bodies of writing will find his collection useful. I am sure they will. But in the end Satlow has succeeded only in making an interesting subject boring. That is because after an enormous labor of collection, arrangement, paraphrase, and recapitulation, Satlow gives us neither history nor consequential analysis of social culture nor anything else; his conclusions prove platitudinous, uncertain, and on the whole, rather obvious, and that brings us to the matter of what he deems "analysis" to require and to yield.

Let us turn to the substance of matters, the claim to analyze "Rabbinic rhetorics of sexuality." Precisely what is the upshot? Satlow begins with ambitious promises to tell us about "what kinds of arguments the rabbis thought would be effective within their own cultures. How did these rabbis attempt to persuade each other...to practice only 'sanctioned' sexual behavior?" (p. xiii). That is what he means by studying "rhetoric," and it is a valid program in the Aristotelian framework, as everyone knows. But what, exactly, does "rhetoric" stand for in this dissertation? So far as I can tell, the answer is, absolutely nothing. That is, after calling something "rhetoric of," as in "rhetoric of definition," "rhetoric of categorization," Satlow just collects whatever he thinks falls into the category, but says nothing about rhetoric in particular, "that is, the language of persuasion. What is fascinating, indeed, is that in his final chapters, he simply drops the language of "rhetoric of," from his sub-titles, but in no way changes his presentation of the materials thereof. That leads to the surmise that all he means by "rhetoric" is "topic," as in, "the topic of...," and he has then confused his Aristotle, *topoi* being the tractate he had in mind.

Readers may well find implausible this judgment that Satlow has utilized a category of "analysis" that he simply does not understand, with the result that he conducts no analysis of any consequence. So let me give a sample of the discussion, chosen randomly from hundreds of candidates in this long and tedious book. Here I provide a precis of Satlow's treatment, within his chapter on incest, of "rhetoric of liability" (pp. 52-56), and I stipulate that I could have duplicated the tone and quality of this discussion at any point start to finish. Satlow is nothing if not methodical, and the reader can then imagine the rest:

> Several legal discussions of incest within Rabbinic literature contains [sic!] rhetoric that (1) seeks to establish the precise 'count' for which one is considered guilty; and (2) discusses [sic!] those factors that mitigate the assignment of guilt.
>
> DETERMINATION OF THE TRANSGRESSION
>
> Most of the rhetoric of liability on incest concentrates on how many and which transgressions are incurred when a single incestuous act falls under more than one rubric.
>
> *Tannaitic Sources*
>
> The Mishnah presents a simple example of this sort of rhetoric:
>
>> A. If one...has intercourse with his mother he is liable on her account both for sexual contact with one's mother and for intercourse with the wife of one's father. Rabbi Yehudah says: he is only liable for the transgression of intercourse with one's mother.
>>
>> B. If one has intercourse with the wife of one's father, he is liable on her account for intercourse with the wife of one's father and for adul-

> tery, whether it is during the life of his father or af-
> ter the death of his father...
>
> C.   If one has intercourse with his daughter-in-
>   law he is liable on her account for sexual con-
>   tact with his daughter-in-law and for adul-
>   tery...

So much for the source, now the discussion of "the rhetoric of," complete as follows:

> Intercourse with one's mother (A), a wife of
> one's father (B), or one's daughter-in-law (C) violates
> more than one sexual restriction. This Mishnah at-
> tempts to clarify exactly which transgressions are com-
> mitted. In another passage, the Mishnah demonstrates
> how a single act of intercourse can violate up to six
> sexual restrictions most of his are violations of incest
> restrictions.

These paraphrastic observations, I maintain, have no bearing whatsoever on rhetorical analysis and, moreover, tell us nothing the source did not already set forth perfectly clearly. Compare Satlow's substance to Aristotle's theory: "the faculty of discovering the possible means of persuasion in reference to any subject whatever." Where Satlow pays attention to "means of persuasion" in this "rhetorics of..." hardly emerges. The shank of the book ignores its theoretical statement, an astonishing failure once more underscored as Satlow continues what adds up to little more than a junior high school book report:

> The Tosefta develops this rhetoric far beyond
> the Mishnah. Several times the Tosefta refocuses
> Mishnaic passages that show little interest in issues of
> liability to this area. According, for example, to m. Ye-
> bam. 3:10:
>> If two men betrothed two women and when they
>> entered the wedding canopy exchanged brides, they
>> are liable for adultery...

> The Mishnah presents a hypothetical case where two men accidentally exchange women to whom they are betrothed. On this, t. Yebam. 5:9 elaborates:
>
>> If two men betrothed two women and when they entered the wedding canopy exchanged brides, they are liable for sixteen transgressions....
>
> In contrast to the Mishnah, this passage begins with the situation that would yield the most transgressions It concludes with another issue of liability, not mentioned in the Mishnah: the effects of age on guilt. In other passages, the Tosefta adds discussions of issues of liability to Mishnaic passages that are not concerned with this issue.
>
> Among the Tannaitic Midrashim there is a single attempt to establish precisely the transgression incurred by sexual contact with a woman to whom more than one prohibition applies...

The footnote directs us to an unanalyzed passage in Sifra. Behind this rubric, subjected to "rhetorical analysis" is a card-file with two items and a note about a third. Out of his files what has Satlow created, if not a slothful report of what is in them?

For, I submit, what Satlow has contributed to the analysis of "Rabbinic rhetorics of sexuality" on the subject, "incest/determination of the transgression" is *nothing whatsoever*. All he has done is identify a passage on the topic and cite it; his comments on the passage are unilluminating space-filler, an unambitious repetition in his own words, "analysis" consisting of paraphrase and not much more. What he means by "rhetoric of" should emerge in the character of his analysis, in the questions that he proposes to answer, in the reasons in the on-going argument and exposition that he formulates. But the "method" of rhetorical analysis does not emerge at all, for before us there is no argument and no exposition. Indeed, the presentation expounds little more than what we see before our naked eyes in the cited source, and so far as there is a proposition that is served, the passage contains not a hint at what it might be. As I said, I could duplicate the same "method" many times over; it fills the pages of the book with vacuity.

The upshot is disheartening. Satlow's promise to analyze the "rhetorics" is not so much ignored as forgotten, and I cannot even imagine what he or his doctoral committee at the Jewish Theological Seminary of America might have had in mind in claiming to undertake such an analysis or award a doctorate for such meretricious pretense. All I see before me is a labor of slogging industry: repeated citation of a passage and then a recapitulation in Satlow's own words of what the passage says. And that is not scholarship by any accepted norm, nor by prevailing standards in successful academic disciplines do people receive doctoral degrees for merely collecting and arranging information. Not only is the passage I gave representative, but the conclusion, given in a moment, underscores the intellectual flaccidity of the whole. Indeed, the flavor of the whole can be conveyed through any one of the parts, because Satlow laboriously says the same thing about everything, which is, if not nothing, then, alas, very little and nothing systematic. It would be unfair to suggest that he has nothing to say about anything; he has a great deal to say, but it is episodic and notional, and what he has to say in no way coheres in a cogent statement of any sort.

My sense is that Satlow chose his topic — a very fashionable one in the USA in the season at which he made his choice, particularly as it extends to unconventional sexual behavior — and determined to find out what the Rabbinic literature says about the topic. This he juxtaposes with what other bodies of evidence, near and far, have to say about the same topic. But as to the focus of his interest, sex in Rabbinic literature ("talmudic erotica"), he brings to the inquiry no large thesis on the character of the literature and the culture it represents, he finds nothing to say on the religion and theology that come to expression, also, in the topic at hand, and he introduces no speculation on any broader intellectual context that might impart consequence to his collection. That explains why he falls silent in the presence of the texts themselves, on the one side, and how at the end he can produce no results of any broad consequence, on the other. I have already cited some of his concluding remarks. Here are the final ones:

> "Rabbinic writings are our primary source for the study of Jews and Judaism in late antiquity. Yet if this study has been successful, it has shown that Rabbinic culture was not monolithic. Rabbinic assumptions about sexuality were as historically as textually determined, to the point where Rabbinic texts created under one set of assumptions were misunderstood when read in societies that held different assumptions. Only in academic writing is it possible to separate sex; the constructions of sexuality; strategies (especially rhetorical) of sexual (and other types of) control; gender assumptions and expectations; social relationships between dominant and minority cultures as well as different classes within the society; and the relationship between texts and real lives and social institutions In reality all of these threads are finely interwoven. The study of Rabbinic sexuality, although only a small part of the complex fabric of which it is a part offers a glimpse of some of these complex relationships."

This paragraph, I maintain, uses a great many words to say of sexuality what one may say as well of pretty much any other subject, which is to say, this paragraph says nothing whatsoever.

Who imagines, who ever has alleged, that Rabbinic culture was monolithic? And who doubts that Rabbinic assumptions about sexuality were historically and textually determined? What a trash-load of banalities! Is this to say I suspect that Satlow has perpetrated a very subtle joke by offering a sustained caricature of scholarship? Not at all. Would that someone meant to fabricate a wonderful hoax, showing how scholarship can neuter a salacious subject! But, alas, nothing in the long and lugubrious work suggests so, and I am confident that the work was done, alas, in a wholly sincere way. That is why I express amazement that Satlow's *Doktorvater* at the Jewish Theological Seminary of America and now at Brown University did not ask some tough questions when Satlow was doing the work. I do not think he has served his disciple very well at all, though, as I said, I am confident he has done his best too.

To summarize: what is needed is less industry and more intellection, for scholarship is just not the same thing as collecting information on a given topic and paraphrasing it for a class report. By the criterion, if I know this, what else do I know? Satlow fails. By his own stated criteria in the self-composed review of the book Satlow includes, he fails. By the criterion, what is at stake in this elaborated, protracted compilation of information? he fails. Why so? Because primitive work of mere hunting and gathering leaves learning in the stone age. Lacking an episteme, absent a paradigm, that form of learning proves both pointless and pretentious. *Die Wissenschaft des Judenthums* in its day attained a high level of sophistication; its historicistic reading of Judaic culture in the name of Reform changed the world it addressed. Now it has come to this.

24.

ELIEZER SEGAL. *THE BABY-
LONIA ESTHER MIDRASH. A
CRITICAL COMMENTARY.*
ATLANTA, 1994: SCHOLARS
PRESS FOR BROWN JUDAIC
STUDIES. BROWN JUDAIC
STUDIES VOLUMES 291, 292,
AND 293. I: *TO THE END OF
ESTHER CHAPTER 1.* II: *TO
THE BEGINNING OF ESTHER
CHAPTER 5* III: *ESTHER
CHAPTER 5 TO THE END.*

A commentary on the commentary on the book of
Esther found at Babylonian Talmud-tractate Megillah 10b-
17a, this compendious work collects an enormous amount of
information, on which the author expresses his opinion
throughout. The work begins with Introductory Remarks, in
which Segal expresses the opinion that the Midrash is an oral
literature (pp. 16-19), in which the book of Esther is retold.
He finds that the retelling "involves a complete overturning
of the thematic structure of the original story. Presumably
this common exegetical tradition [among the various exegeses
to Esther] took shape during the early Tannaitic era or before." The author assembles parallel materials so as to "ex-

plain each passage...within the context of the Esther-Midrash as a whole," assembling references to the Mishnah, Tosefta, Tannaite Midrash-compilations, both Talmuds, Aggadic Midrash-compilations, Targums, and Josephus and Church Fathers. Segal explains, "On a case-by-case basis, each parallel should be allowed to tell us whatever it has to teach us about its relationship with the Babylonian Esther-Midrash. In some instances what will prove important is the similarity between the versions...in many other places, what might strike us at first as essentially similar traditions will prove on closer inspection to have significant differences...." Since Segal takes for granted he deals with an originally oral literature, which has passed through "assorted literary, exegetical, and ideological contexts," he proposes to reconstruct the process of transmission. He gives a new translation, noting variant readings in footnotes, and consulting early printed editions as well. As indicated, Segal then works his way through the composite, step by step. His chapter headings are as follows, for volume I: Prologue; the proems; Ahasuerus; Ahasuerus' calculations; the feast; Vashti; for volume II: Mordecai; Esther; Haman; prophets and prophetesses; fighting back; the tide turns; the sleepless night; Joseph and his brothers; Purim; great is the study of Torah. He concludes with an overview of the text. The work contains a bibliography and excellent indices. The work is commendable for diligence.

But it also adds up to little more than a massive exercise in collecting and arranging facts. The notes amass a huge amount of information, but the text, so far as there is one that the author has provided, is trivial. Indeed, even defining the author's purpose in composing this commentary presents difficulties. Segal has no clear thesis or argument in mind, and, indeed, even what he means by a commentary and why he regards the work as worthwhile emerges with clarity only at the end, in his overview. Here he explains his objective, by which the work must be judged:

> The primary objective of this study has been
> to explain the contents of the Babylonian Esther-
> Midrash in a manner that would approximate the un-
> derstanding, literary appreciation, and emotional impact
> that it would have had for its original audiences during
> the talmudic era. In order to achieve this aim it was
> necessary to maintain distinctions between the individ-
> ual comments and dicta of the rabbis, and the broader
> literary contexts into which they were subsequently
> embedded by the redactors of the Talmud. The Esther-
> Midrash, like almost all Rabbinic documents, presents
> itself to us as a collage of materials that were assembled
> and rearranged in accordance with the concerns and
> requirements of the broader literary contexts into
> which they were incorporated. The task of the modern
> critical commentator is therefore a twofold one: to clar-
> ify the meaning of the final product as it was perceived
> by the redactor, as well as to reconstruct the original in-
> tentions of the dictum's author. Both of these objec-
> tives demand that we pay careful attention to minutiae
> of philological research, including the linguistic usages,
> literary standards, and editorial conventions to which
> the authors and editors were trying to conform, as well
> as whatever other information, assumptions, and realia
> might contribute to a fuller appreciation of the text.
> The above objectives had to be based on the accumula-
> tion and evaluation of the textual evidence, and assisted
> by the efforts of previous traditional and modern
> commentators.

It seems to me that there is less here than meets the eye, since the author leaves us in the dark about the connection between his commentary and those whom he claims to represent, namely, the "original audiences."

The connection between that goal and the means, "maintain distinctions..." is not spelled out, and I see none. More to the point, how distinguishing "the meaning of the final product as perceived by the redactor" and "the original intentions of the dictum's author" demands the massive compilation of this, that, and the other thing pertinent to each word and sentence of the text Segal does not tell us. On the contrary, when we examine the presentation in detail, we are hard put to find systematic attention to the promised questions; all we do find is that mass of information that Segal announces at the end is required to achieve his entirely correct goals. But collecting data is not the same thing as achieving the stated objectives, and, in my view, Segal has not even attempted to do what he promises. That is, I look in vain for his view of "the understanding, literary appreciation, and emotional impact that it would have had for its original audiences during the talmudic era." Segal does not appear to have tried to keep that particular promise. Would that he had, for it is a commendable intent.

What Segal does do is: "The main body of this commentary is made up of my interpretations of the individual pericopes of the Esther-Midrash. I have endeavored in each case to propose the most reasonable and straightforward explanations that can account for the evidence at hand." The net result is a vast amount of entirely commendable work, but also, in the end, an account so prolix and indeterminate as to prove useful only for episodic reference. Segal manages to use a great many words to say very little, for he is constantly giving with one hand and taking away with the other. One sample suffices:

> Following from our hypothesis that the rabbis did not always indulge in aggadic exegesis for its own sake, but used their textual observations for some further purpose, usually in the context of a homiletical discourse, we tried to confront each unit of Midrashic exegesis with such question as: What point is being made here? or: How would this comment be employed in a sermon? In many instances it turned out that there

> was room for more than one plausible explanation, and these explanations would not necessarily be mutually exclusive.

If that qualification were not sufficient, then this footnote after "in a sermon" is added:

> We of course allowed for the possibility of negative answers to such questions, i.e., that a given Rabbinic interpretation arose out of a desire to account for some redundancy or contradiction in the verse, rather than from homiletical needs.

What that leaves of the whole is absolutely nothing: this, not-this, and maybe that or not-that anyhow. Consequently, the work breaks down into a mass of platitudes and banalities, e.g., "The *darshan* was thus regarded as occupying a position midway between the biblical text and his congregation." Who would have thought otherwise, and who has ever claimed otherwise?

Both Segal's diffuse results and his insistence that we have only bits and pieces, but no whole, run contrary to my own approach to the same problems, captured in the documentary method that I have set forth. Segal explicitly rejects this method, stating:

> I have been unsuccessful in my attempts to trace any meaningful basis for his claims, which, in the absence of detailed literary or philological analysis of primary texts, appear to rest on nothing more than a dogmatic faith in their validity...

Segal's "attempts" cannot have required arduous effort, since the elaborate literary analysis that I have conducted Segal obviously does not know. He seems not to have read my *Judaism: The Evidence of the Mishnah, The Integrity of Leviticus Rabbah, The Problem of the Autonomy of a Rabbinic Document*, or *Compara-*

tive Midrash: The Plan and Program of Genesis Rabbah and Leviticus Rabbah. In these and numerous other books I have identified the kind of evidence that would mark a piece of writing as autonomous and systematically examined every document of the Rabbinic canon in accord with the stated criteria. Segal asks for evidence that does not pertain and cannot explain the evidence I set forth that, in my view, does relate to the description, analysis, and interpretation of complete documents.

Repeatedly, Segal maintains that the entire literature of Midrash is oral, and, by definition, the category of the document does not apply. This he states in so many words in contrasting his claim concerning the oral character of the Rabbinic corpus with mine concerning documentary analysis:

> ...as a genre, aggadic Midrash is first and foremost the creation of the synagogue...the classical Palestinian collections drew primarily from a body of oral sermons. As far as I have been able to discern, this feature has been virtually ignored in the many studies of Palestinian aggadah by Jacob Neusner, who treats all Rabbinic compendia as consistent, distinct and individual 'documents' expressing the [theological] positions of their respective authors. [In the more extreme statements of his position, Neusner makes little allowance for any meaningful redaction of earlier units, whether from the synagogues or elsewhere.] I have been unsuccessful in my attempts to trace any meaningful basis for his claims, which, in the absence of detailed literary or philological analysis of primary texts, appear to rest on nothing more than a dogmatic faith in their validity. Neusner's work is almost completely devoid of conventional scholarly annotation or consideration of previous scholarship; he claims to be interested only in the broader external structures of the pericopes, having little to say about the specific details on which

generalizations should normally be based[45]...The theories have been refuted by most students of Midrash;
see, e.g., J. Heinemann, Aggadah and its Development,
44-7; Peter Schaefer, "Research into Rabbinic Literature: An Attempt to Define the Status Quaestionis," JJS
376, 1986, 146-52; Steven D. Fraade, "Interpreting
Midrash 1: Midrash and the History of Judaism,"
Prooftexts 7, 1987, 179-194; Gerald L. Bruns, "The
Hermeneutics of Midrash," in The Book and the
Text....; and "Midrash and Allegory: The Beginnings of
Scripture Interpretation," in *The Literary Guide to the Bi-
ble*; E. P. Sanders, *Jewish Law from Jesus to the Mishnah:
Five Studies.*"

---

[45]This is an astonishing statement on his part. Segal clearly does
not know my systematic book reviewing of the important contributions to
the study of the Rabbinic canon, for example, *The Formation of the Babylonian Talmud. Studies on the Achievements of Late Nineteenth and Twentieth Century
Historical and Literary-Critical Research.* Leiden, 1970: Brill; *The Modern Study
of the Mishnah.* Leiden, 1973: Brill; *Rabbinic Judaism in the Formative Age: Disputes and Debates.* Atlanta, 1994: Scholars Press for South Florida Studies in
the History of Judaism; *Ancient Judaism. Debates and Disputes.* Chico, 1984:
Scholars Press for Brown Judaic Studies; *Ancient Judaism. Debates and Disputes. Second Series.* Atlanta, 1990: Scholars Press for South Florida Studies
in the History of Judaism; *Ancient Judaism. Debates and Disputes. Third Series.
Essays on the Formation of Judaism, Dating Sayings, Method in the History of Judaism, the Historical Jesus, Publishing Too Much, and Other Current Issues.* Atlanta,
1993: Scholars Press for South Florida Studies in the History of Judaism;
*The Public Side of Learning. The Political Consequences of Scholarship in the Context
of Judaism.* Chico, 1985: Scholars Press for the American Academy of Religion *Studies in Religion* Series; *Reading and Believing: Ancient Judaism and Contemporary Gullibility.* Atlanta, 1986: Scholars Press for Brown Judaic Studies;
*Ancient Judaism and Modern Category-Formation. "Judaism," "Midrash," "Messian-
ism," and Canon in the Past Quarter-Century.* Lanham, 1986: University Press
of America *Studies in Judaism* Series. I cannot explain how he can allege I
have not considered "previous scholarship," when I have read and reviewed the received and the newly-published scholarly literature in German, French, Hebrew, English, Italian, Scandinavian (Swedish), and Span-
ish. I credit this judgment to mere malice.

Any informed person who examines the critiques to which Segal make reference will see that his description of them, "the theories have been refuted by most students of Midrash" vastly overstates the facts.[46] What Segal imputes to scholars and what they have actually said cannot even be assumed to correspond in any exact way. Not only has the documentary method not been "refuted," it has scarcely been confronted.

For example, as to the initial reference to Heinemann, Segal's confidence that my "theories" have been refuted proves puzzling, when we consider the exact language that Heinemann uses:

> The Rabbinic editors of the classical Midrashim that have come down to us, especially of the so-called homiletical Midrashim, undoubtedly drew upon material that had first been used in public sermons delivered on Sabbaths and festivals. This is not to say that the Midrashic homilies are identical with the sermons as they were actually preached in public. It appears that the later compilers of the Midrashim made use of a variety of actual sermons, in full or in part, from which they fashioned a new entity that might be called a 'literary homily.' Consequently, we do not know very much, certainly far less than would at first appear, about the forms of the public sermon itself. Nevertheless, some types can be identified with certainty. One rhetorical form found frequently in the Midrash, the proem (petihta), undoubtedly had its origin in the sermon. The proem opens with a quotation from Scripture, taken not from the text read on the day in question but usually from the Hagiographa. From this remote verse the preacher proceeds to evolve a

---

[46] I have addressed the critiques of those he names in *The Documentary Foundation of Rabbinic Culture. Mopping Up after Debates with Gerald L. Bruns, S. J. D. Cohen, Arnold Maria Goldberg, Susan Handelman, Christine Hayes, James Kugel, Peter Schaefer, Eliezer Segal, E. P. Sanders, and Lawrence H. Schiffman.* Atlanta, 1995: Scholars Press for South Florida Studies in the History of Judaism.

> chain of expositions and interpretations, until, at the
> very end, he arrives at the verse of the seder of the
> day... The proem was by no means the only type of
> sermon. A question posed by a member of the audi-
> ence often served as the taking-off point for a ser-
> mon.[47]

Heinemann's claim here is that the Midrash-writings to which
he refers originated in public sermons, but he immediately
distinguishes between the allegedly originally-oral formulation
and the transmission of the materials as we know them; he
says the Midrashic homilies are *not* identical with the sermons
as actually preached. How Segal imagines the relationship between the writings we have and the supposed oral beginnings
need not detain us; it is clear that what he says Heinemann
says and what Heinemann says do not coincide.

Let us turn to Segal's explicit position, which ignores
Heinemann's careful formulation. For Segal is explicit on the
conclusions that he wishes to draw from the allegedly oral
origin — formulation and transmission — to which he for his
part now assigns the entirety of the Rabbinic literature [!]:

> ...the very existence of oral literature demands
> that it be delivered before an audience. This fact holds
> true for both Halakhic and aggadic creations and it has
> a decisive influence on the content and goals of the lit-
> erature. Unlike written or graphic art, which can be in-
> trospective and private and is expressed initially on an
> impersonal piece of paper or parchment, an oral narra-
> tion will almost invariably be delivered within a living
> social setting. It is therefore much less likely to become
> a vehicle for the expression of individual feelings or to
> place contrived obstacles in the way of immediate
> comprehension. We are probably even justified in re-

---

[47]*The Literature of the Synagogue,* edited, with introductions and
notes, by Joseph Heinemann with Jakob J. Petuchowski (NY 1965, Behr-
man House), pp. 110-111.

garding excessive individualism or intimacy as an artistic flaw in an oral creation. At any rate the aggadah, like all Rabbinic literature, speaks in a collective voice of the Jewish people, in which both the literary methods and the conceptual vocabularies become generic, and it is rarely possible to discern individual personalities. There is no evidence that aggadah strives to represent itself as an autonomous profession of Judaism. On the contrary, it is much more likely that each work was composed in the awareness that it constituted a part of the rich constellation of a broader "Oral Law" literature that included the Talmuds, Halakhic Midrash, and other genres that were created by the same community of Rabbinic sages. Each work or genre was designed to collect material appropriate to itself; taken together, they would preserve a full picture of the spectrum of Rabbinic Judaism.[48]

Lest we miss the point, Segal adds the following footnote: "This view should be contrasted that that of Neusner's argument that each Rabbinic 'document' was composed by a single 'author' in order to express a distinct and consistent ideology."

It would be difficult to formulate in a more dogmatic manner a set of more dubious, undemonstrated propositions. For Segal is required by his position to link the issue of documents to the question of orality, and in alleging that the canon comes to us out of a process of oral formulation and oral transmission, he formulates the theory that in the end calls into question the pervasive premises of his commentary, specifically, his egregious and astounding claim to tell us how people "originally" understood what is before us. While documentary analysis, inclusive of the classification of relevant data for documentary differentiation, hardly demands that we attend to issues of mnemonics at all, Segal has linked

---

[48]Segal, p. 17-18:

the two matters.

As soon as we deal with the differentiation of documents, with special reference to formal patterns, we find ourselves facing the matter of mnemonics, which surely provides the data pertinent to the claim of origin in a state of orality. But these are not problems to which Segal has devoted attention in the work at hand. So, alas, *iqqar haser min hassefer* — the author seems to have forgotten the point of his book. The upshot is much hard work, a highly serviceable compendium of information, but, alas, a great deal, also, of sheer confusion and no clear results of any kind.

But the value of the assembly of information vastly outweighs the absence of a well-crafted and carefully-argued, sustained proposition, and, in the balance, I recommend the compilation to every academic library.

25.

HERSHEL SHANKS, ED., *CHRISTIANITY AND RABBINIC JUDAISM. A PARALLEL HISTORY OF THEIR ORIGINS AND EARLY DEVELOPMENT.* WASHINGTON, DC: BIBLICAL ARCHAEOLOGY SOCIETY, 1992.

Mr. Hershel Shanks, a Washington lawyer and publisher of popular magazines on biblical archaeology and on Judaism, has edited and published a book that packages a stylish idea. It appeals to the intriguing premise that in antiquity Judaism and Christianity have had parallel histories and that we may compare and contrast the history of one to the other. In an age in which two religious communities seek to overcome ages of mutual hostility, this is an attractive model. But is it a valid one? It would be if we dealt with two simple entities, and if those entities took shape under roughly comparable conditions, out of a shared set of premises, within a congruent set of historical models. But late antiquity's Judaism was exceptionally rich and complex, so that the data scarcely sustain the premise of a single, uniform, coherent, normative, Jewish religion, much less the cumulative and linear history of such a religion. The history of early Christianity is the story of *rechtglaubigkeit und ketzerei,* in Walter Bauer's felicitous phrase, and even though, in H. E. W. Turner's eloquent response, we may discern *a pattern of Christian truth,* it is not a truth of this world. The simplest facts of what in hindsight scholarship now identifies as "Judaism" and "Christianity" in antiquity makes the design of this book puzzling and renders the collaboration of reputable scholars in this project incomprehensible.

In Shanks's defense, the idea is a appealing. "Parallel lives" — comparing and contrasting lives of persons — yields brilliant speculative essays in the hands of a first-rate mind like Alan Bullock, whose *Parallel Lives: Hitler and Stalin* shows how the principals of Nazism and Communism may be compared and contrasted to carry us deep into the intersection of the pathologies of politics and psychology of our times — a remarkably profound and compelling account of our own times. In principle the notion of "parallel history" could bear promise. But the allegation that histories run parallel, and that the parallel points beyond mere temporal coincidence has to be validated, not just fabricated for the occasion. Otherwise, drawing parallels shades over into what Samuel Sandmel in 1951 first diagnosed as the intellectual disease of parallelomania and labeled as inanity.

To begin, what are the objects of comparison in "parallel histories"? What do we think we are comparing? Everything depends on the arena of analysis. "History" carries so many and diverse predicates — history of astronomy, history of France, history of the corset, history of religious institutions, history of theological disputes, Church history — that by itself the word conveys no clear sense. The claim to discern parallel histories of "Christianity" and "Judaism" in particular requires close clarification and justification, with special attention to the precise traits of the respective religions to be brought into alignment for purposes of study. That requires tough-minded definitions of what is meant by "parallel," "history," not to mention by "religion," "Judaism" and "Christianity."

The title of the book alleges that Christianity and Judaism run along parallel lines and therefore may be compared as to their origins and early development. But even if Judaism and Christianity were monolithic in antiquity, in both origins and development they exhibit nothing in common, despite the shared appeal to some writings of ancient Israel. Look at the obvious points of difference and see which parallels await delineation. Christianity originates in the figure of one man, Jesus. No one has ever claimed that Rabbinic Judaism originates in the work or life of a single holy person (other than Moses, but he is not at issue here). The early development of Christianity took place in small cells of the faithful, sifting the memories of God Incarnate and writing letters to one another about the meaning of that event. The early development of Rabbinic Judaism took place among sages engaged in public administration of an entire nation's affairs. The early development of Christianity yielded Gospels and epistles, and the early writings of Rabbinic Judaism contain neither biographies of named persons nor signed letters. Rabbinic Judaism made its statements in law codes and commentaries thereon and in the exposition of Scripture. Christianity's law codes hardly compare in position or importance, and its modes of exposition of Scripture took quite different form indeed. Christianity sorted out conflict in world councils. Of these, Rabbinic Judaism knew nothing. Rabbinic Judaism appealed to a single type of authority, the sage. Christianity recognized a great many types of authority. Church government and the administration of local communities, such as bishops and sages respectively conducted, bear nothing in common. There is not a single point in their this-worldly origins and early development at which "Christianity" and Rabbinic Judaism afford basis for comparison and contrast, therefore for composing "a parallel history." Even demonstrating that, at some few points for substantive, worldly reasons, they actually did intersect has proven difficult.

To demonstrate the existence of parallel histories of the origins and early development of Christianity and Judaism, Shanks and his authors must explain what they mean by Christianity and Rabbinic Judaism. A generation of scholarship has demolished the simple-minded notion of a uniform, ubiquitous Orthodox Christianity and an Orthodox (Rabbinic) Judaism, each a normative statement of a linear, uniform, accumulative tradition. Both "Rabbinic Judaism" and "Christianity" encompass large, quarreling families of data, so if we compare them, we must ask which component of that Judaism and its imagined counterpart Christianity. I am pained to note that Shanks does not tell us.

Parallels between Christianity and Rabbinic Judaism? Then do we mean the Mishnah and the Gospel of Matthew, or Pesiqta deRab Kahana and Justin Martyr, or Song of Songs Rabbah and Aphrahat, or the Talmud of Babylonia and the Theodosian Code? These Judaic and Christian documents have been systematically differentiated from one another and defined, severally and jointly. Which of them is discussed here for purposes of forming a parallel with which document(s) of the correspondingly complex entity? And if not documentary comparison, then the authors must specify the aspects of Judaism and correspondent traits of Christianity that require comparison and contrast to yield a parallel. The experts assembled here must be expected to identify the evidence out of the Judaism and the Christianity under discussion and validate the comparison, since parallel lines never meet. They are supposed actually to show us that the parallel history that they conceive they can delineate. Since the book speaks of "Christianity," we have to add to the burden of the authors of the Christian parts of the book a task of differentiation. Of which "Christianity" do they speak? All of them? Only a few? Is the Christianity to be that of a given church-community, Matthew's for instance, or the formal system of doctrine set forth at Nicaea? Is it to be Arianism or Gnostic or Catholic, Marcionism or the Church that adopted the Bible, Old and New Testaments together?

To render plausible the project of comparing religions' histories, a large essay of definition, analysis, and interpretation must stand at the head of any concrete work. Not only so, but all parties to the comparison, specialists in the various topics under discussion, must give evidence that they grasp and respond to a single program of thought and inquiry. They should have the benefit of sustained, rigorous conversations among themselves, so that a single coherent agenda may govern the formulation of the various chapters. At the very least, the authors of chapters on the same period should agree on a joint program.

Otherwise, the project undefined, the participants wandering about aimlessly, the result can only be a book lacking all purpose, point, or intelligible program. So let us examine the book in detail. It can then speak for, and classify, itself.

Everything rests on the editor's explanation of his intention and how the several chapters have realized it, so let us turn first to what the editor has contributed, then proceed to the nine chapters that supposedly realize his purpose. Curiously, the editor and publisher of the work, Hershel Shanks, does not participate in the work. He printed his name on the cover, (presumably) selected and paid the writers, and dashed off a two-page preface. But he has done nothing to accomplish the tasks that editing a scholarly book imposes. He neither asks nor answers a single important question about the problem he has asked us to study. An account of what he should have done makes the point. His introduction does not tell us what he had in mind in inviting various scholars to write for his book, and as we shall see in detail, none of their papers suggests that the editor provided much guidance, a definition of a problem, an outline of the treatment, in a given special subfield, of a generative problematic uniting a variety of specialties into a topic of general intelligibility.

Shanks tells us that his book presents "a parallel history of early Christianity and Rabbinic Judaism, an attempt to trace their stories side by side. This is what beckons us to ruminate on larger questions." But Shanks does not tell us what he conceives these larger questions to be, and he never tells us what, if anything, this "parallel history" teaches about anything. Shanks writes:

> Paradoxically, these two histories have a common source; they grew out of the same soil — Second Temple Judaism. Yet their stories are very different. No figure in Rabbinic Judaism is as central to it as Jesus is to Christianity. A chapter in this book is devoted to the life of Jesus. There is no comparable chapter on a figure in Rabbinic Judaism.

Once more, Shanks raises the question of what he can possibly mean by "parallel history." He begins by explaining that there is no such thing. He proceeds:

> Judaism started out as a nation in this story; it twice rebelled against its Roman overlords; twice it was defeated. Early Christians sometimes suffered persecution, but there is no comparable stand of Christian history.
>
> Christianity started out as a little off-beat Jewish sect — and conquered the West. Judaism, from being a nation, became a tiny minority in larger, often hostile cultures.
>
> For Christianity, the questions were of doctrine and institutionalization; for Judaism, of adapting for survival as a people without a place. No wonder their histories — their stories — are so very different. No wonder they took such divergent paths.

Shanks has presented in his two-page introduction a persuasive case against his book. Unfortunately, he did not write up the case *for* it. All he says is this:

> All this cannot help but make us stop and puzzle over how to achieve an understanding of the critical early centuries of Rabbinic Judaism and Christianity. This book — parallel histories — is not simply a compendium of summaries and generalizations. Here the reader will find the details too.....

These random observations do not tell us what a parallel history is, or precisely why Shanks conceives the two entities before us to exhibit parallels at all, or what his authors' nine chapters are supposed to teach us about "parallel histories' of Christianity and Rabbinic Judaism. Whether these histories illuminate one another, afford perspective on one another, somehow so relate as to demand the formation of "parallel histories" — these questions Shanks does not raise, and he also evidently did not instruct his stable of scholars on the track they were to run. We are left with the sinking feeling that all Shanks means by "parallel" histories is "things that took place more or less at the same time," that is, not parallel but merely coincident histories. But surely we all know the difference between events that are parallel and those that are merely coincident.

So Shanks has dumped the entire intellectual burden on the backs of the scholars he has presumably hired to write up his chapters. He promises they will give us "the details...the basic evidence...," but the scholars are on their own when it comes to forming chapters relevant to the program of the book.

To evaluate the nine chapters, let us ask three questions to each author: [1] does this chapter take seriously the promise of the book for which it was written, showing in some detail the alleged parallels between the origins and development of Christianity and Rabbinic Judaism? [2] are the data adduced in reference to Christianity the same types of data as are produced for Rabbinic Judaism? [3] do the chapters tell us anything new, offer us any fresh perspectives, as a result of these parallel histories? Do these parallel histories show us anything at all?

Under better circumstances, we should respond to these questions through a set of general characterizations of the whole. But the nine chapters go in nine directions; each man has defined his own work (the absence of women scholars and attention to the topic of women in the book is an embarrassment), and every chapter must be read on its own. That no single thread of argument holds the whole together forms the book's least dubious distinction. Let us briefly take up the three groups of chapters, in succession. These are, the introduction and conclusion; the chapters on Judaism, then more briefly, the chapters on Christianity.

GEZA VERMES, "PARALLEL HISTORY PREVIEW," AND JAMES H,. CHARLESWORTH, "CHRISTIANS AND JEWS IN THE FIRST SIX CENTURIES:" Vermes simply surveys the contents of the book and passes his opinion on each chapter. He then argues that there was no parallel history: "The relationship between Judaism and Christianity is not fully reciprocal...this basic inequality is manifest throughout the various periods surveyed in this volume...a civilized and peaceful dialogue is a post-Holocaust phenomenon." But Vermes also calls the book "a remarkable achievement," though what makes him think so is hardly clear from his chapter.

Charlesworth is the only writer in this book to attempt to attempt the goal of parallel history or even to pretend that he understands what might qualify for such an account. He alleges that Christianity and Judaism did not develop in isolation from one another. That of course is the crux of the book. But what serves to show that fact is a survey of the following topics: "the age of variety and standardization: 167 B.C.E.-70 C.E.;" "the Qumran community;" "Jewish factionalism and Hellenistic rhetoric;" "Standardization of the content and canon of Scripture;" "the languages of Scripture;" "the age of centralization, 70-132 C.E.;" "the apocryphal gospels;" "the age of canonization and codification, 132-200 C.E.;" "the age of differing Scriptures, 200-313 C.E.;" "the age of councils, 313-451 C.E.;" "relations between churches and synagogues in Palestine;" "the age of final institutionalization, 451-571 C.E." What we have is not "parallel history." And that is for a very good reason. In fact there is no parallel history to be delineated between Judaism and Christianity, no comparison and contrasts of parallel histories to be undertaken. The culmination of the origins and early development of Christianity in politics came with Constantine, and in theology, Augustine. Judaism knew no Constantine, and its monument, the work of a collective authorship and the result of a massive consensus among authorities, the Talmud of Babylonia, bears nothing whatsoever in common with the equally massive writings of Augustine. Coincidence yields the intersection of Augustine's City of God and the Yerushalmi's great re-presentation of the Mishnah, as I have argued in *The Transformation of Judaism. From Philosophy to Religion.* (Champaign, 1992: University of Illinois Press). But "the city of God" is not parallel to the Yerushalmi's vision of holy Israel. Neither Vermes's introduction nor Charlesworth's conclusion solves the riddle of the editor's "parallel histories."

This brings us to the shank of the book. We consider the treatment of each religion separately, and after reviewing the contents of each chapter, systematically raise the definitive questions outlined earlier.

Louis H. Feldman, "Palestinian and Diaspora Judaism in the

First Century;" Lee I. A. Levine, "Judaism from the Destruction of Je-
rusalem to the End of the Second Jewish Revolt: 70-135 C.E.;" "Shaye
J.. D. Cohen, "Judaism to the Mishnah: 135-220 C.E.;" "Isaiah M.
Gafni, "The World of the Talmud: From the Mishnah to the Arab
Conquest:"

The four chapters on Judaism do not address Judaism; they treat the history of Jews here and there, various
events, institutions, and the like. But from these chapters we
should have difficulty reconstructing the fact that Rabbinic
Judaism took shape in the period under discussion, let alone
describing that Judaism as a coherent religious structure. The
Judaism of the volume itself is hardly parallel to Christianity;
the one set of chapters tells about a political entity and its social history and institutions, the other set of chapters takes up
a religious system. The title of the book speaks of "origins,"
and in fact the two religions originated in the same time
frame, but a parallel history that shows how the initial phases
of Rabbinic Judaism and Christianity ran parallel depends
upon discussing Rabbinic Judaism within the same category-
formation as applies to Christianity. If the latter is a religion,
then the former is here portrayed simply as something else.

Feldman does not discuss religion at all. He is explicit
on this point: "political background;" "economic background;" "religious background of the revolt" — meaning,
"two instances...when the Romans offended Jewish religious
sensibilities...." By "religious developments" he means the
high priest, the sanhedrin, and so on. "Judaism" is not defined, but "Jewish sects" are. Feldman does not address the
premise of the book; he finds no parallels to notice. He does
not tell us how the "Judaism" he treats forms a religion comparable to the Christianity, to which he makes reference. The
account, however, is standard and well-informed. If it bears
upon Judaism as a religion only episodically, it does at least
make an attempt at inner coherence.

Levine's picture of "Judaism" after 70 slogs again over well-worn paths: the "aftermath of the destruction," ""Roman reaction in the wake of the revolt;" the sages and the Yabneh academy; "Yohanan ben Zakkai;" "Gamaliel II;" "origins of traditions still observed today;" "Jewish nationalist aspirations;" "causes of the Bar Kokhba revolt;" and so on. Levine offers no material for "parallel histories" but instead a chapter in a narrative history that relies heavily on paraphrased Rabbinic sources. He writes on the period in which, people generally maintain, "Judaism" and "Christianity" parted company. But in his chapter I cannot point to a discussion of the topic that is commensurate to its importance.

It is difficult to find evidence of Cohen's concern with the problem of this book. His chapter defines neither "Judaism" or "religion." Rather, like Levine, he supplies a chapter on "Jewish history," — not Judaism: "...our information about the Jewish history of this period is both scanty and one-sided. Practically all the literary evidence is Rabbinic — which means we hear much about the rabbis and their concerns, but little about non-Rabbinic and Diaspora Jews, and virtually nothing about 'political' events. In short, our sources do not allow us to write a complete history of the Jews and Judaism of the second and early third centuries." Cohen presents his work as a history of the Jews, not of Judaism.

Isaiah Gafni's chapter on the Talmudic period is a major disappointment. For here, a comparison between the situation of the Jews and Christians in the Iranian empire, inclusive of Rabbinic Judaism and Christianity, is certainly feasible; we have the *Demonstrations* of Aphrahat, ca. 340 C.E., who discusses a range of social and theological problems in explicit dialogue with the Judaism of his day. Here, moreover, Christianity was the persecuted religion, Judaism the licit one. So a real parallel, not simply a coincidence — Judaism harassed in the Roman empire, Christianity in the Iranian one —

does yield an opportunity for an instructive comparison. Not only so, but Aphrahat explicitly addresses an Israelite sage and argues about religious beliefs and theological convictions. He presents a theology of history that bears comparison and contrast with the counterpart theology of history set forth by the sages of the fourth century. Of all of this Gafni says nothing — an amazing lacuna.

The failure of Gafni's chapter to address the assignment of the book exacts a considerable price. It in no way concerns itself with a well-defined and carefully, accurately described religion, Rabbinic Judaism, on the other. A rapid survey of his topics speaks for itself: "the Jews of Palestine in the late Roman period, 220-324 C.E.;" "the growth of the patriarchy;" "new forms of taxation;" "the role of the sages in Jewish-Christian confrontations;" "transition to Roman-Byzantine era;" "the Jews under early Roman-Christian rule, 324-361 C.E.;" "clashes between Romans and Jews; the Gallus revolt;" the Jews and Julian, 361-363 C.E.;" "from Julian's death to abolition of patriarchate, 363-425 C.E.;" "the synagogue as a focus of attack;" "the decline of the patriarchy;" the final two centuries of Byzantine rule in Palestine: 425-614 C.E.;" the literary achievement in Palestine: Talmud and Midrash;" "differences between Palestinian and Babylonian Talmudim;" "the aggadic Midrashim;" "Halakhic and liturgical literature;" "late Byzantine rule in Palestine; the Persian invasion and Arab conquest of the Holy Land;" the rise and fall of Jewish fortunes under the Persians;" the defeat of the Persians;" "beyond the Euphrates: the Jews of Babylonia." This tedious sequence of topics, jumping from hither to yon, makes it difficult to reconstruct Gafni's theory of how things fit together. I am sorry to observe that Shanks, for his part, seems to have missed the problem.

But even if such a cogent program can be concocted, what is at stake emerges as trivial, boring, and inconsequential. In Gafni's period the Talmud of Babylonia came into being, surely one of the greatest writings in the history of religion. Gafni does not tell us why. He has not framed for himself or for us a set of important questions. Apart from Feldman's recitation of standard facts, none of the Judaism-chapters conforms to the state of the art, and some of them — Gafni's and Levine's — are simply incoherent. Cohen, Levine, and Gafni still imagine they are supposed to write "narrative history," and their intellectual failure underscores the contrast between their uncritical, mediocre results with the uniformly critical essays on Christianity.

E. P. Sanders, *"The life of Jesus;"* Howard C. Kee, *"After the Crucifixion — Christianity through Paul;"* Harold W. Attridge, *"Christianity from the Destruction of Jerusalem to Constantine's Adoption of the New Religion: 70-312 C.E.;"* Dennis E. Groh, *"The Religion of the Empire: Christianity from Constantine to the Arab Conquest:"*

The counterpart chapters on Christianity derive from a field with high critical standards and a coherent agendum. Problems not addressed in the study of ancient Judaism in this book — precisely what is meant by "religion" and by "Judaism," how are we to know, out of the written sources, what really happened — have been sorted out in the study of Christianity. Each of the writers of the Judaic chapters would have learned much concerning sound method by studying his counterpart on the Christian side. As it is, if the Christianity-chapters represent the state of the art in our day, as I believe they do, then the Judaism-chapters must be consigned to an age gone by, when people believed pretty much everything they read, except what they chose to disbelieve for essentially capricious reasons, when by Judaism people meant anything but a religion — anything at all. No parallel history can be formulated between a religion — Christianity — and an ethnic group — the Jews. They simply are not the same thing. In the contrast between the topical programs of each set of chapters, we shall now see why. The sad result is, the book presents the Christian sources in accord with one scholarly protocol, and the Judaic sources in accord with another.

Best among a uniformly sophisticated set of chapters on the religion, Christianity, we start with Sanders. He opens with a critical statement on the problem of the sources and then follows the outlines of a sound method. Sanders's picture of "the historical" Jesus is as plausible as any and better argued than most. But I cannot explain how this chapter addresses the issue of "parallel histories," especially since, as Shanks himself says, Jesus has no parallel in Rabbinic Judaism.

Kee discusses "the early Christian movement" and the theological issues sorted out therein. Judaism does not figure in this chapter, but as with Sanders, so here, a clear focus upon a religion, its origins and history, defines the program. Read together, the two chapters provide a clear account of Christian origins, and Sanders and Kee (like the others in their group) not only exemplify the state of the art, they define it. But neither chapter turns to address the Judaism of the same period, even the Judaism that ought to have defined the matrix for the Christianity that was coming into being.

Attridge defines the period at hand by reference to the destruction of the Temple and the legalization of Christianity. His picture of Christianity encompasses the development of the institutional church, the Didache, Ignatius, the episcopacy of Rome, and so on and so forth — chapters in the institutional history of Christianity and its theology. Judaism never figures, and Attridge finds no parallel history to examine.

A comparison of Attridge's chapter with Cohen's epitomizes the dismal editorial failure of this book. The simple fact is that Cohen talks about phenomena of one classification, Attridge of another. Cohen presents himself as a historian of the Jews, and Attridge, a historian not of various Christians, here and there, but of *Christianity*. To form comparable chapters, Attridge would have had to write a political history of Christians in the Roman world, or Cohen, a cogent history of Judaism in the period under discussion; but that is not what Cohen did. To work together in the same book, both chapters would have had to speculate on reciprocal points of comparison and contrast. This is the work of elementary editorial vision and discipline that Shanks consistently fails to carry out.

Groh's treatment of the time-frame covered by Gafni follows a linear plan: Constantine's rule, "the new Christian mind of the East," the Arian controversy and Nicaea, doctrinal issues, the New Testament canon, the monastic movement, Augustine, and the like. The result here is a standard rehearsal of conventional subjects. Groh does not discuss alleged parallels between the development of Christianity and Rabbinic Judaism in the period he discusses; the book's premise about the commensurability of the types of evidence plays no role.

"A PARALLEL HISTORY OF THEIR ORIGINS AND EARLY DEVELOPMENT"? I fear not. Since not a single chapter in the shank of the book pretends to address the program of the book, at no point claiming to compose a parallel history of Christianity and Rabbinic Judaism, we have to ask ourselves why the chapters found their way into this particular collection, when they obviously could have served somewhere else, or no where in particular. The answer is that the editor commissioned and then accepted them. They conformed to his wooden and dull conception of the subject, how it should be defined, divided, and discussed. The monumental failure of the parts to accomplish what the book claims they do then points to the question, for whom will this book prove useful? Scholars will find nothing new about these subjects. Lacking all intellectual program, the book also will not speak to students. I fear, therefore, that the book will not keep its promise for many readers.

I fear even more than that. My deeper concern is that the academic study of religion is shown in these pages to have lost sight of itself. In light of the book's systematic and pitiless exposure of stunted editorial vision, we must wonder how colleagues in these pages have failed to live up to our own, shared best aspirations as a field. The very plausibility of the book, the nine participants and the blurbs on the back cover that legitimate it, make me wonder whether this is what people think our field is supposed to produce. Pathetically and incredibly, this book manages to reduce to a set of uninterpreted and on the whole pointless facts the greatest moment in the history of religion in the West, the hour in which Judaism and Christianity as we know them came into being. This book must be judged, with considerable shame, to be unworthy of its sublime subject. Religion is not honored in these pages, and the majesty of humanity, represented in the writings of both synagogue and church, hardly casts a shadow. Imagine, in these centuries, a man walked the earth whom people called God incarnate, and sages formed of Israel a Godly community that would proudly endure through all history. This book tells us nothing of that man or those sages. The origins of Judaism and Christianity are reduced to a hash — and then rehashed.

This is a tired, conventional rerun. On the back cover, figures of such eminence as Robert L. Wilken, Jacob Milgrom, Lawrence H., Schiffman, Alan F. Segal, and John Dominic Crossan, endorse the botched project as a success. Segal stands for them all: "It bristles with interesting perceptions." Name one. Segal is wrong. The book does not "bristle" with new observations, but repeats every standard and well-known thought about the subjects that are discussed. In fact, the book misses every interesting question. Why, for instance, and how the sources of Judaism simply ignore Christianity for the first thousand years of its existence? That strikes me as a question parallel history should take up. When and how did Christians addressed the puzzle of an Israel that clearly was going to persist — and make their peace with Israel and decide not to exterminate either the people or their faith? That seems to me a question demanding attention in a parallel history. For the age of inter-religious dialogue that this book addresses, this book is simply beside the point; by ignoring the other religion in the time of which it speaks, each of the chapters really reinforces abandoned attitudes that lead each religion to ignore the existence of the other.

Nine scholars, all of them clearly indifferent to the notion of "parallel histories" (with the possible exception of Charlesworth) have permitted themselves to be drawn into the project and have contributed to it without asking a single critical question about the work they had been assigned to do. The real problem that fact demands we consider concerns the field of the study of religion. We all claim to study not just religions but religion. But this book calls into question that claim, since it studies two religions but not religion at all. That is amazing, since the two religions that are studied here intersect over the bulk of their sacred literature and theology. This book therefore does not show what our field does, it calls into question whether we form an academic field at all, a discipline, rather than just a set of subjects. That is why I wonder whether we as an academic field oughtn't to feel ashamed of such a book as this. This is not serious and artful and elegant work because it is not worthy of its subject.

Public policy for field of the academic study of religion at some point does enter in. Shanks appears to have done no more than issue invitations and copy-edit the result. For the purpose of the histories of Christianities and Judaisms in antiquity, Shanks defective and deficient knowledge of the primary sources, the original languages, the intellectual issues, the scholarly traditions and controversies, makes it impossible to elicit consequential new writing on established problems. Those who printed their work here are embarrassingly complicit in amateurism. But Shanks's amateurism is not what has here driven out professionalism. The nine scholars who collaborated with Shanks and the five named scholars who blurbed up the back cover, did. Surely it was in everyone's interest for them to protect our field.. They really should have known better — and cared. Through learning void of conscience, they sold us all out.

26.

DAVID STERN, *PARABLES IN MIDRASH. NARRATIVE AND EXEGESIS IN RABBINIC LITERATURE.* CAMBRIDGE, 1991: HARVARD UNIVERSITY PRESS.

The intimidating title, promising to cover four enormous subjects, "parables," "Midrash," "narrative," and "exegesis," the work in fact is a revised dissertation, with the strengths and weaknesses of the genre. It is compendious and very well researched; it contains a large number of interesting observations of detail. But it is more of a collection of information and opinions on a number of topics than a well-argued, thoughtfully-crafted statement of a particular proposition on the general theme at hand. The bridge from the detail to the main point proves shaky. The result is an occasionally-interesting but rather prolix and unfocussed work, a bit pretentiously claiming to accomplish more than is actually achieved, but, still, valuable for what in fact is given.

Dealing with the *mashal* as it occurs in two dozen passages in Lamentations Rabbah, which are given in an appendix in the Hebrew texts in two recensions and in translation as well, the monograph, on the strength of which its author gained a tenured professorship at the University of Pennsylvania, deals with these topics: composition and exegesis, rhetoric, poetics, thematics, the mashal in context, and the mashal in Hebrew literature. The mashal, though represented by a remarkably tiny sample, is treated as uniform, the representations of the form in various, diverse documents not being differentiated; so too "Midrash" is treated as everywhere the same thing, being defined as "the study and interpretation of Scripture by the Rabbis in Late Antiquity." Consequently, the contemporary tools of form-analysis and criticism, on the one side, and of the systematic differentiation of documents by their indicative traits of rhetoric, topic, and logic of coherence, on the other, are denied the author. The result is a rather general and unanalytical treatment of the subject. But that does not deny the book a hearing, since the author provides a full, though somewhat repetitious, account of the scholarly literature and problems, and his treatment of the texts he discusses, if a bit prolix, contains interesting ad hoc observations. A brief survey of the main points yields sound reason to value the book.

COMPOSITION AND EXEGESIS: the mashal or parable is to be distinguished from a table: "a fable utilizes anthropomorphic animals or plants to portray the particularly theriomorphic or phytomorphic features of human behavior. A parable suggests a sort of parallels between an imagined fictional event and an immediate, 'real' situation confronting the parable's author and his audience." Parables in Rabbinic literature are "preserved not in narrative contexts but in exegetical ones, as part of Midrash...There is no important formal or functional difference between meshalim recorded as parts of narratives and those presented as exegeses of Midrashim of verses." Parables are to be distinguished from allegories, on the one side, and the ma'aseh, or precedent ("example or exemplum, an anecdote told to exemplify or illustrate a lesson"). While Stern concedes that the explanation that accompanies the narrative of the mashal., called the nimshal, first occurs only in Medieval documents, he includes in his discussion a full account of that quite distinct development. Indeed, much of the chapter on poetics invokes the nimshal, so we are asked to understand Rabbinic literature of late antiquity only by appeal to literary forms not found in the writings of late antiquity, a rather confusing mode of analysis.

RHETORIC: the occasions of the mashal are spelled out. The mashal serves for three purposes: illustration, "secret speech," and "rhetorical narrative." Stern sees the mashal as "a story that turns allusiveness to effect in order to persuade its audience of the value of a certain idea or approach or feeling." The key word here is "allusiveness," which Stern does not define with clarity.

POETICS: the center of the book is the interest in "the relationship between exegesis and narrative. "The Rabbinic mashal can be defined as a parabolic narrative that claims to be exegesis and serves the purposes of ideology." That definition would prove more compelling if it did not serve equally well a variety of other forms in the Rabbinic literature. Much of the rest of the discussion concerns the nimshal, as I said, leaving open a variety of questions concerning the mashal in late antiquity. But the results are not wholly without interest. Stern's most interesting point is this: "among the most distinctive characteristics of the mashal's poetics is the strategically placed point of discontinuity, technically called a gap." Much of the exposition, alas, proceeds to "disparities between narrative and nimshal," leaving us once more somewhat puzzled as to Stern's program. Lamentations Rabbah is not a medieval document, but much of the exposition of the data spills over into the consideration of kinds of mashal-writing that came to the surface much later than that document; that presents a considerable puzzle, if we want to grasp precisely what Stern wishes to say, indeed, even to define that about which he is writing; sometimes late antique writing, sometimes medieval; sometimes, indeed, the mashal in particular, other times Midrash in general.

Indeed, the confusion is intensified by recurring efforts to define the mashal, each fabricated for its context, thus, later in the same chapter, "the mashal is essentially mimetic narrative. It is about events and characters, and particularly one character — the king, or God. Beyond all else, the mashal represents the greatest effort to imagine God in all Rabbinic literature." That definition bears more enthusiasm than enlightenment, since the conception that the "king" in the Mashal means "God" in particular relies upon the particular cases at hand; the point is not so much demonstrated as alleged with gusto.

THEMATICS: "the Midrashic mashal is a type of ideological narrative, which seeks to impress the truth and validity of a world-view...upon its audience. In any particular mashal, that world-view is refracted within the mashal's specific message, its theme or thesis." This new definition would prove more useful if it did not define equally well every other type of writing in Rabbinic literature. Thus the chapter treats, further, "apologetics, polemics, eulogy and consolation, complaint, regret and warning," and on and on; that is, various mashals are classified in various ways. None of the classifications encompasses only the mashal, so the results are indeterminate and again somewhat puzzling.

THE MASHAL IN CONTEXT: in their seemingly haphazard positions in these collections [Talmud, Midrash], the meshalim are no different from the rest of the contents. The structure and composition of these documents are famously difficult to identify. Despite a few recent attempts to demonstrate the 'integrity' — the formal and thematic coherence — of the various Midrashic collections, they remain to all appearances more like anthologies of traditional Rabbinic interpretations that an anonymous editor has selected and recorded than like self-contained, logically structured books in their own right." Stern does not then see any differences of a general character between, e.g., Sifra and Leviticus Rabbah, both on Leviticus; or the Tosefta and the Talmud of the Land of Israel, both on the Mishnah. This awry view makes difficult for him the determination of the context in which the mashal does, or does not, occur, why here, not there, being questions that, by definition, he finds he cannot answer. That further accounts for his difficulty in seeing formal differences in the mashal as it occurs in the several distinct documents. So he concedes at the outset, "the 'contextual' interpretation of Midrash — reading a Midrashic passage in its literary, documentary context — is a very problematic venture. The larger literary units that we most comfortably use in reading and interpreting the meaning of literary works — the document as a whole, chapters, even subsections in chapters or discrete narrative or legal sections in a work like the Bible — do not constitute significant units of meaning for Midrash."

That explains why Stern sees the units as "fragmentary, miscellaneous, and atomistic." Other views of the documentary character of the Rabbinic corpus are not examined, and the remainder of the chapter replicates in detail the deeply confused character of Stern's reading of the whole. That makes all the more regrettable Stern's failure to understand his own results. After a systematic study, he concludes, "The passages just discussed all show how Midrashic discourse is organized: in recognizable units of discourse, in literary forms like the petihta, the mashal, the enumeration, the series. These forms comprise the genres or subgenres of Midrash. They constitute its language, and they maintain themselves in Midrashic literature formally and rhetorically, even when they combine with one another. The combinatory pattern of these units is essentially additive. The petihta-form provides a frame for the mashal, which in turn is made to serve the special rhetoric of the petihta; but neither form is required to surrender its distinctive structure or formal identity when it joins with the other. Similarly, a mashal can be constructed in the image of an aggadic narrative or ma'aseh, with its own lesson or homily, but it can simultaneously be employed so as to exploit its own parabolic strengths as a paradigmatic, representational narrative." Quite what Stern means to say is not entirely clear, but the main point is precisely that of form-analysis: there are fixed forms, they do govern, and they characterize one kind of writing, rather than some other. Having produced exactly the results that form-analysis of documents has yielded, Stern is left unable to explain his own data. That is because he has not come to grips with the position he rejects without discussion, quite out of hand, that documents make a difference. Once he has declared the literature chaotic, he cannot recognize the points of order he himself identifies. The concluding chapter, the Mashal in Hebrew literature," need not detain us, since it is tacked on, dissertation-style, to cover whatever might have been left out in the substantive chapters.

The strengths of Stern's dissertation are his own. They lie in his ad hoc observations about this and that. In his rambling, sometimes unfocussed discussions of the specific passages in Lamentations Rabbah he has chosen to discuss in detail, he makes numerous interesting observations. Though this is not a work of mature scholarship, it is more than a mere collection and arrangement of information, and we may hope for better things to come from its author.

The weaknesses of the dissertation are those of the genre; the prose I have cited suffices to show that he writes abominably. Stern proves a good graduate student, thorough in compiling opinions on various topic, but embarrassingly selective in dealing with published results that the author does not wish to address at all. He covers a broad range of subjects, but has not got a well crafted thesis to present to make the topical program cohere and form an important proposition and thesis upon a well-crafted problem. So the work is at the same time too general and rambling and altogether too specific, not bridging the gap between the detail and the main point. As a dissertation it certainly is above average; as an account of the parable, this overweight book is more encyclopedic than interesting.

27.

SACHA STERN, *JEWISH IDENTITY IN EARLY RABBINIC WRITINGS*. LEIDEN, 1995: E. J. BRILL. *ARBEITEN ZUR GESCHICHTE DES ANTIKEN JUDENTUMS UND DES URCHRISTENTUMS*. EDITED BY MARTIN HENGEL, PETER SCHÄFER, PIETER W. VAN DER HORST, MARTIN GOODMAN, AND DANIEL R. SCHWARTZ, VOLUME 23.

For reasons I shall explain and illustrate, I find this a very sad book, because the author, obviously a person of ambition, learning, and intelligence, has violated the most basic rules of systematic learning and produced a work of utter confusion. The chaos commences in the opening lines, where Stern declares that he wants to find in ancient legal and theological writings the answers to twentieth-century secular problems of sociology, politics, and theology. The announced topic is "identity in its widest sense: the perception and experience of a person's self in all its lived dimension. 'Jewish identity'...represents therefore the perception by a Jew of his self specifically as Jewish." Stern sees this as not limited to one's "Halakhic or ethnic status," meaning, "a general, subjective feeling of mutual 'belonging.'" He promises "to examine Jewish identity" by "establishing what constitutes the general experience of being Jewish, or 'what it is like to be a

Jew.'"

He admits at the outset that the categories hardly correspond to those that govern the documents he considers" "The evidence I have gleaned...represents a most disparate corpus of intimations, side-lines, and out-of-context quotations which do not correspond as a whole to any sustained systematic piece of Rabbinic writing." Hoping to disarm the critical reader upfront, he adds, "The choice of this topic...may thus appear artificial or anachronistic, but it is inherent to any historical inquiry...the subjective standpoint of the historian is the motivational force behind any historical interpretation. The fact that the authors of Rabbinic sources did not conceptualize the notion of Jewish identity...does not imply that they had no experience at all of being Jewish...their writings are replete with references to their 'Jewishness,' which is to say, to their distinctive features as 'Israel.'"

But Stern defines an odd position for himself, since he asks questions that the writers of the documents not only did not ask but could not have understood. That is why everything he adduces in evidence has been ripped out of its own categorical context and tossed into an alien and incongruent framework. How then are we to know what is "ethnic" and what is theological, what is secular and private, and what is public and normative? Distinctions are in play that make a difference that is never spelled out. Stern wants the sources to tell him about subjects they do not discuss and could not even contemplate. The premises of his inquiry violate the givens of his sources, since he proposes secular, ethnic, individual and personal questions to writings that spoke of the sacred, the holy community, and "Israel" as a component always and everywhere of a supernatural society. "Jewish identity," a secular term pertaining to ethnicity, indeed corresponds to no conception operative in Rabbinic writings, which know "Israel" as a transcendental and holy community.

Quite what Stern can possibly mean in this context by "experience of being Jewish" defies imagining. That is not only because I look in vain for a single reference in the Rabbinic literature to "Jewishness" in its ordinary usage, that is, the secular status of one who is a Jew, as distinct from "Judaism" (in the native category, "Torah"), in everyday terms, the state of practicing the religion and of forming a community with others who do the same. It is also because for people to answer his question, they have also to acknowledge alternatives, to know they face choices and can and should decide for this and against that. Perhaps some Judaisms of the age spoke to Jews who articulated alternatives and affirmed one among them.

But for the Rabbinic writings, what Stern can understand by "experience of being Jewish," the puzzle being, — rather than what else? "Our sages of blessed memory," whose writings Stern trawls for his data, set forth not a single line that suggests they contemplated an alternative to "Israel," that is, in his language, which in common usage does not mean what he wants it to mean, "being Jewish." Where and how our sages would have found it possible to articulate something so profoundly imbedded in the deepest layers of their pre-articulated culture and consciousness surely presents a problem. "Israel" in our sages' writings always means the holy community and never takes place in a this-worldly framework. Our sages of blessed memory produced theology and law to spell out what it means to be "Israel," and "what is it like to be a Jew" in no way corresponds to their meaning.

What has gone wrong here? Stern has brought about the total confusion in category-formation. For to begin with, "Israel" for our sages forms a theological, not a psychological or sociological or political category. "Israel" moreover bears no sense of individuality and of legitimate choices among equally-valid alternatives. When they spoke of "Israel," our sages moreover thought in terms of cosmic events, sacred history, the transactions between God's people and God. What has this to do with "what it is like to be a Jew"! What remarkably trivial language for so elevated a vision of humanity "in our image, after our likeness," that Israel is supposed by our sages to constitute! Not only so, but to make his study congruent to the data, Stern has to show us how the sources with which he deals express "a person," an individual and his consciousness. But the sources represent the consensus of the textual communities that produced and preserved them. They never speak for private persons, except to label schismatic opinion. At the very outset, therefore, Stern has defined for himself a state of formidable confusion.

Stern intensifies the confusion by deciding that all of the Rabbinic literature forms the undifferentiated source of his data: "to analyze the sources as they present themselves to us, namely, in the state of their final redaction...a synchronic study of these sources would aim at presenting...Rabbinic Judaism as it stood in this redactional period." Various incoherent reasons for avoiding all work of differentiation, whether historical, whether documentary, whether even theological, are adduced to excuse Stern from the critical tasks of reflective, analytical scholarship. He gives us only the big picture — taken at the end.

But this picture cannot then be located in the stated period, since "this Judaism depended largely on traditions which had been transmitted from earlier centuries..." And differentiation within the sayings, location of the sayings in any setting more manageable than "Judaism" or "the tradition" or "the literature," prove beyond Stern's intellectual grasp. The result is, he organizes and paraphrases what our sages say, and then introduces various anthropological or philosophical post-modernist gibberish (of which more below) to impart to the result a veneer of intelligent discourse. But we are left with a mass of quotation, paraphrase, and free association, not a coherent and cogent answer to the (dubious) questions that Stern promises to address. The book delivers much less than it promises.

The upshot is, Stern's account deals with an indeterminate time, place, and circumstance; he can then tell us what the sources he has chosen have to say, but he cannot explain how over time various persons responded to a given circumstance, or reflected upon a given age, tried to solve a given problem of doctrine or law, or otherwise tell us something interesting and important. The upshot of a sizable methodological chapter is to validate, to Stern's way of thinking, the familiar "method" of collecting and arranging sayings on various topics. What he gives us is not history, nor, as I explained, is it theology either, though, as we shall see, in the closing lines we may perceive the glimmerings of theological interest, but in language beyond all comprehending. Then what? Alas, Stern is not quite sure: "Much of this study...is based on an extensive survey [of] the majority of Talmudic and Midrashic sources that are now extant. In this process I have constantly faced the difficult task of deciding what was 'relevant' to the experience of Jewish identity. It could be argued...that the whole experience of lived reality, in all its multiple facets, is relevant to some extent to personal identity, and cannot be ignored in such a study. On the other hand, there would be little point in analyzing passages where the experience of identity is only subsidiary, and hence unarticulated and diffused. I have generally given attention...to the more explicit descriptions of the Jews and of the Jewish people...." This rather verbose and chatty account yields little more clarity than the more succinct language cited above.

What, in the end, does Stern deliver? Here are the contents: Israel and the nations: assumptions, images, and representations (self and other, Jews and non-Jews, wicked and the righteous, animals and angels, Israel among the nations and the world); identity, the commandments, and bodily experience (non-Jewish impurity and the experience of revulsion, the bodily features of Israel, the commandments, experience and praxis); the people of Israel: center and periphery (converts, apostates, common people, rabbis and the people)(; the protection of Jewish identity: dissociation and dissimulation (social control: boundaries and dissociation, cultural control: resistance to assimilation); "being Israel: solipsism, introversion, and transcendence" (solipsism, the nations excluded; tzeniut, the ontology of concealment, transcendence, the Almighty and Israel). For all of the differentiation that the contents promise, the treatment of each topic ignores all considerations of analysis, e.g., diverse viewpoints found in various documents. "The Midrash" or "the Halakhah" suffices to tell us who is speaking about what, and diverse sayings are then set side by side in groups, joined by Stern's own category and little more than that. So in the end we are led through his card-files; to his credit, he makes a serious effort to say interesting things about their contents. But the book in the end does little more than paraphrase a great many Rabbinic sayings about the topics the author has selected.

How a given topic is treated may be gauged from the opening unit, "Israel and the nations: Assumptions, images, and representations.: Here Stern begins with "self and other: cultural representations: the dialectics of self and other," yielding the unsurprising observation, "Jews ("Israel") and non-Jews ("the nations" are treated explicitly as radically different entities...This notion is fostered through the weekly liturgical recitation...The Midrash glosses that the difference between light and darkness is the same as between Israel and the nations. The non-Jew is given much attention...but especially in so far as he is contracted with the Jew...In some passages the notion of difference itself is spelled out in full...In a number of passages the clause relating to the non-Jews is no more than the negation of that relating to Israel..." These form the repertoire of generalizations, each joined with an appropriate quotation or two. But to establish the obvious point at hand, Stern commences with the following: "In his study of Herodotus' Histories, Francois Hartog shows how any discourse about others reflects, in a mirror-like fashion, an implicit discourse about oneself." The very same sources that yield Stern's "generalizations" can have lead to that same observation, and invoking a study of Herodotus to show, "...the representation of the 'other' implies a concomitant representation of the 'us'" is hardly required. But when we add up this representative unit, what do we have? Stern's point is little more than a fancy paraphrase of the plain meaning of the sources. What is at stake is hardly clear, for, when we reach the concluding pages, as I shall show, we find little of substance, and nothing surprising. A theology of Judaism sustained by these same sources will have yielded a theologically-appropriate statement about "Israel and the nations." We know that that is the fact, because every systematic theology of Judaism, whether in the idiom of classical or of contemporary discourse, says exactly that. Why package as "Jewish identity" what is in fact a theological theorem I cannot explain, and what is gained by the category "Jewish identity," other than a certain modishness, Stern does not spell out either.

In fact Stern can have developed his ideas in a theological framework, formulating through sound theological method a set of propositions that might have held together in the setting of the Judaism he examines and set forth an interesting proposition and cogent argument. But he sees nothing in the authentic context in which our sages conducted their thought. Instead, he wants his post-modernist context, which has yet to show itself able to take up theological issues and sources. So everything is taken out of its context and forced into an alien and intellectually-paralyzing framework. What has gone wrong here is that Stern takes up topics profoundly embedded within the larger theological structure and system of our sages of blessed memory, but he does not wish to treat them theologically, indeed, systematically in any other way. He prefers constant recourse to post-modernism, which gains in its private, hermetic vocabulary what it loses in clarity and point.

When the sages set forth their teaching on all of the topics that he covers here, the sages determined upon a context and formulated a purpose, a point, and a proposition. But nothing authentic about the Judaism of our sages (their "Torah" to use the native category) emerges here, because Stern has violated the literary system and structure that sages erected but supplied no congruent system or structure of his own. Having deprived himself of all analytical methods, he is left to paraphrase his data in a sequence of stupefyingly obvious observations. A set of topics deemed pertinent to a rather dubious question — dubious because, as Stern admits in the opening pages, it is simply not relevant to the interests of the documents — has ripped out of context every single saying, story, law, and teaching, that is treated in this book. But the new context — the trendy outline cited just now — does not then recast or reorganize but, as I said, produces only chaos. Let me quote the concluding lines, which capture the flavor of the whole:

> Conclusion: Israel and covenantal transcendence
>
> Israel's relationship with the Almighty cannot be restricted...to the function of ensconcing their identity and rendering it...impregnable....an ontological experience such as this cannot be transcribed exclusively in terms of a 'function' or of a 'strategy.' Transcen-

dence must be seen...as a fundamental experience which is characteristic and constitutive of the identity of Israel....This experience is related to the notion...that Jewish identity consists essentially of practices with an explicit covenantal connotation, such as circumcision, Shabbat, and Torah learning, which embody a covenant between the Almighty and Israel...The embodied but transcendental and solipsistic experience of the Almighty...constitutes therefore the ontogenetic essence of the identity of Israel.

...we should not lose sight of the fact that from the perspective of our sources, adhering to the Almighty constitutes a goal in its own right; it is not seen...as a means to constitute the identify of 'Israel.' ...the pursuit of Jewish identity remains...a matter of secondary importance...Jewish identity or 'being Israel' could itself be perceived...as a means towards achieving greater proximity to the Almighty. Indeed, so far as it is ontogenetically related to the Almighty, the notion of 'Israel may represent in itself a powerful, concrete embodiment of Divine transcendence.

Stern has used a great many words — impressively big words at that — to say something, though I am not sure exactly what that may be. But if I may venture a guess and translate this verbose, pretentious screed into ordinary language, Stern seems to want to say that "being Jewish" was not an end in itself, but a byproduct of the love of God. Our sages certainly concur. All Judaisms in ancient, medieval, and modern times, beginning, after all, with Scripture, have said no less. In Judaic religious systems, "being Jewish," that is, "Israel," always is about loving and serving God. "What it is like to be a Jew" — a rather obscure formulation indeed! — is simple: to love the Lord our God with all our heart, with all our soul, and with all our might. That, after all, is what Israel is to hear! But then what is the point of a whole book on "Jewish identity," when the conclusion is, to the sources at hand, "Jewish identity" makes no difference except in relationship to God, made manifest in the Torah. Here I find a confession of intellectual failure: the category imposes a distinction that, in the system, makes no difference whatsoever. Masked in fancy words, plain English suffices for declaring bankruptcy.

For, obviously, the theologically-sound proposition that concludes Stern's book hardly responds to the program announced at the outset. That explains why the entire project strikes me as pretentious. For Stern sets forth neither critical history nor well-crafted theology, nor sociology nor psychology, nor, certainly, an account of a politics. He here prints up little more than a bunch of sayings, neatly arranged, embellished with intimidating and recondite words picked up in a lot of modish post-modernist books, words like ontological and ontogenetic, quotations of Ecco and Merleau-Ponty. But these form merely the window-dressing of post-modernist philosophy, and, so far as rigorous thought and well-crafted propositions form the criterion of authentic scholarship, not mere learning, I find scholarship lacking. For so far as scholarship makes coherent and important observations about data, Stern argues none. Indeed, he illustrates, in the end, the sad truth that ambition, erudition, and a modicum of intelligence require the catalyst of a well-crafted question and a well-considered category-formation to formulate an answer of weight and consequence. This light-weight Oxford dissertation does not win much confidence in the taste and judgment of its sponsors, who themselves do not work along these lines — and, we see here, with very good reason.

28.

TAL ILAN, *JEWISH WOMEN IN GRECO-ROMAN PALESTINE. AN INQUIRY INTO IMAGE AND STATUS. TEXTE UND STUDIEN ZUM ANTIKEN JUDENTUM 44. TÜBINGEN, 1995: J. C. B. MOHR (PAUL SIEBECK)*

Another dreary Israeli dissertation consisting of a collection and arrangement of information masquerading as scholarship, this dull book asks no important questions and conducts no penetrating analyses. Dr. Tal Ilan of the Hebrew University covers these topics: daughters (birth, relations between father and daughter, the daughter as only child, etc.); marriage (the virtuous wife, the bad wife; marriage and spinsterhood, polygamy, economic and legal arrangements, etc.); a woman's biology (virginity, menstruation, sexual relations, etc.); preserving a woman's chastity (talking with a woman, looking at a woman, etc.); crises in married life and the breakdown of marriage (adultery, divorce, widowhood, levirate marriage); women and the legal system (punishments and judgments, women as witnesses, inheritance); women in public (commandments, occupations and professions, study of Torah); other women (maidservants, proselytes, prostitutes, witches). There is a conclusion of exactly three and a half pages; as usual with Israeli dissertations, we may say, *iqqar haser min hassefer,* that is to say, the book misses the point. To state matters in more accessible terms, as we shall see, after assembling diverse facts out of diverse and incoherent sources, the author finds nothing to say about them.

The sources that supply the data scarcely intersect. They are formulated at different times and set forth different propositions and perspectives. All that they have in common is that, here or there, they contain allusions to topics of interest to Dr. Ilan, and what interests her is anything to do with women. She brings to the sources no interesting questions, and she derives from them no data pertinent to the testing of important hypotheses. In the same paragraph we will find the Book of Jubilees, a citation of Sifré Zuta, a passage of the Fathers According to Rabbi Nathan; the next paragraph is devoted to Josephus, and the prior one to Palestinian and Babylonian Talmudic passages on a given them. In fact, the whole conveys little more than a paraphrase, if that. Any passage, chosen at random, yields the same conceptual chaos. So the whole adds up to little more than a report of what is in a variety of writings, lacking all coherence, whether social, whether theological, whether legal. What, indeed, are we supposed to learn from this sequence of paragraphs on "relations between father and daughter" (pp. 48-50):

> A girl was brought up in her father's house until she was married. The longest comment on father-daughter relations can be found in ben Sira [followed by various sayings]...Thus in Ben Sira's eyes a daughter is a constant aggravation to her father...
>
> A slightly different picture emerges from parables in Rabbinic literature. Clearly the fathers and daughters in these parables are usually allegorical representations of God and Israel, but still the authors were describing reality as they saw it when they depicted mutual feelings of love and respect between father and daughter...[here the citations are to "the Tannaim" meaning Song of Songs Rabbah [sic!], and to Leviticus Rabbah].
>
> The halakhah, too, exhibits a double standard

regarding boys and girls, imposing many obligations on a father in connection with his son but awarding rights and benefits in the case of a daughter [here the references are to the Mishnah];'

A similar picture arises from the Halakhic discussion of whether a father is required to provide for his daughters [here: Yerushalmi Ketubot]...

In sum, the various sources treated affection between a father and daughter as exceptional and worthy of note. Even the halakhah treated daughters as less valuable than songs. But the propounders of the halakhah changed their minds on this matter,. at least in one place where it seemed to them that the standard Halakhic attitude was liable to endanger the lives of daughters.

Not a single question of a theoretical character, not a single initiative in relating text to context, an isolated fact to a larger conceptual or social theory, enlivens this tiresome, yet shallow and superficial, collection of topically-pertinent data. All Dr. Ilan has done is collect card-files, arrange them, then empty the box into neat piles and copy down what she found. Yet even here, in a mass of platitudes and banalities, she misses even the simplest opportunity to compare and contrast, so seek context and meaning, for her data. She observes, in a footnote in context, "Father-daughter relations in Judaism — if our sources present a true picture — are quite the opposite of father-daughter relations pictured by Roman sources of the same period, at least as presented by Judith P. Hallet, *Fathers and Daughters in Roman Society: Women and the Elite Family.*" An alert scholar will have turned to another body of data to ask, if I know this, what else do I know? If these facts characterize the social order before me, then what more do I know about that social order, about the larger theory of the world and of woman in that world?

And raising tough questions in the quest of interesting hypotheses and suggestive theses begins in an exercise of comparison and contrast, first among the sources of the data that are surveyed (what indeed do Ben Sira, Leviticus Rabbah, Song of Songs Rabbah, and the like, have in common, other than that circumcised males made them up and wrote them down? For Dr. Ilan, "Jewish" imposes on diverse data a single point of origin and interest; failure to differentiate among sources as to time and place of origin, social status and economic interest of authors and sponsors, theological position and moral perspective of the framers of documents — that failure bears devastating consequences for Dr. Ilan's work. It leaves her, as is clear, simply with nothing to say.

And so at the end, she produces commonplaces, generalizations so stupefyingly obvious as to make one wonder, upon what demonstration of intellectual merit was a doctoral degree conferred, if this is all Dr. Ilan has claimed to prove [pp. 226-229]:

> a.   All sources surviving from the Second Temple period were written by groups who maintained very high moral standards and viewed licentiousness as one of the most serious threats to those standards...
>
> b.   These social norms were anchored in law, as it is laid out in Halakhic literature. Yet here we are able to make a clear distinction between the law of the pietists and the more pragmatic Tannaitic-Pharisaic law. The laws of the pietist circles resemble the requirements for an ideal society, and thus make severe demands...By contrast, the Tannaitic-Pharisaic halakhah takes into consideration both real conditions which depart from the ideal picture of society, and human nature, which is much more complicated than that of the ideal member of society...
>
> c.   Yet we may ask whether the lenient Tannaitic-Pharisaic halakhah was in fact equal for every person, and whether Jewish society of the Second Temple period did in fact follow it. reality turns out to be different from the legislated ideal...

Dr. Ilan has labored to collect and arrange over two hundred pages of passages on her chosen topic only to present platitudes as insight, banalities as worthy of attention. Who can find any of this surprising — or provocative?

In the same concluding pages, she has two more major conclusions in the same setting, each with its own subhead:

> ### The Heterogeneity of Jewish Society in Palestine
>
> In the Second Temple period, Jewish society was highly heterogeneous. Different groups lived by different versions of Jewish law. Tannaitic halakhah was not fully adhered to in that period, both because it was not yet fully developed, part of it being written after the destruction of the Temple, and because only a particular group attempted to live by it before the Destruction...
>
> ### Social Class and Tannaitic Literature
>
> In contrast to the heterogeneity of Jewish society, the authors of Tannaitic literature and of most of the other surviving sources like Josephus and Ben Sira belong to the upper-middle and aristocratic classes...Thus the requirement that men and women be kept separate comes from social circles whose members had the means to put this into practice. Likewise, only a social class whose women could hire wet-nurses in order to save themselves the trouble and possible deterioration of the body would determine that nursing was neither an obligation nor a religious duty. Only families worried about preserving their own property would place great importance on the family backgrounds of the husbands for their daughters, and in fact would make every effort to ensure that the husbands came from related families or families of similar social position. Poor families, by comparison, would have preferred to marry up into wealthier classes. Yet as we have seen, laws made by only these upper social classes were not always appropriate for the lower classes: "A decree cannot be made for the people un-

unless most of the people can endure it" (b BB 60b).

And that is the concluding paragraph of the book — a wild farrago of self-evident but pointless observations (who is going to find surprising that the poor try to marry into money) and undigested, inarticulate yearnings for a theory and a point (who will wonder at the — unsubstantiated — claim that upper class law in general does no favor for lower class life)! The pity is, the glimmerings of speculative thought, e.g., on the relationship of gender to class, could have illumined the discussion throughout and turned a collection of inert facts into a purposeful and constructive argument. What we have here is no book, nor even a monograph, but what is no more than a collection of notes lacking a text — a primitive and intellectually flaccid research report, and the editors of the series, Martin Hengel and Peter Schaefer, have done the author no favor by printing undigested data in book-form. I very much doubt that they made the effort to suggest how she should revise and recast her findings into a systematic statement; they serve as mere gate-keepers.

Now let me say a word in apologia for this obvious failure of intellect. Dr. Ilan clearly has done the best she could, given the retrograde circumstances of her work. She has undertaken a project in feminist studies in a setting in which the entire enterprise is prohibited. She worked with no model, an autodidact, doing her best with what she had. Her first dissertation director was the late Menahem Stern, the classicist, and the second, Y. Gafni, who works on what is called in the State of Israel "the period of the Mishnah and the Talmud," and who wrote a history of the Jews in Babylonia that has yet to be translated into a Western language. Neither has published in feminist studies, nor have they worked even in the realm of social and intellectual history; they are garden-variety, hard-core positivists, who collect and arrange what they conceive to be historical facts.

As a young doctoral student, Ilan had not only to qualify and make a contribution to learning; she had also to invent the field in which she would pursue learning. Her opening paragraph is the one passionate and compelling statement in the entire book and deserves respectful attention to its honesty:

> This book began its career as a Ph. D. dissertation in the Hebrew University of Jerusalem. Although it was written in the late 1980s, when feminism and women studies [sic!] were making enormous strides in many disciplines the world over, working in Jerusalem was like working on another planet. The works of feminists were both unknown and viewed with suspicion as devoid of sound scientific methodology. The literature on the subject of women in the Greco-Roman period was not systematically collected by any of the libraries. Some of the most important books...were not found in any library in the country.

As the author of books that have been proscribed in Jerusalem for thirty-five years, indeed, even kept under lock and key in the Hebrew University Library until the death of E. E. Urbach scarcely a decade ago, my heart goes out to Dr. Ilan. For she took on a scholarly community that, in its way, aped the academic ethics of Bolshevik universities. In the vulnerable position of a doctoral student, depending on the good will of omnipotent masters to validate her work and allow her entry into the profession, she nonetheless chose a forbidden subject and made her way without teachers, without colleagues, without access to a scholarly tradition at home — and yet fully aware that, elsewhere in the world, teachers, colleagues, scholarship and intellectual tradition flourished. The book is a work of remarkable courage and tenacity, and if it is an utter failure as a contribution to learning, it succeeds in revealing that human side of scholarship that does not always dare to show its face. Here is a truly great woman, and I hope that in future work of a more mature and penetrating character, she will prove worthy of her subject. Her book, in its negative, but also in its positive, aspect, forms an indictment of the setting in which it was written.

29.

PIERRE VIDAL-NAQUET, *THE JEWS. HISTORY, MEMORY, AND THE PRESENT.* TRANSLATED AND EDITED BY DAVID AMES CURTIS. WITH A FOREWORD BY PAUL BERMAN AND A NEW PREFACE BY THE AUTHOR. NEW YORK, 1996: COLUMBIA UNIVERSITY PRESS. IN *EUROPEAN PERSPECTIVES. A SERIES IN SOCIAL THOUGHT AND CULTURAL PERSPECTIVES.* EDITED BY LAWRENCE D. KRITZMAN.

Here, in a collection of miscellaneous essays that present considerably less than meets the eye, a distinguished classicist demonstrates that he has nothing interesting to say about "the Jews, history, memory, and the present" — nor much that is even coherent. This pretentious and empty book calls to mind the strange phenomenon of the leaders from the periphery, who come to Jewry with qualifications (mostly financial) attained somewhere else and on the basis of accomplishments with no bearing on Jewish community life demand a hearing and finance what is simply assimilationist policy. Here before us stands the counterpart: the intellectual from the periphery. He is a scholar of Greek who is a Jew and now comes with a great name achieved outside of the realm of Jewish learning and thought and demands a sober hearing for his insights and wisdom on matters Jewish, insights that are, in fact, quite dubious, and thoughts made up of uncomprehending banalities.

The leaders from the periphery make their money and form their values among gentiles and bring their money and their aspirations back to organized Jewry — an observation we owe to Kurt Lewin. Now in the action consisting of this book we see the how the intellectual from the periphery makes his name in one area of learning and decides to pretend to know another, which he has not, in fact, studied at all, and for which, as this book shows, he has remarkably little taste. What Vidal-Naquet, a great scholar in Classics I am told, shows us is that when it comes to the Jews and Judaism, he has no interesting ideas and precious little learning. What makes the book not implausible but contemptible is that Vidal-Naquet treats Judaism with supercilious indifference and the State of Israel and Zionism with unremitting hauteur, — sustained self-righteousness really.

The book covers the Jewish state in ancient times, with special interest in Josephus — chosen as a way of comparing the ancient Zealots with the Zionists, and of condemning both; the emancipation of the Jews in Europe, especially France; and the Holocaust. In moving from the field in which he has distinguished himself to one in which he is a rank amateur — scarcely even a beginner — Vidal-Naquet invokes in his own behalf the rather dubious name of the late Arnaldo Momigliano. Another classicist who in later life decided to study the Jews, among academicians Momigliano also exploited credentials attained elsewhere to declare himself an expert on Jewish subjects, in the theory that he was both an expert on ancient times and also a Jew, so he must be an expert on the Jews of ancient times. It is thus an appropriate, if infelicitous, model that Vidal-Naquet adduces to explain himself, for Momigliano fatuously pontificated with mighty ignorance but much self-confidence on a wide range of problems in the study of the history of the Jews and Judaism in ancient times. Most of Momigliano's writing based on issues that depend upon sources in Hebrew and Aramaic is derivative and ignorant. Alas, Vidal-Naquet comes up significantly short even of the flawed model he has chosen for himself. Both highly opinionated men illustrate what I mean by "intellectuals from the periphery."

Secular, leftist, with a mere smattering of Jewish knowledge and still less of systematic Judaic learning (I doubt he has ever opened a text of Judaism, and the footnotes suggest he has not), Vidal-Naquet gives us three papers on Josephus, which demonstrate that he does not keep up with Josephus scholarship. The chapters also show an astounding lack of learning about the history of the first century; Vidal-Naquet still treats us to the gullible reading of Rabbinic fables as concrete history (missing a great shot at reflecting on history and memory!), he still gives us the hoary notion of a canonical consistory at Yabneh, he still conceives of a Scriptural canon established there, utterly discredited notions in contemporary scholarship. Nor does Vidal-Naquet even know the dozen or so important works — both dissertations and major books on Josephus — that have appeared in the very years in which he was writing these papers. Consequently, his impressionistic, marginally-coherent chapters would embarrass a scholar of the subject; passing his opinion about everything and knowing not too much about anything, Vidal-Naquet meretriciously asks us to believe what he has to say demands a hearing. That is what I mean, in concrete terms, by an intellectual from the periphery: he doesn't know the territory. His footnotes tell us that he does not (to his credit) even pretend to.

Specialists in French and French-Jewish history will

have to tell us whether his chapters on France and the Jews, the Dreyfus affair, and the like, bear any consequence for learning. These chapters run on at some length, and whether or not he contributes to knowledge of the history of French Jewry in the nineteenth and twentieth centuries and in the Dreyfus affair is not for me to say.

But no specialist is needed to assess the wild incoherence of the shank of the book, which is comprised by an interminable sequence of Vidal-Naquet's prefaces to various books, joined with some trivial, brief reviews of still others. What to make of these prefaces and lazy, self-important book reviews I cannot say, not knowing the books he introduces, not finding any coherent line of argument or even perspective that links his preface to book B to his preface to book U to his 800-word review of book L. But that makes me wonder what makes a book out of his episodic, random prefaces to other books! Why someone needs to collect and print as a group not systematic reviews of, but mere introductions to other, diverse books, none can say who does not prize every word written by Vidal-Naquet. Seen whole the collected prefaces by Vidal-Naquet add up to still less than the sum of the parts — for the superficiality and subjectivism emerge only when we see them as a group. Here is a man with a very high opinion of his opinions.

What, concerning "the Jews," concerns Vidal-Naquet? Not very much. He adheres to the thin and acutely contemporary agendum of secular, assimilated (and assimilationist) Jews today, who have no roots in Judaism and no deep knowledge of the Jews in any dimension of their existence. That leaves only what he learns not from tradition or study but only from the world at large, the newspapers for instance, with the predictable result that the Holocaust, Zionism, and the State of Israel and its foreign policy exhaust this man's secular-Jewish agendum. What Vidal-Naquet has to say about the Holocaust has been said better and more profoundly, with greater art and eloquence; his knowledge of Zionism consists of the rejection of Zionist aspirations conventionally expressed by a totally-assimilated French patriot; and his perspective on the State of Israel is — predictably — shaped by a singularly inappropriate analogy: he sees the State of Israel as equivalent to a settler-state, like the French in Algeria.

It is not surprising, then, that Vidal-Naquet simply does not understand the State of Israel as a Jew, because he has no Jewish roots. He dismisses without even discussion the substantive, historic claim of the Jewish People to the Land of Israel (an amazing lacuna in a book that claims to discuss history and memory!). But that is symptomatic of the whole: in writing the essays collected here, he evinces no interest in ever putting down Jewish roots; he boasts about his ignorance, making the reader wonder why he then wants a hearing for it in these pages. He tells us he attended a seder for the first time in Tel Aviv in his mature years; his family was militantly secular ("my grandfather...had declared that if a rabbi appeared at his funeral, he would rise from his coffin to strangle the man"). His knowledge of Israeli affairs proves so flawed as to be implausible; one minor mistake tells the story: he tells us about a march called by "Shalom Archav, (Peace Now)." And his persistent comparisons between the State of Israel and South Africa leave no doubt as to his hostile take on Jewish affairs. Why would a tone-deaf man write a book of music criticism?

Then what of this murky babble about "history, memory, and the present" that, evoking the prestige of French philosophy, the title promises in order to purchase for the book some privileged hearing? We have already noted where "history, memory, and the present" are to have been anticipated but make no appearance. Still, discourse of that kind, invoking Proust for instance, reliably gains for French intellectuals a deferential hearing on our shores. Embodying our nation's humility before its European betters, we bow and scrape before obscurity and verbosity. Then what does Vidal-Naquet have to tell us, systematically or episodically, about "history, memory, and the present," how, in English, does his message come across. I state flatly that if he were not French, Jewish, leftist, and secular, he would have found himself no hearing at all at Columbia University Press. A few sentences, selected more or less at random, convey the flavor of this discourse and explain that judgment:

> A historian is not a prophet. But perhaps it will be understood that, if this book is indeed a torn fabric, that is because the situation [the Arab-Israeli conflict] itself is torn — not only torn but heartrending (p. xxiii).
>
> Remarkable is the fact that, as obvious as it may be, the connection between history and memory is far from always expressed...Work after work has been published during the past thirty years, all of them trying to tell us what, according to the memories of the young and the old preserved on audiotape, happened that day. Yet these works do not represent the kind of reflection on memory I am speaking about, but precisely the opposite. In such books, indeed, it is not a matter of making explicit our relationship to the past, but of suppressing the distance that separates us from it, of acting as if the representation of it rendered it actually present (p. 131).
>
> Between time lost and time rediscovered lies the work of art. The challenge to which *Shoah* [the film] subjects historians lies in the obligation it places on them to be at once scholars and artists. If they do not face up to this challenge, historians will lose, irremediably, a portion of the truth they are pursuing (p. 150).

In the first statement I see nothing but words, certainly no proposition of weight; in the second, merely a mysterious allusion to "reflection on memory" that the essay at hand does not even pretend to instantiate; and in the third I find nothing very startling — or interesting for that matter. Who doubts that historians generally write history; the good ones — and the *Shoah* has attracted a few — write artfully. So what's his point? Readers may stipulate that I could readily adduce in evidence numerous other banal statements of the same kind. Hidden in a cloud of words (in French it may sound profound and wonderful, but in English it comes over as both shallow and verbose) is remarkably little substantive thought.

That leaves the question, not why Vidal-Naquet wished to advertise his ignorance, but why Columbia University Press, publisher of the authentic history of Salo W. Baron, agreed to print — of all places, in its series on "social thought and cultural criticism" — a collection of self-celebratory vacuities? The obvious answer is that they have relied on poor referees, and they would do well now to turn to their distinguished specialists in the religion, Judaism, and in the history of the Jews, to help them raise their standards to an acceptable norm. Professors David Halivni and Yosef H. Yerushalmi will have to weigh in to retrieve the reputation of their University's Press, once made truly formidable in publishing their own Salo W. Baron, but now ruined.

30.

Shaye J. D. Cohen. The Beginnings of Jewishness. Boundaries, Varieties, Uncertainties. *Berkeley and Los Angeles, 1999: University of California Press.*

In this collection of papers on the general theme of defining who is a Jew, most of them already in print, some dating back to the early 1980s, Shaye J. D. Cohen, Ungerleider Professor of Judaic Studies at Brown University, pursues the question, "What is it that makes us us and them them?...Can one of 'them' become one of 'us." He (plausibly) does not claim "to have penetrated to the inner mystery of Jewish identity or 'Jewishness,' the qualities that make a Jew a Jew" (pp. 2-3). But he also does not explain what the term "Jewishness" can possibly have meant in antiquity, and what its counterparts at that time might have been ("Roman-ness"? "Christian-ness"? for instance). So the category that he proposes to impose and illuminate proves remarkably obtuse. But, as I shall explain, the essays exhibit a uniform failure of discernment, start to finish.

Within his probably anachronistic, but surely theological, framework, Cohen divides the book into these parts:

first, Who was a Jew?, with the chapters, "Was Herod Jewish?" "Those Who Say They are Jews and Are Not: How Do you Know a Jew in Antiquity When you See One?" "Judaean, Jew;"

part two: The Boundary Crossed: Becoming a Jew: "from ethnos to ethno-religion;" "crossing the boundary and becoming a Jew;" "to Judaize," "the Rabbinic conversion ceremony;" and

Part Three: The boundary violated: the Union of Diverse Kings: "the prohibition of intermarriage;" "the matrilineal principle;" "Israelite mothers, Israelite fathers: matrilineal descent and the inequality of the convert." There is an epilogue: "Jews, Judaism, and Jewishness: Us and Them," and then come four appendices: Was Martial's slave Jewish? Was Menophilus Jewish? Was Trophimus Jewish? Was Timothy Jewish?

We note, first of all, what we do not find, which is, a systematic account of how Rabbinic Judaism answered the question, how does a gentile become an Israelite?

Since Cohen presents himself as a scholar of Rabbinic Judaism, I find puzzling his omission of the book of Ruth as the Rabbinic sages read the work in Ruth Rabbah. That is where Rabbinic Judaism makes its statement on the issues at hand, and omitting that central evidence renders this collection unbalanced — and unreliable for Judaism (though presumably quite reliable for the evidence Cohen does encompass). Because of this startling omission, I would say, iqqar haser min hasefer.

What about what Cohen does cover? Read in sequence, start to finish, the essays tend to a certain banality: lots of recondite information, yielding unimportant or unsurprising conclusions, the academic equivalent to busy-work. For example, asking about the ethnic traits of the Jews, if any, he spends a fair amount of time on "social mechanisms that did not make Jews distinctive," such as looks, clothing, speech, names, occupations, and the like. At each point he cites a mixture of this and that. Much work goes into few conclusions. The argument follows a simple (some might say, simple-minded) outline, and at each point there is a survey of references in classical and Rabbinic writings that pertain, always with a large serving of sometimes not very nice opinion-passing. All this labor leads nowhere: "How did you know a Jew in antiquity? The answer is that you did not." Wow!

So the upshot is, a great many sources are cited, from diverse times and places and settings, to amass evidence relevant to a topic, but not probative of a proposition. To put it simply, he collects a lot of information and has trouble making it make sense. This is low-brow scholarship: labored erudition about very little. Yet even here, a certain selectivity governs whom he will quote and whom not. The omission of well-known works of scholarship is puzzling, for instance, circumcision as an indicator of "being Jewish" without reference to Jonathan Z. Smith's classic essay on the subject (among many). So the upshot is, to prove a pretty obvious point, he cites a massive amount of information — yet he misses fundamental works of learning, in fields he does not deign to address.

In reading these essays, therefore, the adjectives that come to mind are slipshod, superficial, above all, solipsistic: lightweight and incoherent. The book announces a problem but does not solve it, or even analyze its components. The topic is just an excuse for Cohen just to heave up piles of information on this and that. He comes up with everything loosely relevant to the announced topic, with nothing tightly linked to a proposition. Stated simply: an unsympathetic reader might conclude that Cohen does not have an idea in his head. But then, as I say, for all the erudition, he keeps missing the classics. His key-problem is, as he himself states, how people move from outside to inside. Yet, when it comes to conversion, for example, he is in trouble defining his category, because the classic work is lost to him: Nock's book on the subject! If he had read Arthur Darby Nock's *Conversion* (1933), he would have started at the state of knowledge, especially with precise definitions of the terms he uses casually and loosely. But for someone who presents himself as knowledgeable in Rabbinic Judaism, the omission of Ruth Rabbah presents a stunning lapse, for it is where the Rabbinic sages of the formative age answer all of Cohen's questions, and do so systematically and cogently.

That explains Cohen's most serious failing in this unfortunate book. It is the ubiquitous imprecision about precisely which Jews and which Judaism, which time, place, circumstance, he means at any given point. We never know that concerning which his cited bit of evidence attests, or why that evidence, about a given time and place and condition or type of Jew, bears significance for some other time, place, and type of Jew. The imprecision of his thought is simply staggering. He turns into a pastiche, a mishmash, this mass of discrete evidence concerning a great many diverse times and places and circumstances. At any given point, he draws on anything that pertains to his topic, never asking whether or how his evidence coheres. So we just don't know which Jews he means, though his basic category-formation suggests he thinks they all look alike anyhow (or: they don't look alike and haven't got much in common, depending on where he is standing at that particular minute). His social model differentiates not at all. No wonder he presents such a confusing picture of incompatible facts! And in the end, he wants the facts to illuminate a category-formation that to begin with represents pure anachronism: our categories applied to those times.

Lest readers think I exaggerate the confusion and ob-
fuscation that prevail, here is the repertoire that he invokes to
discuss "problems in defining 'conversion:'" a story from a
Rabbinic source, a story from Sozomen, a Christian historian
of the fifth century, and a homily of Antiochus the Monk, of
the seventh century. These yield this generalization: "they
show that the category of 'conversion' covers a wide variety
of phenomena." Surprise, surprise! What did he expect? Time
and again, once Cohen has assembled and laboriously chatted
up his evidence, he ends up with conclusions of stupefying
banality. For one example, and not the worst, his protracted
account of "the Rabbinic conversion ceremony," runs on for
forty dull pages and reaches no conclusion of any weight.

The epilogue attempts to unify the free-standing
chapters, but only reprises their main points. In a couple of
pages of superficial summary, Cohen then shifts to medieval
and modern times: "Jewishness became an issue when…Jews
emerged from their ghettos and entered western society."
Zounds! Who would have thunk it? This leads to the observation that in the nineteenth and twentieth centuries matters of
identity became complex for the Jews! Cohen claims, "The
uncertainty of Jewishness in antiquity curiously prefigures the
uncertainty of Jewishness in modern times." But that is only
if all lines of structure and order that divide Jews into diverse
Judaisms are ignored, and all the diverse evidence is made to
describe one and the same social group. And that is only if we
read contemporary category-formations of social and cultural
description into antiquity. That is to say, the uncertainty lies
in Cohen's own incapacity to define categories and to differentiate among diverse evidence, locating the point to which
each pertains, eliminating the points to which that evidence
just does not pertain.

In conclusion, Cohen finds it necessary to introduce
himself: "all scholarship is conditioned by the setting and

identity of its authors." So he tells us, "I am white, middle-class, middle-aged, heterosexual, right-handed, American, Jewish, male, married, and father of four." This unilluminating information is supposed to tell us how to make sense of his scholarship. That by-now-not-very-surprising confession leads to two pages that gloss over what Cohen has already revealed about himself in this work of utter confusion. That is not part of his confession. But what he shows us here is that he cannot sustain a piece of systematic research beyond the level of a fairly brief journal article.

Apart from some edited items of uneven quality, Cohen personally, in his own right, has published exactly three titles on his own: a (pretty good) dissertation (1979), a (dubious) text book (1987), and this rather sad collection of essays (1999) — not much for more than twenty years — and that *oeuvre* adds up to a whole lot less than appears on the surface. But what we learn in this collection of occasional essays is why what he has published is not much and not awfully good. I would like to be shown wrong, but by this point, nearly a quarter-century beyond the dissertation he wrote with a teacher's help, I simply doubt he can carry off a serious, substantial, sustained and well-crafted work of scholarship, with an argument, a beginning, a middle, and an end. Instead, he does what he can, which is collect information and make remarks about this and that, not a few of them snide. But there is always hope, and no scholarly career need fizzle, even in the third quarter.

WITHDRAWN